10º

THE DANCE OF LIFE

THE DANCE OF LIFE

BY

HAVELOCK ELLIS

AUTHOR OF "IMPRESSIONS AND COMMENTS," "AFFIRMATIONS"
"ESSAYS IN WAR-TIME," ETC.

TOUT BIEN OU RIEN

BOSTON AND NEW YORK
HOUGHTON MIFFLIN COMPANY
The Riverside Press Cambridge
1923

The Riverside Press
CAMBRIDGE · MASSACHUSETTS
PRINTED IN THE U.S.A.

PREFACE

THIS book was planned many years ago. As to the idea running through it, I cannot say when that arose. My feeling is, it was born with me. On reflection, indeed, it seems possible the seeds fell imperceptibly in youth — from F. A. Lange, maybe, and other sources — to germinate unseen in a congenial soil. However that may be, the idea underlies much that I have written. Even the present book began to be written, and to be published in a preliminary form, more than fifteen years ago. Perhaps I may be allowed to seek consolation for my slowness, however vainly, in the saying of Rodin that "slowness is beauty," and certainly it is the slowest dances that have been to me most beautiful to see, while, in the dance of life, the achievement of a civilisation in beauty seems to be inversely to the rapidity of its pace.

Moreover, the book remains incomplete, not merely in the sense that I would desire still to be changing and adding to each chapter, but even incomplete by the absence of many chapters for which I had gathered material, and twenty years ago should have been surprised to find missing. For there are many arts, not among those we conventionally call "fine," which seem to me fundamental for living. But now I put forth the book

as it stands, deliberately, without remorse, well content
so to do.

Once that would not have been possible. A book
must be completed as it had been originally planned,
finished, rounded, polished. As a man grows older his
ideals change. Thoroughness is often an admirable
ideal. But it is an ideal to be adopted with discrimina-
tion, having due reference to the nature of the work in
hand. An artist, it seems to me now, has not always to
finish his work in every detail; by not doing so he may
succeed in making the spectator his co-worker, and put
into his hands the tool to carry on the work which, as it
lies before him, beneath its veil of yet partly unworked
material, still stretches into infinity. Where there is
most labour there is not always most life, and by doing
less, provided only he has known how to do well, the
artist may achieve more.

He will not, I hope, achieve complete consistency.
In fact a part of the method of such a book as this,
written over a long period of years, is to reveal a continual slight inconsistency. That is not an evil, but
rather the avoidance of an evil. We cannot remain con-
sistent with the world save by growing inconsistent
with our own past selves. The man who consistently
— as he fondly supposes "logically" — clings to an un-
changing opinion is suspended from a hook which has
ceased to exist. "I thought it was she, and she thought
it was me, and when we come near it were n't neither
one of us" — that metaphysical statement holds, with

a touch of exaggeration, a truth we must always bear in mind concerning the relation of subject and object. They can neither of them possess consistency; they have both changed before they come up with one another. Not that such inconsistency is a random flux or a shallow opportunism. We change, and the world changes, in accordance with the underlying organisation, and inconsistency, so conditioned by truth to the whole, becomes the higher consistency of life. I am therefore able to recognise and accept the fact that, again and again in this book, I have come up against what, superficially regarded, seemed to be the same fact, and each time have brought back a slightly different report, for it had changed and I had changed. The world is various, of infinite iridescent aspect, and until I attain to a correspondingly infinite variety of statement I remain far from anything that could in any sense be described as "truth." We only see a great opal that never looks the same this time as when we looked last time. "He never painted to-day quite the same as he had painted yesterday," Élie Faure says of Renoir, and it seems to me natural and right that it should have been so. I have never seen the same world twice. That, indeed, is but to repeat the Heraclitean saying — an imperfect saying, for it is only the half of the larger, more modern synthesis I have already quoted — that no man bathes twice in the same stream. Yet — and this opposing fact is fully as significant — we really have to accept a continuous stream as constituted in our minds; it flows in the same direction; it coheres in what is more or less the same shape. Much the same may be said of the ever-changing bather whom the stream receives. So that, after all, there is not only variety, but also unity. The diversity of the Many is balanced by the stability of the One. That is why life must always be a dance, for that is what a dance is: perpetual slightly varied movements which are yet always held true to the shape of the whole.

We verge on philosophy. The whole of this book is on the threshold of philosophy. I hasten to add that it remains there. No dogmas are here set forth to claim any general validity. Not that even the technical philosopher always cares to make that claim. Mr. F. H. Bradley, one of the most influential of modern English philosophers, who wrote at the outset of his career, "On all questions, if you push me far enough, at present I end in doubts and perplexities," still says, forty years later, that if asked to define his principles rigidly, "I become puzzled." For even a cheese-mite, one imagines, could only with difficulty attain an adequate metaphysical conception of a cheese, and how much more difficult the task is for Man, whose everyday intelligence seems to move on a plane so much like that of a cheese-mite and yet has so vastly more complex a web of phenomena to synthetise.

It is clear how hesitant and tentative must be the attitude of one who, having found his life-work elsewhere than in the field of technical philosophy, may incidentally feel the need, even if only playfully, to speculate concerning his function and place in the universe. Such speculation is merely the instinctive impulse of the ordinary person to seek the wider implications bound up with his own little activities. It is philosophy only in the simple sense in which the Greeks understood philosophy, merely a philosophy of life, of one's own life, in the wide world. The technical philosopher does something quite different when he passes over the threshold and shuts himself up in his study—

"Veux-tu découvrir le monde,
Ferme tes yeux, Rosemonde"—

and emerges with great tomes that are hard to buy, hard to read, and, let us be sure, hard to write. But of Socrates, as of the English philosopher Falstaff, we are not told that he wrote anything.

So that if it may seem to some that this book reveals the expansive influence of that great classico-mathematical Renaissance in which it is our high privilege to live, and that they find here "relativity" applied to life, I am not so sure. It sometimes seems to me that, in the first place, we, the common herd, mould the great movements of our age, and only in the second place do they mould us. I think it was so even in the great earlier classico-mathematical Renaissance. We associate it with Descartes. But Descartes could have effected nothing if an innumerable crowd in many fields had not created the atmosphere by which he was en-

abled to breathe the breath of life. We may here profitably bear in mind all that Spengler has shown concerning the unity of spirit underlying the most diverse elements in an age's productivity. Roger Bacon had in
him the genius to create such a Renaissance three centuries earlier; there was no atmosphere for him to live
in and he was stifled. But Malherbe, who worshipped
Number and Measure as devoutly as Descartes, was
born half a century before him. That silent, colossal,
ferocious Norman — vividly brought before us by
Tallement des Réaux, to whom, rather than to Saint-
Simon, we owe the real picture of seventeenth-century
France — was possessed by the genius of destruction,
for he had the natural instinct of the Viking, and he
swept all the lovely Romantic spirit of old France so
completely away that it has scarcely ever revived since
until the days of Verlaine. But he had the Norman
classico-mathematical architectonic spirit — he might
have said, like Descartes, as truly as it ever can be said
in literature, *Omnia apud me mathematica fiunt* — and
he introduced into the world a new rule of Order.
Given a Malherbe, a Descartes could hardly fail to
follow, a French Academy must come into existence
almost at the same time as the "Discours de la Mé-
thode," and Le Nôtre must already be drawing the geometrical designs of the gardens of Versailles. Descartes,
it should be remembered, could not have worked without support; he was a man of timid and yielding character, though he had once been a soldier, not of the

heroic temper of Roger Bacon. If Descartes could have been put back into Roger Bacon's place, he would have thought many of Bacon's thoughts. But we should never have known it. He nervously burnt one of his works when he heard of Galileo's condemnation, and it was fortunate that the Church was slow to recognise how terrible a Bolshevist had entered the spiritual world with this man, and never realised that his books must be placed on the Index until he was already dead.

So it is to-day. We, too, witness a classico-mathematical Renaissance. It is bringing us a new vision of the universe, but also a new vision of human life. That is why it is necessary to insist upon life as a dance. This is not a mere metaphor. The dance is the rule of number and of rhythm and of measure and of order, of the controlling influence of form, of the subordination of the parts to the whole. That is what a dance is. And these same properties also make up the classic spirit, not only in life, but, still more clearly and definitely, in the universe itself. We are strictly correct when we regard not only life but the universe as a dance. For the universe is made up of a certain number of elements, less than a hundred, and the "periodic law" of these elements is metrical. They are ranged, that is to say, not haphazard, not in groups, but by number, and those of like quality appear at fixed and regular intervals. Thus our world is, even fundamentally, a dance, a single metrical stanza in a poem which will be for ever hidden from us, except in so far as the philosophers, who are to-day even here applying the methods of mathematics, may believe that they have imparted to it the character of objective knowledge.

I call this movement of to-day, as that of the seventeenth century, classico-mathematical. And I regard the dance (without prejudice to a distinction made later in this volume) as essentially its symbol. This is not to belittle the Romantic elements of the world, which are equally of its essence. But the vast exuberant energies and immeasurable possibilities of the first day may perhaps be best estimated when we have reached their final outcome on the sixth day of creation.

However that may be, the analogy of the two historical periods in question remains, and I believe that we may consider it holds good to the extent that the strictly mathematical elements of the later period are not the earliest to appear, but that we are in the presence of a process that has been in subtle movement in many fields for half a century. If it is significant that Descartes appeared a few years after Malherbe, it is equally significant that Einstein was immediately preceded by the Russian ballet. We gaze in admiration at the artist who sits at the organ, but we have been blowing the bellows; and the great performer's music would have been inaudible had it not been for us.

This is the spirit in which I have written. We are all engaged — not merely one or two prominent persons here and there — in creating the spiritual world. I have never written but with the thought that the reader, even though he may not know it, is already on my side. Only so could I write with that sincerity and simplicity without which it would not seem to me worth while to write at all. That may be seen in the saying which I set on the forefront of my earliest book, "The New Spirit": he who carries farthest his most intimate feelings is simply the first in file of a great number of other men, and one becomes typical by being to the utmost degree one's self. That saying I chose with much deliberation and complete conviction because it went to the root of my book. On the surface it obviously referred to the great figures I was there concerned with, representing what I regarded — by no means in the poor sense of mere modernity — as the New Spirit in life. They had all gone to the depths of their own souls and thence brought to the surface and expressed — audaciously or beautifully, pungently or poignantly — intimate impulses and emotions which, shocking as they may have seemed at the time, are now seen to be those of an innumerable company of their fellow men and women. But it was also a book of personal affirmations. Beneath the obvious meaning of that motto on the title-page lay the more private meaning that I was myself setting forth secret impulses which might some day be found to express the emotions also of others. In the thirty-five years that have since passed, the saying has often recurred to my mind, and if I have sought in

vain to make it mine I find no adequate justification
for the work of my life.

And now, as I said at the outset, I am even prepared
to think that that is the function of all books that are
real books. There are other classes of so-called books:
there is the class of history books and the class of foren-
sic books, that is to say, the books of facts and the
books of argument. No one would wish to belittle
either kind. But when we think of a book proper, in
the sense that a Bible means a book, we mean more
than this. We mean, that is to say, a revelation of
something that had remained latent, unconscious, perhaps even more or less intentionally repressed, within
the writer's own soul, which is, ultimately, the soul of
mankind. These books are apt to repel; nothing, indeed, is so likely to shock us at first as the manifest revelation of ourselves. Therefore, such books may have
to knock again and again at the closed door of our
hearts. "Who is there?" we carelessly cry, and we
cannot open the door; we bid the importunate stranger,
whatever he may be, to go away; until, as in the apo-
logue of the Persian mystic, at last we seem to hear the
voice outside saying: "It is thyself."

H. E.

CONTENTS

I. Introduction   1

II. The Art of Dancing   36

III. The Art of Thinking   68

IV. The Art of Writing   141

V. The Art of Religion   191

VI. The Art of Morals   244

VII. Conclusion   285

Index   359

THE DANCE OF LIFE

.:.

CHAPTER I

INTRODUCTION

I

It has always been difficult for Man to realise that his life is all an art. It has been more difficult to conceive it so than to act it so. For that is always how he has more or less acted it. At the beginning, indeed, the primitive philosopher whose business it was to account for the origin of things usually came to the conclusion that the whole universe was a work of art, created by some Supreme Artist, in the way of artists, out of material that was practically nothing, even out of his own excretions, a method which, as children sometimes instinctively feel, is a kind of creative art. The most familiar to us of these primitive philosophical statements — and really a statement that is as typical as any — is that of the Hebrews in the first chapter of their Book of Genesis. We read there how the whole cosmos was fashioned out of nothing, in a measurable period of time by the art of one Jehovah, who proceeded methodically by first forming it in the rough, and gradually working in the details, the finest and most delicate last, just as a sculptor might fashion a statue. We may find many statements of the like kind even as far away as the Pacific.[1] And — also even at the same distance — the artist and the craftsman, who resembled the divine creator of the world by making the most beautiful and useful things for Mankind, himself also partook of the same divine nature. Thus, in Samoa, as also in Tonga, the carpenter, who built canoes, occupied a high and almost sacred position, approaching that of the priest. Even among ourselves, with our Roman traditions, the name Pontiff, or Bridge-Builder, remains that of an imposing and hieratic personage.

But that is only the primitive view of the world. When Man developed, when he became more scientific and more moralistic, however much his practice remained essentially that of the artist, his conception became much less so. He was learning to discover the mystery of measurement; he was approaching the beginnings of geometry and mathematics; he was at the same time becoming warlike. So he saw things in straight lines, more rigidly; he formulated laws and commandments. It was, Einstein assures us, the right way. But it was, at all events in the first place, most unfavourable to the view of life as an art. It remains so even to-day.

Yet there are always some who, deliberately or by instinct, have perceived the immense significance in

[1] See, for instance, Turner's *Samoa*, chap. I. Usually, however, in the Pacific, creation was accomplished, in a more genuinely evolutionary manner, by a long series of progressive generations.

life of the conception of art. That is especially so as regards the finest thinkers of the two countries which, so far as we may divine, — however difficult it may here be to speak positively and by demonstration, — have had the finest civilisations, China and Greece. The wisest and most recognisably greatest practical philosophers of both these lands have believed that the whole of life, even government, is an art of definitely like kind with the other arts, such as that of music or the dance. We may, for instance, recall to memory one of the most typical of Greeks. Of Protagoras, calumniated by Plato, — though, it is interesting to observe that Plato's own transcendental doctrine of Ideas has been regarded as an effort to escape from the solvent influence of Protagoras' logic, — it is possible for the modern historian of philosophy to say that "the greatness of this man can scarcely be measured." It was with measurement that his most famous saying was concerned: "Man is the measure of all things, of those which exist and of those which have no existence." It was by his insistence on Man as the active creator of life and knowledge, the artist of the world, moulding it it to his own measure, that Protagoras is interesting to us to-day. He recognised that there are no absolute criteria by which to judge actions. He was the father of relativism and of phenomenalism, probably the initiator of the modern doctrine that the definitions of geometry are only approximately true abstractions from empirical experiences. We need not, and probably should not, suppose that in undermining dogmatism he was setting up an individual subjectivism. It was the function of Man in the world, rather than of the individual, that he had in mind when he enunciated his great principle, and it was with the reduction of human activity and conduct to art that he was mainly concerned. His projects for the art of living began with speech, and he was a pioneer in the arts of language, the initiator of modern grammar. He wrote treatises on many special arts, as well as the general treatise "On the Art" among the pseudo-Hippocratic writings, — if we may with Gomperz attribute it to him, — which embodies the spirit of modern positive science.[1]

Hippias, the philosopher of Elis, a contemporary of Protagoras, and like him commonly classed among the "Sophists," cultivated the largest ideal of life as an art which embraced all arts, common to all mankind as a fellowship of brothers, and at one with natural law which transcends the convention of human laws. Plato made fun of him, and that was not hard to do, for a philosopher who conceived the art of living as so large could not possibly at every point adequately play at it. But at this distance it is his ideal that mainly concerns us, and he really was highly accomplished, even a pioneer, in many of the multifarious activities he undertook. He was a remarkable mathematician; he was an astronomer and geometer; he was a copious

[1] Gomperz, *Greek Thinkers*, vol. I, book III, chap. VI.

poet in the most diverse modes, and, moreover, wrote on phonetics, rhythm, music, and mnemonics; he discussed the theories of sculpture and painting; he was both mythologist and ethnologist, as well as a student of chronology; he had mastered many of the artistic crafts. On one occasion, it is said, he appeared at the Olympic gathering in garments which, from the sandals on his feet to the girdle round his waist and the rings on his fingers, had been made by his own hands. Such a being of kaleidoscopic versatility, Gomperz remarks, we call contemptuously a Jack-of-all-trades. We believe in subordinating a man to his work. But other ages have judged differently. The fellow citizens of Hippias thought him worthy to be their ambassador to the Peloponnesus. In another age of immense human activity, the Renaissance, the vast-ranging energies of Leo Alberti were honoured, and in yet a later like age, Diderot—Pantophile as Voltaire called him—displayed a like fiery energy of wide-ranging interests, although it was no longer possible to attain the same level of wide-ranging accomplishment. Of course the work of Hippias was of unequal value, but some of it was of firm quality and he shrank from no labour. He seems to have possessed a gracious modesty, quite unlike the conceited pomposity Plato was pleased to attribute to him. He attached more importance than was common among the Greeks to devotion to truth, and he was cosmopolitan in spirit. He was famous for his distinction between Convention and Nature, and Plato put into his mouth the words: "All of you who are here present I reckon to be kinsmen and friends and fellow citizens, and by nature, not by law; for by nature like is akin to like, whereas law is the tyrant of mankind, and often compels us to do many things that are against nature." Hippias was in the line of those whose supreme ideal is totality of existence. Ulysses, as Benn remarks, was in Greek myth the representative of the ideal, and its supreme representative in real life has in modern times been Goethe.[1]

II

BUT, in actual fact, is life essentially an art? Let us look at the matter more closely, and see what life is like, as people have lived it. This is the more necessary to do since, to-day at all events, there are simple-minded people — well-meaning honest people whom we should not ignore — who pooh-pooh such an idea. They point to the eccentric individuals in our Western civilisation who make a little idol they call "Art," and fall down and worship it, sing incomprehensible chants in its honour, and spend most of their time in pouring

[1] I have here mainly followed Gomperz (*Greek Thinkers*, vol. I, pp. 430–34); there is not now, however, much controversy over the position of Hippias, which there is now, indeed, rather a tendency to exaggerate, considering how small is the basis of knowledge we possess. Thus Dupréel (*La Légende Socratique*, p. 432), regarding him as the most misunderstood of the great Sophists, declares that Hippias is "the thinker who conceived the universality of science, just as Prodicus caught glimpses of the synthesis of the social sciences. Hippias is the philosopher of science, the Great Logician, just as Prodicus is the Great Moralist." He compares him to Pico della Mirandola as a Humanist and to Leibnitz in power of wide synthesis.

contempt on the people who refuse to recognise that this worship of "Art" is the one thing needed for what they may or may not call the "moral uplift" of the age they live in. We must avoid the error of the good simple-minded folk in whose eyes these "Arty" people loom so large. They are not large, they are merely the morbid symptoms of a social disease; they are the fantastic reaction of a society which as a whole has ceased to move along the true course of any real and living art. For that has nothing to do with the eccentricities of a small religious sect worshipping in a Little Bethel; it is the large movement of the common life of a community, indeed simply the outward and visible form of that life.

Thus the whole conception of art has been so narrowed and so debased among us that, on the one hand, the use of the word in its large and natural sense seems either unintelligible or eccentric, while, on the other hand, even if accepted, it still remains so unfamiliar that its immense significance for our whole vision of life in the world is scarcely at first seen. This is not altogether due to our natural obtusity, or to the absence of a due elimination of subnormal stocks among us, however much we may be pleased to attribute to that dysgenic factor. It seems largely inevitable. That is to say that, so far as we in our modern civilisation are concerned, it is the outcome of the social process of two thousand years, the result of the break-up of the classic tradition of thought into various parts

which under post-classic influences have been pursued
separately.[1] Religion or the desire for the salvation of
our souls, "Art" or the desire for beautification,
Science or the search for the reasons of things —
these conations of the mind, which are really three
aspects of the same profound impulse, have been
allowed to furrow each its own narrow separate
channel, in alienation from the others, and so they
have all been impeded in their greater function of
fertilising life.

It is interesting to observe, I may note in passing,
how totally new an aspect a phenomenon may take on
when transformed from some other channel into that
of art. We may take, for instance, that remarkable
phenomenon called Napoleon, as impressive an individualistic manifestation as we could well find in
human history during recent centuries, and consider
two contemporary, almost simultaneous, estimates of
it. A distinguished English writer, Mr. H. G. Wells, in
a notable and even famous book, his "Outline of
History," sets down a judgment of Napoleon throughout a whole chapter. Now Mr. Wells moves in the
ethico-religious channel. He wakes up every morning,
it is said, with a rule for the guidance of life; some of his

[1] Strictly speaking, in the technical sense of that much-abused word,
this is "decadence." (I refer to the sense in which I defined "decadence"
many years ago in *Affirmations*, pp. 175–87.) So that while the minor
arts have sometimes been classic and sometimes decadent, the major art
of living during the last two thousand years, although one can think of
great men who have maintained the larger classic ideal, has mainly been
decadent.

critics say that it is every morning a new rule, and others that the rule is neither ethical nor religious; but we are here concerned only with the channel and not with the direction of the stream. In the "Outline" Mr. Wells pronounces his ethico-religious anathema of Napoleon, "this dark little archaic personage, hard, compact, capable, unscrupulous, imitative, and neatly vulgar." The "archaic" — the old-fashioned, out-worn — element attributed to Napoleon, is accentuated again later, for Mr. Wells has an extremely low opinion (hardly justifiable, one may remark in passing) of primitive man. Napoleon was "a reminder of ancient evils, a thing like the bacterium of some pestilence"; "the figure he makes in history is one of almost incredible self-conceit, of vanity, greed, and cunning, of callous contempt and disregard of all who trusted him." There is no figure, Mr. Wells asserts, so completely antithetical to the figure of Jesus of Nazareth. He was "a scoundrel, bright and complete."

There is no occasion to question this condemnation when we place ourselves in the channel along which Mr. Wells moves; it is probably inevitable; we may even accept it heartily. Yet, however right along that line, that is not the only line in which we may move. Moreover — and this is the point which concerns us — it is possible to enter a sphere in which no such merely negative, condemnatory, and dissatisfying a conclusion need be reached. For obviously it is dissatisfying. It is not finally acceptable that so supreme a protagonist of humanity, acclaimed by millions, of whom many gladly died for him, and still occupying so large and glorious a place in the human imagination, should be dismissed in the end as merely an unmitigated scoundrel. For so to condemn him is to condemn Man who made him what he was. He must have answered some lyric cry in the human heart. That other sphere in which Napoleon wears a different aspect is the sphere of art in the larger and fundamental sense. Élie Faure, a French critic, an excellent historian of art in the ordinary sense, is able also to grasp art in the larger sense because he is not only a man of letters but of science, a man with medical training and experience, who has lived in the open world, not, as the critic of literature and art so often appears to be, a man living in a damp cellar. Just after Wells issued his "Outline," Élie Faure, who probably knew nothing about it since he reads no English, published a book on Napoleon which some may consider the most remarkable book on that subject they have ever come across. For to Faure Napoleon is a great lyric artist.

It is hard not to believe that Faure had Wells's chapter on Napoleon open before him, he speaks so much to the point. He entitled the first chapter of his "Napoléon" "Jesus and He," and at once pierces to what Wells, too, had perceived to be the core of the matter in hand: "From the point of view of morality he is not to be defended and is even incomprehensible.

In fact he violates law, he kills, he sows vengeance and death. But also he dictates law, he tracks and crushes crime, he establishes order everywhere. He is an assassin. He is also a judge. In the ranks he would deserve the rope. At the summit he is pure, distributing recompense and punishment with a firm hand. He is a monster with two faces, like all of us perhaps, in any case like God, for those who have praised Napoleon and those who have blamed him have alike not understood that the Devil is the other face of God." From the moral point of view, Faure says (just as Wells had said), Napoleon is Antichrist. But from this standpoint of art, all grows clear. He is a poet of action, as Jesus was, and like him he stands apart. These two, and these two alone among the world's supremely great men of whom we have any definite knowledge, "acted out their dream instead of dreaming their action." It is possible that Napoleon himself was able to estimate the moral value of that acted dream. As he once stood before the grave of Rousseau, he observed: "It would have been better for the repose of France if that man and I had never existed." Yet we cannot be sure. "Is not repose the death of the world?" asks Faure. "Had not Rousseau and Napoleon precisely the mission of troubling that repose? In another of the profound and almost impersonal sayings that sometimes fell from his lips, Napoleon observed with a still deeper intuition of his own function in the world: "I love power. But it is as an artist that

I love it. I love it as a musician loves his violin, to draw out of it sounds and chords and harmonies. I love it as an artist." As an artist! These words were the inspiration of this finely illuminating study of Napoleon, which, while free from all desire to defend or admire, yet seems to explain Napoleon, in the larger sense to justify his right to a place in the human story, so imparting a final satisfaction which Wells, we feel, could he have escaped from the bonds of the narrow conception of life that bound him, had in him the spirit and the intelligence also to bestow upon us.

But it is time to turn from this aside. It is always possible to dispute about individuals, even when so happy an illustration chances to come before us. We are not here concerned with exceptional persons, but with the interpretation of general and normal human civilisations.

III

I TAKE, almost at random, the example of a primitive people. There are many others that would do as well or better. But this happens to come to hand, and it has the advantage not only of being a primitive people, but one living on an island, so possessing until lately its own little-impaired indigenous culture, as far as possible remote in space from our own; the record also has been made, as carefully and as impartially as one can well expect, by a missionary's wife who speaks from a knowledge covering over twenty years.[1] It is almost needless to add that she is as little concerned with any theory of the art of life as the people she is describing.

The Loyalty Islands lie to the east of New Caledonia, and have belonged to France for more than half a century. They are thus situated in much the same latitude as Egypt is in the Northern hemisphere, but with a climate tempered by the ocean. It is with the Island of Lifu that we are mainly concerned. There are no streams or mountains in this island, though a ridge of high rocks with large and beautiful caves contains stalactites and stalagmites and deep pools of fresh water; these pools, before the coming of the Christians, were the abode of the spirits of the departed, and therefore greatly reverenced. A dying man would say to his friends: "I will meet you all again in the caves where the stalactites are."

The Loyalty Islanders, who are of average European stature, are a handsome race, except for their thick lips and dilated nostrils, which, however, are much less pronounced than among African negroes. They have soft large brown eyes, wavy black hair, white teeth, and rich brown skin of varying depth. Each tribe has its own well-defined territory and its own chief. Al-

[1] Emma Hadfield, *Among the Natives of the Loyalty Group.* 1920. It would no doubt have been more satisfactory to select a people like the Fijians rather than the Lifuans, for they represented a more robust and accomplished form of a rather similar culture, but their culture has receded into the past,— and the same may be said of the Marquesans of whom Melville left, in *Typee,* a famous and delightful picture which other records confirm, — while that of the Lifuans is still recent.

though possessing high moral qualities, they are a
laughter-loving people, and neither their climate nor
their mode of life demands prolonged hard labour, but
they can work as well as the average Briton, if need be,
for several consecutive days, and, when the need is
over, lounge or ramble, sleep or talk. The basis of their
culture — and that is doubtless the significant fact for
us — is artistic. Every one learned music, dancing,
and song. Therefore it is natural for them to regard
rhythm and grace in all the actions of life, and almost
a matter of instinct to cultivate beauty in all social
relationships. Men and boys spent much time in
tattooing and polishing their brown skins, in dyeing
and dressing their long wavy hair (golden locks, as
much admired as they always have been in Europe,
being obtained by the use of lime), and in anointing
their bodies. These occupations were, of course, confined to the men, for man is naturally the ornamental
sex and woman the useful sex. The women gave no
attention to their hair, except to keep it short. It was
the men also who used oils and perfumes, not the
women, who, however, wore bracelets above the elbow
and beautiful long strings of jade beads. No clothing
is worn until the age of twenty-five or thirty, and then
all dress alike, except that chiefs fasten the girdle differently and wear more elaborate ornaments. These
people have sweet and musical voices and they cultivate them. They are good at learning languages and
they are great orators. The Lifuan language is soft and

liquid, one word running into another pleasantly to the ear, and it is so expressive that one may sometimes understand the meaning by the sound. In one of these islands, Uvea, so great is the eloquence of the people that they employ oratory to catch fish, whom indeed they regard in their legends as half human, and it is believed that a shoal of fish, when thus politely plied with compliments from a canoe, will eventually, and quite spontaneously, beach themselves spellbound.

For a primitive people the art of life is necessarily of large part concerned with eating. It is recognised that no one can go hungry when his neighbour has food, so no one was called upon to make any great demonstration of gratitude on receiving a gift. Help rendered to another was help to one's self, if it contributed to the common weal, and what I do for you to-day you will do for me to-morrow. There was implicit trust, and goods were left about without fear of theft, which was rare and punishable by death. It was not theft, however, if, when the owner was looking, one took an article one wanted. To tell a lie, also, with intent to deceive, was a serious offence, though to tell a lie when one was afraid to speak the truth was excusable. The Lifuans are fond of food, but much etiquette is practised in eating. The food must be conveyed to the mouth gracefully, daintily, leisurely. Every one helped himself to the food immediately in front of him, without hurry, without reaching out for dainty morsels (which were often offered to women), for every one looked

after his neighbour, and every one naturally felt that
he was his brother's keeper. So it was usual to invite
passers-by cordially to share in the repast. "In the
matter of food and eating," Mrs. Hadfield adds, "they
might put many of our countrymen to shame." Not
only must one never eat quickly, or notice dainties
that are not near one, but it would be indelicate to eat
in the presence of people who are not themselves eating. One must always share, however small one's portion, and one must do so pleasantly; one must accept
also what is offered, but slowly, reluctantly; having
accepted it, you may, if you like, openly pass it on to
some one else. In old days the Lifuans were, occasionally, cannibals, not, it would seem, either from necessity or any ritual reason, but because, like some peoples
elsewhere, they liked it, having, indeed, at times, a
kind of craving for animal food. If a man had twenty
or thirty wives and a large family, it would be quite
correct if, now and then, he cooked one of his own children, although presumably he might prefer that some
one else's child was chosen. The child would be cooked
whole, wrapped in banana or coconut leaves. The
social inconveniences of this practice have now been
recognised. But they still feel the utmost respect and
reverence for the dead and fail to find anything offen-
sive or repulsive in a corpse. "Why should there be,
seeing it was once our food?" Nor have they any fear
of death. To vermin they seem to have little objection, but otherwise they have a strong love of cleanli-

ness. The idea of using manure in agricultural operations seems to them disgusting, and they never do use it. "The sea was the public playground." Mothers take their little ones for sea-baths long before they can walk, and small children learn to swim as they learn to walk, without teaching. With their reverence for death is associated a reverence for old age. "Old age is a term of respect, and every one is pleased to be taken for older than he is since old age is honoured." Still, regard for others was general — not confined to the aged. In the church nowadays the lepers are seated on a separate bench, and when the bench is occupied by a leper healthy women will sometimes insist on sitting with him; they could not bear to see the old man sitting alone as though he had no friends. There was much demonstration on meeting friends after absence. A Lifuan always said "Olea" ("Thank you") for any good news, though not affecting him personally, as though it were a gift, for he was glad to be able to rejoice with another. Being divided into small tribes, each with its own autocratic chief, war was sometimes inevitable. It was attended by much etiquette, which was always strictly observed. The Lifuans were not acquainted with the civilised custom of making rules for warfare and breaking them when war actually broke out. Several days' notice must be given before hostilities were commenced. Women and children, in contrast to the practice of civilised warfare, were never molested. As soon as half a dozen fighters were put out of action on one side, the chief of that side would give the command to cease fighting and the war was over. An indemnity was then paid by the conquerors to the vanquished, and not, as among civilised peoples, by the vanquished to the conquerors. It was felt to be the conquered rather than the conqueror who needed consolation, and it also seemed desirable to show that no feeling of animosity was left behind. This was not only a delicate mark of consideration to the vanquished, but also very good policy, as, by neglecting it, some Europeans may have had cause to learn. This whole Lifuan art of living has, however, been undermined by the arrival of Christianity with its usual accompaniments. The Lifuans are substituting European vices for their own virtues. Their simplicity and confidence are passing away, though, even yet, Mrs. Hadfield says, they are conspicuous for their honesty, truthfulness, good-humour, kindness, and politeness, remaining a manly and intelligent people.

IV

THE Lifuans furnish an illustration which seems decisive. But they are savages, and on that account their example may be invalidated. It is well to take another illustration from a people whose high and long-continued civilisation is now undisputed.

The civilisation of China is ancient: that has long been a familiar fact. But for more than a thousand years it was merely a legend to Western Europeans;

none had ever reached China, or, if they had, they had never returned to tell the tale; there were too many fierce and jealous barbarians between the East and the West. It was not until the end of the thirteenth century, in the pages of Marco Polo, the Venetian Columbus of the East, — for it was an Italian who discovered the Old World as well as the New, — that China at last took definite shape alike as a concrete fact and a marvellous dream. Later, Italian and Portuguese travellers described it, and it is interesting to note what they had to say. Thus Perera in the sixteenth century, in a narrative which Willes translated for Hakluyt's "Voyages," presents a detailed picture of Chinese life with an admiration all the more impressive since we cannot help feeling how alien that civilisation was to the Catholic traveller and how many troubles he had himself to encounter. He is astonished, not only by the splendour of the lives of the Chinese on the material side, alike in large things and in small, but by their fine manners in all the ordinary course of life, the courtesy in which they seemed to him to exceed all other nations, and in the fair dealing which far surpassed that of all other Gentiles and Moors, while in the exercise of justice he found them superior even to many Christians, for they do justice to unknown strangers, which in Christendom is rare; moreover, there were hospitals in every city and no beggars were ever to be seen. It was a vision of splendour and delicacy and humanity, which he might have seen, here and there, in the courts of princes in Europe, but nowhere in the West on so vast a scale as in China.

The picture which Marco Polo, the first European to reach China (at all events in what we may call modern times), presented in the thirteenth century was yet more impressive, and that need not surprise us, for when he saw China it was still in its great Augustan age of the Sung Dynasty. He represents the city of Hang-Chau as the most beautiful and sumptuous in the world, and we must remember that he himself belonged to Venice, soon to be known as the most beautiful and sumptuous city of Europe, and had acquired no small knowledge of the world. As he describes its life, so exquisite and refined in its civilisation, so humane, so peaceful, so joyous, so well ordered, so happily shared by the whole population, we realise that here had been reached the highest point of urban civilisation to which Man has ever attained. Marco Polo can think of no word to apply to it — and that again and again — but Paradise.

The China of to-day seems less strange and astonishing to the Westerner. It may even seem akin to him — partly through its decline, partly through his own progress in civilisation — by virtue of its direct and practical character. That is the conclusion of a sensitive and thoughtful traveller in India and Japan and China, G. Lowes Dickinson. He is impressed by the friendliness, the profound humanity, the gaiety, of the Chinese, by the unequalled self-respect, independence, and courtesy of the common people. "The fundamental attitude of the Chinese towards life is, and has always been, that of the most modern West, nearer to us now than to our mediæval ancestors, infinitely nearer to us than India."[1]

So far it may seem scarcely as artists that these travellers regard the Chinese. They insist on their cheerful, practical, social, good-mannered, tolerant, peaceable, humane way of regarding life, on the remarkably educable spirit in which they are willing, and easily able, to change even ancient and deep-rooted habits when it seems convenient and beneficial to do so; they are willing to take the world lightly, and seem devoid of those obstinate conservative instincts by which we are guided in Europe. The "Resident in Peking" says they are the least romantic of peoples. He says it with a *nuance* of dispraise, but Lowes Dickinson says precisely the same thing about Chinese poetry, and with no such *nuance:* "It is of all poetry I know the most human and the least symbolic or romantic. It contemplates life just as it presents itself, without any veil of ideas, any rhetoric or sentiment; it simply clears away the obstruction which habit has

[1] G. Lowes Dickinson, *An Essay on the Cilivisations of India, China, and Japan* (1914), p. 47. No doubt there are shades to be added to this picture. They may be found in a book, published two years earlier, *China as it Really Is*, by "a Resident in Peking" who claims to have been born in China. Chinese culture has receded, in part swamped by over-population, and concerning a land where to-day, it has lately been said, "magnificence, crudity, delicacy, fetidity, and fragrance are blended," it is easy for Westerners to show violent difference of opinion.

built up between us and the beauty of things and leaves that, showing in its own nature." Every one who has learnt to enjoy Chinese poetry will appreciate the delicate precision of this comment. The quality of their poetry seems to fall into line with the simple, direct, childlike quality which all observers note in the Chinese themselves. The unsympathetic "Resident in Peking" describes the well-known etiquette of politeness in China: "A Chinaman will inquire of what noble country you are. You return the question, and he will say his lowly province is so-and-so. He will invite you to do him the honour of directing your jewelled feet to his degraded house. You reply that you, a discredited worm, will crawl into his magnificent palace." Life becomes all play. Ceremony — the Chinese are unequalled for ceremony, and a Government Department, the Board of Rites and Ceremonies, exists to administer it — is nothing but more or less crystallised play. Not only is ceremony here "almost an instinct," but, it has been said, "A Chinese thinks in theatrical terms." We are coming near to the sphere of art.

The quality of play in the Chinese character and Chinese civilisation has impressed alike them who have seen China from afar and by actual contact. It used to be said that the Chinese had invented gunpowder long before Europeans and done nothing with it but make fireworks. That seemed to the whole Western world a terrible blindness to the valuable uses of gunpowder,

and it is only of late years that a European com-
mentator has ventured to remark that "the proper use
of gunpowder is obviously to make fireworks, which
may be very beautiful things, not to kill men." Certainly the Chinese, at all events, appreciate to the full
this proper use of gunpowder. "One of the most
obvious characteristics of the Chinese is their love of
fireworks," we are told. The gravest people and the
most intellectual occupy themselves with fireworks,
and if the works of Bergson, in which pyrotechnical
allusions are so frequent, are ever translated into
Chinese, one can well believe that China will produce
enthusiastic Bergsonians. All toys are popular; everybody, it is said, buys toys of one sort or another: paper
windmills, rattles, Chinese lanterns, and of course
kites, which have an almost sacred significance. They
delight, also, in more complicated games of skill, including an elaborate form of chess, far more difficult
than ours.[1] It is unnecessary to add that to philosophy, a higher and more refined form of play, the Chinese
are peculiarly addicted, and philosophic discussion is
naturally woven in with an "art of exquisite enjoyment" — carried probably to greater perfection than
anywhere else in the world. Bertrand Russell, who
makes this remark, in the suggestive comments on his

[1] See, for instance, the chapter on games in Professor E. H. Parker's
China: Past and Present. Reference may be made to the same author's
important and impartial larger work, *China: Its History,* with a discriminating chapter on Chinese personal characteristics. Perhaps, the
most penetrating study of Chinese psychology is, however, Arthur H.
Smith's *Chinese Characteristics.*

own visit to China, observes how this simple, child-like, yet profound attitude towards life results in a liberation of the impulses to play and enjoyment which "makes Chinese life unbelievably restful and delightful after the solemn cruelties of the West." We are reminded of Gourmont's remark that "pleasure is a human creation, a delicate art, to which, as for music or painting, only a few are apt."

The social polity which brings together the people who thus view life is at once singular and appropriate. I well remember how in youth a new volume of the Sacred Books of the East Series, a part of the Confucian Lî-kî, came into my hands and how delighted I was to learn that in China life was regulated by music and ceremony. That was the beginning of an interest in China that has not ceased to grow, though now, when it has become a sort of fashion to exalt the spiritual qualities of the Chinese above those of other peoples, one may well feel disinclined to admit any interest in China. But the conception itself, since it seems to have had its beginning at least a thousand years before Christ, may properly be considered independently of our Western fashions. It is Propriety — the whole ceremony of life — in which all harmonious intercourse subsists; it is "the channel by which we apprehend the ways of Heaven," in no supernatural sense, for it is on the earth and not in the skies that the Confucian Heaven lies concealed. But if human feelings, the instincts — for in this matter the ancient

Chinese were at one with our modern psychologists, — are the field that has to be cultivated, and it is ceremony that ploughs it, and the seeds of right action that are to be planted on it, and discipline that is to weed it, and love that is to gather in the fruits, it is in music, and the joy and peace that accompany music, that it all ends. Indeed, it is also in music that it all begins. For the sphere in which ceremonies act is Man's external life; his internal life is the sphere of music. It is music that moulds the manners and customs that are comprised under ceremony, for Confucius held that there can be music without sound where "virtue is deep and silent"; and we are reminded of the "Crescendo of Silences" on the Chinese pavilion in Villiers de l'Isle Adam's story, "Le Secret de l'ancienne Musique." It is music that regulates the heart and mind and with that development brings joy, and joy brings repose. And so "Man became Heaven." "Let ceremonies and music have their course until the earth is filled with them!"

It is sometimes said that among Chinese moralists and philosophers Lao-tze, the deepest of them all, alone stands aside from the chorus in praise of music and ceremony. When once Confucius came to consult Lao-tze concerning the rules of propriety, and reverence for the teaching of the sages of antiquity, we are told, Lao-tze replied: "The men of whom you speak, sir, have, if you please, together with their bones, mouldered." Confucius went away, puzzled if not dissatisfied. He was willing to work not only from within outwards, but from without inwards, because he allowed so large a place for social solidity, for traditionalism, for paternalism, though he recognised that ceremony is subordinate in the scheme of life, as colour is in a painting, the picture being the real thing. Lao-tze was an individualist and a mystic. He was little concerned with moralities in the ordinary sense. He recognised no action but from within outwards. But though Confucius could scarcely have altogether grasped his conception, he was quite able to grasp that of Confucius, and his indifference to tradition, to rule and propriety was simply an insistence on essential reality, on "music." "Ceremonies," he said, "are the outward expression of inward feeling." He was no more opposed to the fundamental Chinese conception than George Fox was opposed to Christianity in refusing to observe the mere forms and ceremonies of the Church. A sound Confucianism is the outward manifestation of Taoism (as Lao-tze himself taught it), just as a sound socialism is the outward manifestation of a genuine individualism. It has been well said that Chinese socialistic solidarity rests on an individualistic basis, it is not a bureaucratic State socialism; it works from within outward. (One of the first European visitors to China remarked that there a street was like a home.) This is well shown by so great and typical a Chinese philosopher as Meh-ti,[1] who lived shortly

[1] His ideas have been studied by Madame Alexandra David, *Le Philosophe Meh-ti et l'Idée de Solidarité*. London, 1907.

after Confucius, in the fifth century B.C. He taught
universal love, with universal equality, and for him to
love meant to act. He admitted an element of self-
interest as a motive for such an attitude. He desired to
universalise mutual self-help. Following Confucius,
but yet several centuries before Jesus, he declared that
a man should love his neighbour, his fellow man, as
himself. "When he sees his fellow hungry, he feeds
him; when he sees him cold, he clothes him; ill, he
nurses him; dead, he buries him." This, he said, was
by no means opposed to filial piety; for if one cares for
the parents of others, they in turn will care for his.
But, it was brought against him, the power of egoism?
The Master agreed. Yet, he said, Man accepts more
difficult things. He can renounce joy, life itself, for
even absurd and ridiculous ends. A single generation,
he added, such is the power of imitation, might suffice
to change a people's customs. But Meh-ti remained
placid. He remarked that the great ones of the earth
were against human solidarity and equality; he left it
at that. He took no refuge in mysticism. Practical
social action was the sole end he had in view, and we
have to remember that his ideals are largely embodied
in Chinese institutions.[1]

We may understand now how it is that in China,
and in China alone among the great surviving civilisations, we find that art animates the whole of life, even
its morality. "This universal presence of art," remarks

[1] Eugène Simon, *La Cité Chinoise.*

an acute yet discriminating observer, Émile Hovelaque, whom I have already quoted,[1] "manifested in the smallest utensil, the humblest stalls, the notices on the shops, the handwriting, the rhythm of movement, always regular and measured, as though to the tune of unheard music, announces a civilisation which is complete in itself, elaborated in the smallest detail, penetrated by one spirit, which no interruption ever breaks, a harmony which becomes at length a hallucinatory and overwhelming obsession." Or, as another writer has summed up the Chinese attitude: "For them the art of life is one, as this world and the other are one. Their aim is to make the Kingdom of Heaven here and now."

It is obvious that a natural temperament in which the art-impulse is so all-embracing, and the æsthetic sensibility so acute, might well have been of a perilous instability. We could scarcely have been surprised if, like that surpassing episode in Egyptian history of which Akhenaten was the leader and Tell-el-Amarna the tomb, it had only endured for a moment. Yet Chinese civilisation, which has throughout shown the dominating power of this sensitive temperament, has lasted longer than any other. The reason is that the very excesses of their temperament forced the Chinese to fortify themselves against its perils. The Great Wall, built more than two thousand years ago, and still to-day almost the most impressive work of man on

[1] E. Hovelaque, *La Chine* (Paris, 1920), p. 47.

the earth, is typical of this attitude of the Chinese. They have exercised a stupendous energy in fortifying themselves against the natural enemies of their own temperament. When one looks at it from this point of view, it is easy to see that, alike in its large outlines and its small details, Chinese life is always the art of balancing an æsthetic temperament and guarding against its excesses. We see this in the whole of the ancient and still prevailing system of Confucian morality with its insistence on formal ceremony, even when, departing from the thought of its most influential founder, — for ceremonialism in China would have existed even if Confucius had not lived, — it tended to become merely an external formalism. We see it in the massive solidarity of Chinese life, the systematic social organisation by which individual responsibility, even though leaving individuality itself intact, is merged in the responsibility of the family and the still larger group. We see it in the whole drift of Chinese philosophy, which is throughout sedative and contemplative. We see it in the element of stoicism on the one hand and cruelty on the other which in so genuinely good-natured a people would otherwise seem puzzling. The Chinese love of flowers and gardens and landscape scenery is in the same direction, and indeed one may say much the same of Chinese painting and Chinese poetry.[1] That is why it is only to-day that we in the

[1] This point has not escaped the more acute students of Chinese civilisation. Thus Dr. John Steele, in his edition of the *I-Li*, remarks

West have reached the point of nervous susceptibility which enables us in some degree to comprehend the æsthetic supremacy which the Chinese reached more than a thousand years ago.

Thus, during its extremely long history — for the other great civilisations with which it was once contemporary have passed away or been disintegrated and transformed — Chinese civilisation has borne witness to the great fact that all human life is art. It may be because they have realised this so thoroughly that the Chinese have been able to preserve their civilisation so long, through all the violent shocks to which it has been subjected. There can be no doubt, however, that, during the greater part of the last thousand years, there has been, however slow and gradual, a decline in the vitality of Chinese civilisation, largely due, it may well be, to the crushing pressure of an excessive population. For, however remarkable the admiration which China arouses even to-day, its finest flowering periods in the special arts lie far in the past, while in the art of living itself the Chinese have long grown languid. The different reports of ancient and modern travellers

that "ceremonial was far from being a series of observances, empty and unprofitable, such as it degenerated into in later time. It was meant to inculcate that habit of self-control and ordered action which was the expression of a mind fully instructed in the inner meaning of things, and sensitive to every impression." Still more clearly, Reginald Farrer wrote, in *On the Eaves of the World*, that "the philosophic calm that the Chinese deliberately cultivate is their necessary armour to protect the excessive susceptibility to emotion. The Chinese would be for ever the victims of their nerves had they not for four thousand years pursued reason and self-control with self-protective enthusiasm."

regarding one definite social manifestation, the prevalence of beggary, cannot fail to tell us something regarding the significant form of their social life. Modern travellers complain of the plague constituted by the prevalence of beggars in China; they are even a fixed and permanent institution on a trades-union basis. But in the sixteenth century Galeotto Perera noticed with surprise in China the absence of beggars, as Marco Polo had before him, and Friar Gaspar de Cruz remarked that the Chinese so abhorred idleness that they gave no alms to the poor and mocked at the Portuguese for doing so: "Why give alms to a knave? Let him go and earn it." Their own priests, he adds, they sometimes whipped as being knaves. (It should be noted at the same time that it was considered reasonable only to give half the day to work, the other half to joy and recreation.) But they built great asylums for the helpless poor, and found employment for blind women, gorgeously dressed and painted with ceruse and vermilion, as prostitutes, who were more esteemed in early China than they have been since. That is a curious instance of the unflinching practicality still shown by the Chinese in endless ways. The undoubted lassitude in the later phases of this long-lived Chinese culture has led to features in the art of life, such as beggary and dirt among the poor, not manifested in the younger offshoot of Chinese and Korean culture in Japan, though it is only fair to point out that impartial English observers, like Parker, consider this prevalence of vermin and dirt as simply due to the prevalence of poverty, and not greater than we find among the poor in England and elsewhere in the West. Marco Polo speaks of three hundred public baths in one city alone in his time. We note also that in the more specialised arts the transcendence of China belongs to the past, and even sometimes a remote past. It is so in the art of philosophy, and the arts of poetry and painting. It is so also in the art of pottery, in which Chinese supremacy over the rest of the world has been longest recognised — has not the word "china" for centuries been our name for the finest pottery? — and is most beyond measure. Our knowledge of the pottery of various cultures excels that of any other human products because of all it is the most perdurable. We can better estimate their relative æsthetic worth now than in the days when a general reverence for Greek antiquity led to a popular belief in the beauty of Greek pottery, though scarcely a single type of its many forms can fairly be so considered or even be compared to the products of the Minoan predecessors of Greek culture, however interesting they may still remain for us as the awkward and inappropriate foundation for exquisite little pictures. The greatest age of this universal human art was in China and was over many centuries ago. But with what devotion, with what absolute concentration of the spirit, the Chinese potters of the great period struggled with the problem of art is finely illustrated by the well-known story which an old Chinese historian tells of the sacrifice of the divine T'ung, the spirit who protects potters. It happened that a complicated problem had baffled the potters. T'ung laid down his life to serve them and to achieve the solution of the problem. He plunged into the fire and the bowl came out perfect. "The vessel's perfect glaze is the god's fat and blood; the body material is the god's body of flesh; the blue of the decoration, with the brilliant lustre of gems, is the essence of the god's pure spirit." That story embodies the Chinese symbol of the art of living, just as we embody our symbol of that art in the Crucifixion of Jesus. The form is diverse; the essence is the same.

V

It will be seen that when we analyse the experiences of life and look at it simply, in the old-fashioned way, liberated from the artificial complexities of a temporary and now, it may be, departing civilisation, what we find is easy to sum up. We find, that is to say, that Man has forced himself to move along this line, and that line, and the other line. But it is the same water of life that runs in all these channels. Until we have ascended to a height where this is clear, to see all our little dogmatisms will but lead us astray.

We may illuminatingly change the analogy and turn to the field of chemistry. All these various elements of life are but, as it were, allotropic forms of the same element. The most fundamental among these forms is that of art, for life in all its forms, even morality in the narrowest sense, is, as Duprat has argued, a matter of technique, and technique at once brings us to the elements of art. If we would understand what we are dealing with, we may, therefore, best study these forms under that of art.

There is, however, a deeper chemical analogy than this to be seen. It may well be, indeed, that it is more than an analogy. In chemistry we are dealing, not merely with the elements of life, but with the elements of the world, even of what we call our universe. It is not unreasonable to think that the same law holds good for both. We see that the forms of life may all be found, and then better understood, in one form. Some day, perhaps, we shall also see that that fact is only a corollary of the larger fact — or, if any one prefers so to regard it, the smaller fact — that the chemical elements of our world can be regarded as all only transmutations of one element. From of old, men instinctively divined that this might be so, though they were merely concerned to change the elements into gold, the element which they most highly valued. In our own times this transmutation is beginning to become, on a minute scale, a demonstrable fact, though it would seem easier to transmute elements into lead than into gold. Matter, we are thus coming to see, may not be a confused variety of separate substances, but simply a different quantitative arrangement of a single fundamental stuff, which might possibly be identical with hydrogen or some other already known element. Similarly we may now believe that the men of old who thought that all human life was made of one stuff were not altogether wrong, and we may, with greater assurance than they were able to claim, analyse the modes of human action into different quantitative or other arrangements of which the most fundamental may well be identical with art.

This may perhaps become clearer if we consider more in detail one of the separate arts, selecting the most widely symbolic of all, the art that is most clearly made of the stuff of life, and so able to translate most truly and clearly into beautiful form the various modalities of life.

CHAPTER II
THE ART OF DANCING

I

DANCING and building are the two primary and essential arts. The art of dancing stands at the source of all the arts that express themselves first in the human person. The art of building, or architecture, is the beginning of all the arts that lie outside the person; and in the end they unite. Music, acting, poetry proceed in the one mighty stream; sculpture, painting, all the arts of design, in the other. There is no primary art outside these two arts, for their origin is far earlier than man himself; and dancing came first.[1]

That is one reason why dancing, however it may at times be scorned by passing fashions, has a profound and eternal attraction even for those one might suppose farthest from its influence. The joyous beat of the feet of children, the cosmic play of philosophers' thoughts rise and fall according to the same laws of rhythm. If we are indifferent to the art of dancing, we have failed to understand, not merely the supreme manifestation of physical life, but also the supreme symbol of spiritual life.

[1] It is even possible that, in earlier than human times, dancing and architecture may have been the result of the same impulse. The nest of birds is the chief early form of building, and Edmund Selous has suggested (*Zoölogist*, December, 1901) that the nest may first have arisen as an accidental result of the ecstatic sexual dance of birds.

The significance of dancing, in the wide sense, thus lies in the fact that it is simply an intimate concrete appeal of a general rhythm, that general rhythm which marks, not life only, but the universe, if one may still be allowed so to name the sum of the cosmic influences that reach us. We need not, indeed, go so far as the planets or the stars and outline their ethereal dances. We have but to stand on the seashore and watch the waves that beat at our feet, to observe that at nearly regular intervals this seemingly monotonous rhythm is accentuated for several beats, so that the waves are really dancing the measure of a tune. It need surprise us not at all that rhythm, ever tending to be moulded into a tune, should mark all the physical and spiritual manifestations of life. Dancing is the primitive expression alike of religion and of love — of religion from the earliest human times we know of and of love from a period long anterior to the coming of man. The art of dancing, moreover, is intimately entwined with all human tradition of war, of labour, of pleasure, of education, while some of the wisest philosophers and the most ancient civilisations have regarded the dance as the pattern in accordance with which the moral life of men must be woven. To realise, therefore, what dancing means for mankind — the poignancy and the many-sidedness of its appeal — we must survey the whole sweep of human life, both at its highest and at its deepest moments.

II

"WHAT do you dance?" When a man belonging to one branch of the great Bantu division of mankind met a member of another, said Livingstone, that was the question he asked. What a man danced, that was his tribe, his social customs, his religion; for, as an anthropologist has put it, "a savage does not preach his religion, he dances it."

There are peoples in the world who have no secular dances, only religious dances; and some investigators believe with Gerland that every dance was of religious origin. That view may seem too extreme, even if we admit that some even of our modern dances, like the waltz, may have been originally religious. Even still (as Skene has shown among the Arabs and Swahili of Africa) so various are dances and their functions among some peoples that they cover the larger part of life. Yet we have to remember that for primitive man there is no such thing as religion apart from life, for religion covers everything. Dancing is a magical operation for the attainment of real and important ends of every kind. It was clearly of immense benefit to the individual and to society, by imparting strength and adding organised harmony. It seemed reasonable to suppose that it attained other beneficial ends, that were incalculable, for calling down blessings or warding off misfortunes. We may conclude, with Wundt, that the dance was, in the beginning, the expression of the whole man, for the whole man was religious.[1]

Thus, among primitive peoples, religion being so large a part of life, the dance inevitably becomes of supreme religious importance. To dance was at once both to worship and to pray. Just as we still find in our Prayer Books that there are divine services for all the great fundamental acts of life, — for birth, for marriage, for death, — as well as for the cosmic procession of the world as marked by ecclesiastical festivals, and for the great catastrophes of nature, such as droughts, so also it has ever been among primitive peoples. For all the solemn occasions of life, for bridals and for funerals, for seed-time and for harvest, for war and for peace, for all these things there were fitting dances. To-day we find religious people who in church pray for rain or for the restoration of their friends to health. Their forefathers also desired these things, but, instead of praying for them, they danced for them the fitting dance which tradition had handed down, and which the chief or the medicine-man solemnly conducted. The gods themselves danced, as the stars dance in the sky — so at least the Mexicans, and we may be sure many other peoples, have held; and to dance is there-

[1] "Not the epic song, but the dance," Wundt says (*Völkerpsychologie*, 3d ed. 1911, Bd. i, Teil i, p. 277), "accompanied by a monotonous and often meaningless song, constitutes everywhere the most primitive, and, in spite of that primitiveness, the most highly developed art. Whether as a ritual dance, or as a pure emotional expression of the joy in rhythmic bodily movement, it rules the life of primitive men to such a degree that all other forms of art are subordinate to it."

fore to imitate the gods, to work with them, perhaps to persuade them to work in the direction of our own desires. "Work for us!" is the song-refrain, expressed or implied, of every religious dance. In the worship of solar deities in various countries, it was customary to dance round the altar, as the stars dance round the sun. Even in Europe the popular belief that the sun dances on Easter Sunday has perhaps scarcely yet died out. To dance is to take part in the cosmic control of the world. Every sacred dionysian dance is an imitation of the divine dance.

All religions, and not merely those of primitive character, have been at the outset, and sometimes throughout, in some measure saltatory. That was recognised even in the ancient world by acute observers, like Lucian, who remarks in his essay on dancing that "you cannot find a single ancient mystery in which there is no dancing; in fact most people say of the devotees of the Mysteries that 'they dance them out.'" This is so all over the world. It is not more pronounced in early Christianity, and among the ancient Hebrews who danced before the ark, than among the Australian aborigines whose great corroborees are religious dances conducted by the medicine-men with their sacred staves in their hands. Every American Indian tribe seems to have had its own religious dances, varied and elaborate, often with a richness of meaning which the patient study of modern investigators has but slowly revealed. The Shamans in the remote steppes of Northern Siberia have their ecstatic religious dances, and in modern Europe the Turkish dervishes — perhaps of related stock — still dance in their cloisters similar ecstatic dances, combined with song and prayer, as a regular part of devotional service.

These religious dances, it may be observed, are sometimes ecstatic, sometimes pantomimic. It is natural that this should be so. By each road it is possible to penetrate towards the divine mystery of the world. The auto-intoxication of rapturous movement brings the devotees, for a while at least, into that self-forgetful union with the not-self which the mystic ever seeks. The ecstatic Hindu dance in honour of the pre-Aryan hill god, afterwards Siva, became in time a great symbol, "the clearest image of the *activity* of God," it has been called, "which any art or religion can boast of."[1] Pantomimic dances, on the other hand, with their effort to heighten natural expression and to imitate natural process, bring the dancers into the divine sphere of creation and enable them to assist vicariously in the energy of the gods. The dance thus becomes the presentation of a divine drama, the vital reënactment of a sacred history, in which the worshipper is enabled to play a real part.[2] In this way ritual arises.

[1] See an interesting essay in *The Dance of Siva: Fourteen Indian Essays*, by Ananda Coomaraswamy. New York, 1918.

[2] This view was clearly put forward, long ago, by W. W. Newell at the International Congress of Anthropology at Chicago in 1893. It has become almost a commonplace since.

It is in this sphere — highly primitive as it is — of pantomimic dancing crystallised in ritual, rather than in the sphere of ecstatic dancing, that we may to-day in civilisation witness the survivals of the dance in religion. The divine services of the American Indian, said Lewis Morgan, took the form of "set dances, each with its own name, songs, steps, and costume." At this point the early Christian, worshipping the Divine Body, was able to join in spiritual communion with the ancient Egyptian or the later Japanese [1] or the modern American Indian. They are all alike privileged to enter, each in his own way, a sacred mystery, and to participate in the sacrifice of a heavenly Mass.

What by some is considered to be the earliest known Christian ritual — the "Hymn of Jesus" assigned to the second century — is nothing but a sacred dance. Eusebius in the third century stated that Philo's description of the worship of the Therapeuts agreed at all points with Christian custom, and that meant the prominence of dancing, to which indeed Eusebius often refers in connection with Christian worship. It has been supposed by some that the Christian Church was originally a theatre, the choir being the raised stage, even the word "choir," it is argued, meaning an enclosed space for dancing. It is certain that at the

---

[1] See a charming paper by Marcella Azra Hincks, "The Art of Dancing in Japan," *Fortnightly Review*, July, 1906. Pantomimic dancing, which has played a highly important part in Japan, was introduced into religion from China, it is said, in the earliest time, and was not adapted to secular purposes until the sixteenth century.

Eucharist the faithful gesticulated with their hands, danced with their feet, flung their bodies about. Chrysostom, who referred to this behaviour round the Holy Table at Antioch, only objected to drunken excesses in connection with it; the custom itself he evidently regarded as traditional and right.

While the central function of Christian worship is a sacred drama, a divine pantomime, the associations of Christianity and dancing are by no means confined to the ritual of the Mass and its later more attenuated transformations. The very idea of dancing had a sacred and mystic meaning to the early Christians, who had meditated profoundly on the text, "We have piped unto you and ye have not danced." Origen prayed that above all things there may be made operative in us the mystery "of the stars dancing in Heaven for the salvation of the Universe." So that the monks of the Cistercian Order, who in a later age worked for the world more especially by praying for it ("orare est laborare"), were engaged in the same task on earth as the stars in Heaven; dancing and praying are the same thing. St. Basil, who was so enamoured of natural things, described the angels dancing in Heaven, and later the author of the "Dieta Salutis" (said to have been St. Bonaventura), which is supposed to have influenced Dante in assigning so large a place to dancing in the "Paradiso," described dancing as the occupation of the inmates of Heaven, and Christ as the leader of the dance. Even in more modern times an ancient

Cornish carol sang of the life of Jesus as a dance, and represented him as declaring that he died in order that man "may come unto the general dance." [1]

This attitude could not fail to be reflected in practice. Genuine dancing, not merely formalised and unrecognisable dancing, such as the traditionalised Mass, must have been frequently introduced into Christian worship in early times. Until a few centuries ago it remained not uncommon, and it even still persists in remote corners of the Christian world. In English cathedrals dancing went on until the fourteenth century. At Paris, Limoges, and elsewhere in France, the priests danced in the choir at Easter up to the seventeenth century, in Roussillon up to the eighteenth century. Roussillon is a Catalan province with Spanish traditions, and it is in Spain, where dancing is a deeper and more passionate impulse than elsewhere in Europe, that religious dancing took firmest root and flourished longest. In the cathedrals of Seville, Toledo, Valencia, and Jeres there was formerly dancing, though it now only survives at a few special festivals in the first.[2] At Alaro in Mallorca, also at the present day, a dancing

[1] I owe some of these facts to an interesting article by G. R. Mead, "The Sacred Dance of Jesus," *The Quest*, October, 1910.

[2] The dance of the Seises in Seville Cathedral is evidently of great antiquity, though it was so much a matter of course that we do not hear of it until 1690, when the Archbishop of the day, in opposition to the Chapter, wished to suppress it. A decree of the King was finally obtained permitting it, provided it was performed only by men, so that evidently, before that date, girls as well as boys took part in it. Rev. John Morris, "Dancing in Churches," *The Month*, December, 1892; also a valuable article on the Seises by J. B. Trend, in *Music and Letters*, January, 1921.

company called Els Cosiers, on the festival of St. Roch, the patron saint of the place, dance in the church in fanciful costumes with tambourines, up to the steps of the high altar, immediately after Mass, and then dance out of the church. In another part of the Christian world, in the Abyssinian Church — an offshoot of the Eastern Church — dancing is also said still to form part of the worship.

Dancing, we may see throughout the world, has been so essential, so fundamental, a part of all vital and un-degenerate religion, that, whenever a new religion appears, a religion of the spirit and not merely an anæmic religion of the intellect, we should still have to ask of it the question of the Bantu: "What do you dance?"

III

DANCING is not only intimately associated with religion, it has an equally intimate association with love. Here, indeed, the relationship is even more primitive, for it is far older than man. Dancing, said Lucian, is as old as love. Among insects and among birds it may be said that dancing is often an essential part of love. In courtship the male dances, sometimes in rivalry with other males, in order to charm the female; then, after a short or long interval, the female is aroused to share his ardour and join in the dance; the final climax of the dance is the union of the lovers. Among the mammals most nearly related to man, indeed, dancing is but little developed: their energies are more variously diffused, though a close observer of the apes, Dr. Louis Robinson, has pointed out that the "spasmodic jerking of the chimpanzee's feeble legs," pounding the partition of his cage, is the crude motion out of which "the heavenly alchemy of evolution has created the divine movements of Pavlova"; but it must be remembered that the anthropoid apes are offshoots only from the stock that produced Man, his cousins and not his ancestors. It is the more primitive love-dance of insects and birds that seems to reappear among human savages in various parts of the world, notably in Africa, and in a conventionalised and symbolised form it is still danced in civilisation to-day. Indeed, it is in this aspect that dancing has so often aroused reprobation, from the days of early Christianity until the present, among those for whom the dance has merely been, in the words of a seventeenth-century writer, a series of "immodest and dissolute movements by which the cupidity of the flesh is aroused."

But in nature and among primitive peoples it has its value precisely on this account. It is a process of courtship and, even more than that, it is a novitiate for love, and a novitiate which was found to be an admirable training for love. Among some peoples, indeed, as the Omahas, the same word meant both to dance and to love. By his beauty, his energy, his skill, the male must win the female, so impressing the image of himself on her imagination that finally her desire is aroused to overcome her reticence. That is the task of the male throughout nature, and in innumerable species besides Man it has been found that the school in which the task may best be learnt is the dancing-school. Those who have not the skill and the strength to learn are left behind, and, as they are probably the least capable members of the race, it may be in this way that a kind of sexual selection has been embodied in unconscious eugenics, and aided the higher development of the race. The moths and the butterflies, the African ostrich and the Sumatran argus pheasant, with their fellows innumerable, have been the precursors of man in the strenuous school of erotic dancing, fitting themselves for selection by the females of their choice as the most splendid progenitors of the future race.[1]

From this point of view, it is clear, the dance performed a double function. On the one hand, the tendency to dance, arising under the obscure stress of this impulse, brought out the best possibilities the individual held the promise of; on the other hand, at the moment of courtship, the display of the activities thus acquired developed on the sensory side all the latent possibilities of beauty which at last became conscious in man. That this came about we cannot easily escape concluding. How it came about, how it happens that some of the least intelligent of creatures thus developed a beauty and a grace that are enchanting even to our

[1] See, for references, Havelock Ellis, *Studies in the Psychology of Sex*, vol. III; *Analysis of the Sexual Impulse*, pp. 29, etc.; and Westermarck, *History of Human Marriage*, vol. I, chap. XIII, p. 470.

human eyes, is a miracle, even if not affected by the mystery of sex, which we cannot yet comprehend.

When we survey the human world, the erotic dance of the animal world is seen not to have lost, but rather to have gained, influence. It is no longer the males alone who are thus competing for the love of the females. It comes about by a modification in the earlier method of selection that often not only the men dance for the women, but the women for the men, each striving in a storm of rivalry to arouse and attract the desire of the other. In innumerable parts of the world the season of love is a time which the nubile of each sex devote to dancing in each other's presence, sometimes one sex, sometimes the other, sometimes both, in the frantic effort to display all the force and energy, the skill and endurance, the beauty and grace, which at this moment are yearning within them to be poured into the stream of the race's life.

From this point of view we may better understand the immense ardour with which every part of the wonderful human body has been brought into the play of the dance. The men and women of races spread all over the world have shown a marvellous skill and patience in imparting rhythm and measure to the most unlikely, the most rebellious regions of the body, all wrought by desire into potent and dazzling images. To the vigorous races of Northern Europe in their cold damp climate, dancing comes naturally to be dancing of the legs, so naturally that the English poet, as a matter of course, assumes that the dance of Salome was a "twinkling of the feet." [1] But on the opposite side of the world, in Japan and notably in Java and Madagascar, dancing may be exclusively dancing of the arms and hands, in some of the South Sea Islands of the hands and fingers alone. Dancing may even be carried on in the seated posture, as occurs at Fiji in a dance connected with the preparation of the sacred drink, ava. In some districts of Southern Tunisia dancing, again, is dancing of the hair, and all night long, till they perhaps fall exhausted, the marriageable girls will move their heads to the rhythm of a song, maintaining their hair, in perpetual balance and sway. Elsewhere, notably in Africa, but also sometimes in Polynesia, as well as in the dances that had established themselves in ancient Rome, dancing is dancing of the body, with vibratory or rotatory movements of breasts or flanks. The complete dance along these lines is, however, that in which the play of all the chief muscle-groups of the body is harmoniously interwoven. When both sexes take part in such an exercise, developed into an idealised yet passionate pantomime of love, we have the complete erotic dance. In the beautiful ancient civilisation of the Pacific, it is probable that this ideal was

[1] At an earlier period, however, the dance of Salome was understood much more freely and often more accurately. As Enlart has pointed out, on a capital in the twelfth-century cloister of Moissac, Salome holds a kind of castanets in her raised hands as she dances; on one of the western portals of Rouen Cathedral, at the beginning of the sixteenth century, she is dancing on her hands; while at Hemelverdeghem she is really executing the *morisco*, the "*danse du ventre.*"

sometimes reached, and at Tahiti, in 1772, an old voyager crudely and summarily described the native dance as "an endless variety of posturings and wagglings of the body, hands, feet, eyes, lips, and tongue, in which they keep splendid time to the measure." In Spain the dance of this kind has sometimes attained its noblest and most harmoniously beautiful expression. From the narratives of travellers, it would appear that it was especially in the eighteenth century that among all classes in Spain dancing of this kind was popular. The Church tacitly encouraged it, an Aragonese Canon told Baretti in 1770, in spite of its occasional indecorum, as a useful safety-valve for the emotions. It was not less seductive to the foreign spectator than to the people themselves. The grave traveller Peyron, towards the end of the century, growing eloquent over the languorous and flexible movements of the dance, the bewitching attitude, the voluptuous curves of the arms, declares that, when one sees a beautiful Spanish woman dance, one is inclined to fling all philosophy to the winds. And even that highly respectable Anglican clergyman, the Reverend Joseph Townsend, was constrained to state that he could "almost persuade myself" that if the fandango were suddenly played in church the gravest worshippers would start up to join in that "lascivious pantomime." There we have the rock against which the primitive dance of sexual selection suffers shipwreck as civilisation advances. And that prejudice of civilisation becomes so ingrained that it is brought to bear even on the primitive dance. The pygmies of Africa are described by Sir H. H. Johnston as a very decorous and highly moral people, but their dances, he adds, are not so. Yet these dances, though to the eyes of Johnston, blinded by European civilisation, "grossly indecent," he honestly, and inconsistently, adds, are "danced reverently."

IV

FROM the vital function of dancing in love, and its sacred function in religion, to dancing as an art, a profession, an amusement, may seem, at the first glance, a sudden leap. In reality the transition is gradual, and it began to be made at a very early period in diverse parts of the globe. All the matters that enter into courtship tend to fall under the sway of art; their æsthetic pleasure is a secondary reflection of their primary vital joy. Dancing could not fail to be first in manifesting this tendency. But even religious dancing swiftly exhibited the same transformation; dancing, like priesthood, became a profession, and dancers, like priests, formed a caste. This, for instance, took place in old Hawaii. The hula dance was a religious dance; it required a special education and an arduous training; moreover, it involved the observance of important taboos and the exercise of sacred rites; by the very fact of its high specialisation it came to be carried out by paid performers, a professional caste. In India, again, the Devadasis, or sacred dancing girls, are at once both religious and professional dancers. They are married to gods, they are taught dancing by the Brahmins, they figure in religious ceremonies, and their dances represent the life of the god they are married to as well as the emotions of love they experience for him. Yet, at the same time, they also give professional performances in the houses of rich private persons who pay for them. It thus comes about that to the foreigner the Devadasis scarcely seem very unlike the Ramedjenis, the dancers of the street, who are of very different origin, and mimic in their performances the play of merely human passions. The Portuguese conquerors of India called both kinds of dancers indiscriminately Balheideras (or dancers) which we have corrupted in Bayaderes.[1]

In our modern world professional dancing as an art has become altogether divorced from religion, and even, in any biological sense, from love; it is scarcely even possible, so far as Western civilisation is concerned, to trace back the tradition to either source. If we survey the development of dancing as an art in Europe, it seems to me that we have to recognise two streams of tradition which have sometimes merged, but yet remain in their ideals and their tendencies essentially distinct. I would call these traditions the Classical, which is much the more ancient and fundamental, and may be said to be of Egyptian origin, and

---

[1] For an excellent account of dancing in India, now being degraded by modern civilisation, see Otto Rothfeld, *Women of India*, chap. VII, "The Dancing Girl," 1922.

the Romantic, which is of Italian origin, chiefly known to us as the ballet. The first is, in its pure form, solo dancing — though it may be danced in couples and many together — and is based on the rhythmic beauty and expressiveness of the simple human personality when its energy is concentrated in measured yet passionate movement. The second is concerted dancing, mimetic and picturesque, wherein the individual is subordinated to the wider and variegated rhythm of the group. It may be easy to devise another classification, but this is simple and instructive enough for our purpose.

There can scarcely be a doubt that Egypt has been for many thousands of years, as indeed it still remains, a great dancing centre, the most influential dancing-school the world has ever seen, radiating its influence to south and east and north. We may perhaps even agree with the historian of the dance who terms it "the mother-country of all civilised dancing." We are not entirely dependent on the ancient wall-pictures of Egypt for our knowledge of Egyptian skill in the art. Sacred mysteries, it is known, were danced in the temples, and queens and princesses took part in the orchestras that accompanied them. It is significant that the musical instruments still peculiarly associated with the dance were originated or developed in Egypt; the guitar is an Egyptian instrument and its name was a hieroglyph already used when the Pyramids were being built; the cymbal, the tambourine, triangles, castanets, in one form or another, were all familiar to the ancient Egyptians, and with the Egyptian art of dancing they must have spread all round the shores of the Mediterranean, the great focus of our civilisation, at a very early date.[1] Even beyond the Mediterranean, at Cadiz, dancing that was essentially Egyptian in character was established, and Cadiz became the dancing-school of Spain. The Nile and Cadiz were thus the two great centres of ancient dancing, and Martial mentions them both together, for each supplied its dancers to Rome. This dancing, alike whether Egyptian or Gaditanian, was the expression of the individual dancer's body and art; the garments played but a small part in it, they were frequently transparent, and sometimes discarded altogether. It was, and it remains, simple, personal, passionate dancing, classic, therefore, in the same sense as, on the side of literature, the poetry of Catullus is classic.[2]

[1] I may hazard the suggestion that the gypsies may possibly have acquired their rather unaccountable name of Egyptians, not so much because they had passed through Egypt, the reason which is generally suggested, — for they must have passed through many countries, — but because of their proficiency in dances of the recognised Egyptian type.

[2] It is interesting to observe that Egypt still retains, almost unchanged through fifty centuries, its traditions, technique, and skill in dancing, while, as in ancient Egyptian dancing, the garment forms an almost or quite negligible element in the art. Loret remarks that a charming Egyptian dancer of the Eighteenth Dynasty, whose picture in her transparent gauze he reproduces, is an exact portrait of a charming Almeh of to-day whom he has seen dancing in Thebes with the same figure, the same dressing of the hair, the same jewels. I hear from a physician, a gynæcologist now practising in Egypt, that a dancing-girl can lie on her back, and with a full glass of water standing on one side of her abdomen

Ancient Greek dancing was essentially classic dancing, as here understood. On the Greek vases, as reproduced in Emmanuel's attractive book on Greek dancing and elsewhere, we find the same play of the arms, the same sideward turn, the same extreme backward extension of the body, which had long before been represented in Egyptian monuments. Many supposedly modern movements in dancing were certainly already common both to Egyptian and Greek dancing, as well as the clapping of hands to keep time which is still an accompaniment of Spanish dancing. It seems clear, however, that, on this general classic and Mediterranean basis, Greek dancing had a development so refined and so special — though in technical elaboration of steps, it seems likely, inferior to modern dancing — that it exercised no influence outside Greece. Dancing became, indeed, the most characteristic and the most generally cultivated of Greek arts. Pindar, in a splendid Oxyrhynchine fragment, described Hellas, in what seemed to him supreme praise, as "the land of lovely dancing," and Athenæus pointed out that he calls Apollo the Dancer. It may well be that the Greek drama arose out of dance and song, and that the dance throughout was an essential and plastic element in it. Even if we reject

and an empty glass on the other, can by the contraction of the muscles on the side supporting the full glass, project the water from it, so as to fill the empty glass. This, of course, is not strictly dancing, but it is part of the technique which underlies classic dancing and it witnesses to the thoroughness with which the technical side of Egyptian dancing is still cultivated.

the statement of Aristotle that tragedy arose out of the Dionysian dithyramb, the alternative suppositions (such as Ridgeway's theory of dancing round the tombs of the dead) equally involve the same elements. It has often been pointed out that poetry in Greece demanded a practical knowledge of all that could be included under "dancing." Æschylus is said to have developed the technique of dancing and Sophocles danced in his own dramas. In these developments, no doubt, Greek dancing tended to overpass the fundamental limits of classic dancing and foreshadowed the ballet.[1]

The real germ of the ballet, however, is to be found in Rome, where the pantomime with its concerted and picturesque method of expressive action was developed, and Italy is the home of Romantic dancing. The same impulse which produced the pantomime produced, more than a thousand years later in the same Italian region, the modern ballet. In both cases, one is inclined to think, we may trace the influence of the same Etruscan and Tuscan race which so long has had its seat there, a race with a genius for expressive, dramatic, picturesque art. We see it on the walls of Etruscan tombs and again in pictures of Botticelli and his fellow Tuscans. The modern ballet, it is generally believed, had its origin in the spectacular pageants at

[1] "We must learn to regard the form of the Greek drama as a dance form," says G. Warre Cornish in an interesting article on "Greek Drama and the Dance" (*Fortnightly Review*, February, 1913), "a musical symphonic dance-vision, through which the history of Greece and the soul of man are portrayed."

the marriage of Galeazzo Visconti, Duke of Milan, in 1489. The fashion for such performances spread to the other Italian courts, including Florence, and Catherine de' Medici, when she became Queen of France, brought the Italian ballet to Paris. Here it speedily became fashionable. Kings and queens were its admirers and even took part in it; great statesmen were its patrons. Before long, and especially in the great age of Louis XIV, it became an established institution, still an adjunct of opera but with a vital life and growth of its own, maintained by distinguished musicians, artists, and dancers. Romantic dancing, to a much greater extent than what I have called Classic dancing, which depends so largely on simple personal qualities, tends to be vitalised by transplantation and the absorption of new influences, provided that the essential basis of technique and tradition is preserved in the new development. Lulli in the seventeenth century brought women into the ballet; Camargo discarded the complicated costumes and shortened the skirt, so rendering possible not only her own lively and vigorous method, but all the freedom and airy grace of later dancing. It was Noverre who by his ideas worked out at Stuttgart, and soon brought to Paris by Gaetan Vestris, made the ballet a new and complete art form; this Swiss-French genius not only elaborated plot revealed by gesture and dance alone, but, just as another and greater Swiss-French genius about the same time brought sentiment and emotion into the novel, he brought it into the ballet. In the French ballet of the eighteenth century a very high degree of perfection seems thus to have been reached, while in Italy, where the ballet had originated, it decayed, and Milan, which had been its source, became the nursery of a tradition of devitalised technique carried to the finest point of delicate perfection. The influence of the French school was maintained as a living force into the nineteenth century, — when it was renovated afresh by the new spirit of the age and Taglioni became the most ethereal embodiment of the spirit of the Romantic movement in a form that was genuinely classic, — overspreading the world by the genius of a few individual dancers. When they had gone, the ballet slowly and steadily declined. As it declined as an art, so also it declined in credit and in popularity; it became scarcely respectable even to admire dancing. Thirty or forty years ago, those of us who still appreciated dancing as an art — and how few they were! — had to seek for it painfully and sometimes in strange surroundings. A recent historian of dancing, in a book published so lately as 1906, declared that "the ballet is now a thing of the past, and, with the modern change of ideas, a thing that is never likely to be resuscitated." That historian never mentioned Russian ballet, yet his book was scarcely published before the Russian ballet arrived to scatter ridicule over his rash prophecy by raising the ballet to a pitch of perfection it can rarely have surpassed, as an expressive, emotional, even passionate form of living art.

The Russian ballet was an offshoot from the French
ballet and illustrates once more the vivifying effect of
transplantation on the art of Romantic dancing. The
Empress Anna introduced it in 1735 and appointed a
French ballet-master and a Neapolitan composer to
carry it on; it reached a high degree of technical perfection during the following hundred years, on the
traditional lines, and the principal dancers were all imported from Italy. It was not until recent years that
this firm discipline and these ancient traditions were
vitalised into an art form of exquisite and vivid beauty
by the influence of the soil in which they had slowly
taken root. This contact, when at last it was effected,
mainly by the genius of Fokine and the enterprise of
Diaghilev, involved a kind of revolution, for its outcome, while genuine ballet, has yet all the effect of delicious novelty. The tradition by itself was in Russia
an exotic without real life, and had nothing to give
to the world; on the other hand, a Russian ballet
apart from that tradition, if we can conceive such a
thing, would have been formless, extravagant, bizarre,
not subdued to any fine æsthetic ends. What we see
here, in the Russian ballet as we know it to-day, is a
splendid and arduous technical tradition, brought at
last — by the combined skill of designers, composers,
and dancers — into real fusion with an environment
from which during more than a century it had been
held apart; Russian genius for music, Russian feeling
for rhythm, Russian skill in the use of bright colour,

and, not least, the Russian orgiastic temperament, the Russian spirit of tender poetic melancholy, and the general Slav passion for folk-dancing, shown in other branches of the race also, Polish, Bohemian, Bulgarian, and Servian. At almost the same time what I have termed Classic dancing was independently revived in America by Isadora Duncan, bringing back what seemed to be the free naturalism of the Greek dance, and Ruth St. Denis, seeking to discover and revitalise the secrets of the old Indian and Egyptian traditions. Whenever now we find any restored art of theatrical dancing, as in the Swedish ballet, it has been inspired more or less, by an eclectic blending of these two revived forms, the Romantic from Russia, the Classic from America. The result has been that our age sees one of the most splendid movements in the whole history of the ballet.

V

DANCING as an art, we may be sure, cannot die out, but will always be undergoing a rebirth. Not merely as an art, but also as a social custom, it perpetually emerges afresh from the soul of the people. Less than a century ago the polka thus arose, extemporised by the Bohemian servant girl Anna Slezakova out of her own head for the joy of her own heart, and only rendered a permanent form, apt for world-wide popularity, by the accident that it was observed and noted down by an artist. Dancing has for ever been in existence as a spontaneous custom, a social discipline. Thus it is, finally, that dancing meets us, not only as love, as religion, as art, but also as morals.

All human work, under natural conditions, is a kind of dance. In a large and learned book, supported by an immense amount of evidence, Karl Bücher has argued that work differs from the dance, not in kind, but only in degree, since they are both essentially rhythmic. There is a good reason why work should be rhythmic, for all great combined efforts, the efforts by which alone great constructions such as those of megalithic days could be carried out, must be harmonised. It has even been argued that this necessity is the source of human speech, and we have the so-called Yo-heave-ho theory of languages. In the memory of those who have ever lived on a sailing ship — that loveliest of human creations now disappearing from the world — there will always linger the echo of the chanties which sailors sang as they hoisted the topsail yard or wound the capstan or worked the pumps. That is the type of primitive combined work, and it is indeed difficult to see how such work can be effectively accomplished without such a device for regulating the rhythmic energy of the muscles. The dance rhythm of work has thus acted socialisingly in a parallel line with the dance rhythms of the arts, and indeed in part as their inspirer. The Greeks, it has been too fancifully suggested, by insight or by intuition understood this when they fabled that Orpheus, whom they regarded as the earliest poet, was specially concerned with moving stones and trees. Bücher has pointed out that even poetic metre may be conceived as arising out of work; metre is the rhythmic stamping of feet, as in the technique of verse it is still metaphorically called; iambics and trochees, spondees and anapæsts and dactyls, may still be heard among blacksmiths smiting the anvil or navvies wielding their hammers in the streets. In so far as they arose out of work, music and singing and dancing are naturally a single art. A poet must always write to a tune, said Swinburne. Herein the ancient ballad of Europe is a significant type. It is, as the name indicates, a dance as much as a song, performed by a singer who sang the story and a chorus who danced and shouted the apparently meaningless refrain; it is absolutely the chanty of the sailors and is equally apt for the purposes of concerted work.[1] Yet our most complicated musical forms are evolved from similar dances. The symphony is but a development of a dance suite, in the first place folk-dances, such as Bach and Handel composed. Indeed a dance still lingers always at the heart of music and even the heart of the composer. Mozart, who was himself an accomplished dancer, used often to say, so his wife stated, that it was dancing, not music, that he really cared for. Wagner believed that Beethoven's Seventh

[1] It should perhaps be remarked that in recent times it has been denied that the old ballads were built up on dance songs. Miss Pound, for instance, in a book on the subject, argues that they were of aristocratic and not communal origin, which may well be, though the absence of the dance element does not seem to follow.

Symphony — to some of us the most fascinating of them and the most purely musical — was an apotheosis of the dance, and, even if that belief throws no light on the intention of Beethoven, it is at least a revelation of Wagner's own feeling for the dance.

It is, however, the dance itself, apart from the work and apart from the other arts, which, in the opinion of many to-day, has had a decisive influence in socialising, that is to say in moralising, the human species. Work showed the necessity of harmonious rhythmic coöperation, but the dance developed that rhythmic coöperation and imparted a beneficent impetus to all human activities. It was Grosse, in his "Beginnings of Art," who first clearly set forth the high social significance of the dance in the creation of human civilisation. The participants in a dance, as all observers of savages have noted, exhibit a wonderful unison; they are, as it were, fused into a single being stirred by a single impulse. Social unification is thus accomplished. Apart from war, this is the chief factor making for social solidarity in primitive life; it was indeed the best training for war. It has been a twofold influence; on the one hand, it aided unity of action and method in evolution: on the other, it had the invaluable function — for man is naturally a timid animal — of imparting courage; the universal drum, as Louis Robinson remarks, has been an immense influence in human affairs. Even among the Romans, with their highly developed military system, dancing and war were definitely allied; the Salii constituted a college of sacred military dancers; the dancing season was March, the war-god's month and the beginning of the war season, and all through that month there were dances in triple measure before the temples and round the altars, with songs so ancient that not even the priests could understand them. We may trace a similar influence of dancing in all the coöperative arts of life. All our most advanced civilisation, Grosse insisted, is based on dancing. It is the dance that socialised man.

Thus, in the large sense, dancing has possessed peculiar value as a method of national education. As civilisation grew self-conscious, this was realised. "One may judge of a king," according to ancient Chinese maxim, "by the state of dancing during his reign." So also among the Greeks; it has been said that dancing and music lay at the foundation of the whole political and military as well as religious organisation of the Dorian states.

In the narrow sense, in individual education, the great importance of dancing came to be realised, even at an early stage of human development, and still more in the ancient civilisations. "A good education," Plato declared in the "Laws," the final work of his old age, "consists in knowing how to sing and dance well." And in our own day one of the keenest and most enlightened of educationists has lamented the decay of dancing; the revival of dancing, Stanley Hall declares, is imperatively needed to give poise to the nerves, schooling to the emotions, strength to the will, and to harmonise the feelings and the intellect with the body which supports them.

It can scarcely be said that these functions of dancing are yet generally realised and embodied afresh in education. For, if it is true that dancing engendered morality, it is also true that in the end, by the irony of fate, morality, grown insolent, sought to crush its own parent, and for a time succeeded only too well. Four centuries ago dancing was attacked by that spirit, in England called Puritanism, which was then spread over the greater part of Europe, just as active in Bohemia as in England, and which has, indeed, been described as a general onset of developing Urbanism against the old Ruralism. It made no distinction between good and bad, nor paused to consider what would come when dancing went. So it was that, as Remy de Gourmont remarks, the drinking-shop conquered the dance, and alcohol replaced the violin.

But when we look at the function of dancing in life from a higher and wider standpoint, this episode in its history ceases to occupy so large a place. The conquest over dancing has never proved in the end a matter for rejoicing, even to morality, while an art which has been so intimately mixed with all the finest and deepest springs of life has always asserted itself afresh. For dancing is the loftiest, the most moving, the most beautiful of the arts, because it is no mere translation or abstraction from life; it is life itself. It is the only

art, as Rahel Varnhagen said, of which we ourselves
are the stuff. Even if we are not ourselves dancers,
but merely the spectators of the dance, we are still —
according to that Lippsian doctrine of *Einfühlung* or
"empathy" by Groos termed "the play of inner
imitation" — which here, at all events, we may accept
as true — feeling ourselves in the dancer who is manifesting and expressing the latent impulses of our own
being.

It thus comes about that, beyond its manifold
practical significance, dancing has always been felt to
possess also a symbolic significance. Marcus Aurelius
was accustomed to regard the art of life as like the
dancer's art, though that Imperial Stoic could not resist adding that in some respects it was more like the
wrestler's art. "I doubt not yet to make a figure in the
great Dance of Life that shall amuse the spectators in
the sky," said, long after, Blake, in the same strenuous
spirit. In our own time, Nietzsche, from first to last,
showed himself possessed by the conception of the art
of life as a dance, in which the dancer achieves the
rhythmic freedom and harmony of his soul beneath
the shadow of a hundred Damoclean swords. He said
the same thing of his style, for to him the style and the
man were one: "My style," he wrote to his intimate
friend Rohde, "is a dance." "Every day I count
wasted," he said again, "in which there has been no
dancing." The dance lies at the beginning of art, and
we find it also at the end. The first creators of civi-

lisation were making the dance, and the philosopher of a later age, hovering over the dark abyss of insanity, with bleeding feet and muscles strained to the breaking point, still seems to himself to be weaving the maze of the dance.

CHAPTER III
THE ART OF THINKING

I

HERBERT SPENCER pointed out, in his early essay on "The Genesis of Science," that science arose out of art, and that even yet the distinction is "purely conventional," for "it is impossible to say when art ends and science begins." Spencer was here using "art" in the fundamental sense according to which all practice is of the nature of art. Yet it is of interest to find a thinker now commonly regarded as so prosaic asserting a view which to most prosaic people seems fanciful. To the ordinary solid man, to any would-be apostle of common sense, science — and by "science" he usually means applied science — seems the exact opposite of the vagaries and virtuosities that the hard-headed *homme moyen sensuel* is accustomed to look upon as "art."

Yet the distinction is modern. In classic times there was no such distinction. The "sciences" — reasonably, as we may now see, and not fancifully as was afterwards supposed — were "the arts of the mind." In the Middle Ages the same liberal studies — grammar, logic, geometry, music, and the rest — could be spoken of either as "sciences" or as "arts," and for Roger Bacon, who in the thirteenth century was so genuine a man of science, every branch of study or learning was a "scientia." I am inclined to think that it was the Mathematical Renaissance of the seventeenth century which introduced the undue emphasis on the distinction between "science" and "art." "All the sciences are so bound together," wrote Descartes, the banner-bearer of that Renaissance, in his "Règles pour la Direction de l'Esprit," "that it is much easier to learn them all at once than to learn one alone by detaching it from the others." He added that we could not say the same of the arts. Yet we might perhaps say of arts and sciences that we can only understand them all together, and we may certainly say, as Descartes proceeded to say of the sciences alone, that they all emanate from the same focus, however diversely coloured by the media they pass through or the objects they encounter. At that moment, however, it was no doubt practically useful, however theoretically unsound, to overemphasise the distinction between "science," with its new instrumental precision, and "art." [1] At the same time the tradition of the old usage was not completely put aside, and a Master of "Arts" remained a master of such sciences as the directors of education succeeded in recognising until the middle of the nineteenth century. By that time

[1] It would not appear that the pioneers of the Mathematical Renaissance of the twentieth century are inclined to imitate Descartes in this matter. Einstein would certainly not, and many apostles of physical science to-day (see, e.g., Professor Smithells, *From a Modern University: Some Aims and Aspirations of Science*) insist on the æsthetic, imaginative, and other "art" qualities of science.

the development of the sciences, and especially of the physical sciences, as "the discovery of truth," led to a renewed emphasis on them which resulted in the practical restriction of the term "art" to what are ordinarily called the fine arts. More formally, science became the study of what were supposed to be demonstrable and systematically classifiable truths regarding the facts of the world; art was separated off as the play of human impulses in making things. Sir Sidney Colvin, in the "Encyclopædia Britannica," after discussing the matter (which Mill had already discussed at length in his "Logic" and decided that the difference is that Science is in the Indicative Mood and Art in the Imperative Mood), concluded that science is "ordered knowledge of natural phenomena and of the relations between them," or that "Science consists in knowing, Art consists in doing." Men of science, like Sir E. Ray Lankester, accepted this conclusion. That was as far as it was possible to go in the nineteenth century.

But the years pass, and the progress of science itself, especially the sciences of the mind, has upset this distinction. The analysis of "knowing" showed that it was not such a merely passive and receptive method of recognising "truth" as scientists had innocently supposed. This is probably admitted now by the Realists among philosophers as well as by the Idealists. Dr. Charles Singer, perhaps our most learned historian of science, now defines science, no longer as a body of organized knowledge, but as "the process which makes knowledge," as "knowledge in the making"; that is to say, "the growing edge between the unknown and the known." [1] As soon as we thus regard it, as a *making* process, it becomes one with art. Even physical science is perpetually laying aside the "facts" which it thought it knew, and learning to replace them by other "facts" which it comes to know as more satisfactory in presenting an intelligible view of the world. The analysis of "knowing" shows that this is not only a legitimate but an inevitable process. Such a process is active and creative. It clearly partakes at least as much of the nature of "doing" as of "knowing." It involves qualities which on another plane, sometimes indeed on the same plane, are essentially those involved in doing. The craftsman who moulds conceptions with his mind cannot be put in a fundamentally different class from the craftsman who moulds conceptions with his hand, any more than the poet can be put in a totally different class from the painter. It is no longer possible to deny that science is of the nature of art.

[1] C. Singer. "What is Science?" *British Medical Journal*, 25th June, 1921. Singer refuses the name of "science" in the strict sense to fields of completely organised knowledge which have ceased growing, like human anatomy (though, of course, the anatomist still remains a man of science by working outwards into adjoining related fields), preferring to term any such field of completed knowledge a *discipline*. This seems convenient and I should like to regard it as sound. It is not, however, compatible with the old doctrine of Mill and Colvin and Ray Lankester, for it excludes from the field of science exactly what they regarded as most typically science, and some one might possibly ask whether in other departments, like Hellenic sculpture or Sung pottery, a completed art ceases to be art.

So it is that in the fundamental sense, and even, it will
have to be added, in a sense that comprehends the extravagancies of wild variations from the norm, we have
to recognise that the true man of science is an artist.
Like the lunatic, the lover, the poet (as a great physician, Sir William Osler, has said), the student is "of
imagination all compact." It was by his "wonderful
imagination," it has been well pointed out, that Newton was constantly discovering new tracks and new
processes in the region of the unknown. The extraordinary various life-work of Helmholtz, who initiated
the valuation of beauty on a physiological basis,
scientifically precise as it was, had, as Einstein has
remarked, an æsthetic colouring. "There is no such
thing as an unimaginative scientific man," a distinguished professor of mechanics and mathematics declared some years ago, and if we are careful to remember that not every man who believes that his life
is devoted to science is really a "scientific man," that
statement is literally true.[1]   It is not only true of the
scientific man in the special sense; it is also true of the
philosopher.   In every philosopher's work, a philosophic writer has remarked, "the construction of a
complete system of conceptions is not carried out
simply in the interests of knowledge. Its underlying

[1] It has often been pointed out that the imaginative application of
science — artistic ideas like that of the steam locomotive, the flying-
machine heavier than air, the telegraph, the telephone, and many others
— were even at the moment of their being achieved, elaborately shown
to be "impossible" by men who had been too hastily hoisted up to posi-
tions of "scientific" eminence.

motive is æsthetic. It is the work of a creative artist." [1] The intellectual lives of a Plato or a Dante,
Professor Graham Wallas from a different standpoint
has remarked, "were largely guided and sustained by
their delight in the sheer beauty of the rhythmic relation between law and instance, species and individual, or cause and effect."[2]

That remark, with its reference to the laws and
rhythm in the universe, calls to mind the great initiator, so far as our knowledge extends back, of scientific research in our European world. Pythagoras is a
dim figure, and there is no need here to insist unduly
on his significance. But there is not the slightest doubt
about the nature of that significance in its bearing on
the point before us. Dim and legendary as he now
appears to us, Pythagoras was no doubt a real person,
born in the sixth century before Christ, at Samos, and
by his association with that great shipping centre
doubtless enabled to voyage afar and glean the wisdom
of the ancient world. In antiquity he was regarded,
Cicero remarks, as the inventor of philosophy, and
still to-day he is estimated to be one of the most
original figures, not only of Greece, but the world.
He is a figure full of interest from many points of view,

[1] J. B. Baillie, *Studies in Human Nature* (1921), p. 221. This point
has become familiar ever since F. A. Lange published his almost epoch-
marking work, *The History of Materialism*, which has made so deep an
impress on many modern thinkers from Nietzsche to Vaihinger; it is indeed a book which can never be forgotten (I speak from experience) by
any one who read it in youth.
[2] G. Wallas, *The Great Society*, p. 107.

however veiled in mist, but he only concerns us here because he represents the beginning of what we call "science" — that is to say, measurable knowledge at its growing point— and because he definitely represents it as arising out of what we all conventionally recognise as "art," and as, indeed, associated with the spirit of art, even its most fantastic forms, all the way. Pythagoras was a passionate lover of music, and it was thus that he came to make the enormously fruitful discovery that pitch of sound depends upon the length of the vibrating chord. Therein it became clear that law and spatial quantity ruled even in fields which had seemed most independent of quantitative order. The beginning of the great science of mechanics was firmly set up. The discovery was no accident. Even his rather hostile contemporary Heraclitus said of Pythagoras that he had "practised research and inquiry beyond all other men." He was certainly a brilliant mathematician; he was, also, not only an astronomer, but the first, so far as we know, to recognise that the earth is a sphere, — so setting up the ladder which was to reach at last to the Copernican conception, — while his followers took the further step of affirming that the earth was not the centre of our cosmic system, but concentrically related. So that Pythagoras may not only be called the Father of Philosophy, but, with better right the Father of Science in the modern exact sense. Yet he remained fundamentally an artist even in the conventional sense. His free play of imagination and emotion, his delight in the ravishing charm of beauty and of harmony, however it may sometimes have led him astray, — and introduced the reverence for Number which so long entwined fancy too closely with science, — yet, as Gomperz puts it, gave soaring wings to the power of his severe reason.[1]

One other great dim figure of early European antiquity shares with Pythagoras the philosophic dominance over our world, and that is the Platonic Socrates, or, as we might perhaps say, the Socratic Plato. And here, too, we are in the presence of a philosopher, if not a scientist, who was a supreme artist. Here again, also, we encounter a legendary figure concealing a more or less real human person. But there is a difference. While all are agreed that, in Pythagoras we have a great and brilliant figure dimly seen, there are many who consider that in Socrates we have a small and dim figure grown great and brilliant in the Platonic medium through which alone he has been really influential in our world, for without Plato the name of Socrates would have scarcely been mentioned. The problem of the Pythagorean legend may be said to be settled. But the problem of the Socratic legend is still under discussion. We cannot, moreover, quite put it aside as merely of academic interest, for its solution, if ever reached, would touch that great vital problem of art

[1] Gomperz, *Greek Thinkers*, vol. I, chap. III, where will be found an attractive account of Pythagoras' career and position.

in the actual world with which we are here throughout concerned.

If one examines any large standard history of Greece, like Grote's to mention one of the oldest and best, one is fairly sure to find a long chapter on the life of Socrates. Such a chapter is inserted, without apology, without explanation, without compunction, as a matter of course, in a so-called "history," and nearly every one, even to-day, still seems to take it as a matter of course. Few seem to possess the critical and analytical mind necessary for the examination of the documents on which the "history" rests. If they approached this chapter in a questioning spirit, they might perhaps discover that it was not until about half a century after the time of the real Socrates that any "historical" evidence for the existence of our legendary Socrates begins to appear.[1] Few people seem to realise that even of Plato himself we know nothing certain that

[1] Always, it may perhaps be noted in passing, it seems to have been difficult for the sober and solemn Northerner, especially of England, to enter into the Greek spirit, all the more since that spirit was only the spirit of a sprinkling of people amid a hostile mass about as unlike anything we conventionally call "Greek" as could well be imagined, so that, as Élie Faure, the historian of art, has lately remarked, Greek art is a biological "monstrosity." (Yet, I would ask, might we not say the same of France or of England?) That is why it is usually so irritating to read books written about the Greeks by barbarians; they slur over or ignore what they do not like and, one suspects, they instinctively misinterpret what they think they do like. Better even the most imperfect knowledge of a few original texts, better even only a few days on the Acropolis, than the second-hand opinions of other people. And if we must have a book about the Greeks, there is always Athenæus, much nearer to them in time and in spirit, with all his gossip, than any Northern barbarian, and an everlasting delight.

could not be held in a single sentence. The "biographies" of Plato began to be written four hundred years after his death. It should be easy to estimate their value.

There are three elements — one of them immeasurably more important than the other two — of which the composite portrait of our modern Socrates is made up: Xenophon, Plato, the dramatists. To the contribution furnished by the first, not much weight is usually attached. Yet it should really have been regarded as extremely illuminating. It suggests that the subject of "Socrates" was a sort of school exercise, useful practice in rhetoric or in dialectics. The very fact that Xenophon's Socrates was so reminiscent of his creator ought to have been instructive.[1] It has, however, taken scholars some time to recognise this, and Karl Joël, who spent fifteen of the

---

[1] Along another line it should have been clear that the dialogues of the philosophers were drama and not history. It would appear (Croiset, *Littérature Grecque*, vol. III, pp. 448 *et seq.*) that with Epicharmus of Cos, who was settled in Megara at the beginning of the fifth century, philosophic comedy flourished brilliantly at Syracuse, and indeed fragments of his formal philosophic dialogue survive. Thus it is suggested that Athenian comedy and sophistic prose dialogues may be regarded as two branches drawn from the ancient prototype of such Syracusan comedy, itself ultimately derived from Ionian philosophy. It is worth noting, I might add, that when we first hear of the Platonic dialogues they were being grouped in trilogies and tetralogies like the Greek dramas; that indicates, at all events, what their earliest editors thought about them. It is also interesting to note that the writer of, at the present moment, the latest handbook to Plato, Professor A. E. Taylor (*Plato*, 1922, pp. 32–33), regards the "Socrates" of Plato as no historical figure, not even a mask of Plato himself, but simply "the hero of the Platonic drama," which we have to approach in much the same way as the work of "a great dramatist or novelist."

best years of his life over the Xenophontic Socrates,
to discover that the figure was just as much a fiction
as the Platonic Socrates, has lately confessed that he
thinks those years rather wasted. It might have been
clear earlier that what Plato had done was really just the
same thing so far as method was concerned, though
a totally different thing in result because done by the
most richly endowed of poet-philosophers, the most
consummate of artists. For that is probably how we
ought to regard Plato, and not, like some, as merely a
great mystificator. It is true that Plato was the master
of irony, and that "irony," in its fundamental meaning, is, as Gomperz points out, "pleasure in mystify-
ing." But while Plato's irony possesses a significance
which we must always keep before us, it is yet only one
of the elements of his vast and versatile mind.

It is to the third of these sources that some modern
investigators are now inclined to attach primary significance. It was on the stage — in the branch of drama
that kept more closely in touch with life than that
which had fallen into the hands of the prose dialecti-
cians and rhetoricians — that we seem to find the
shadow of the real Socrates. But he was not the Socrates of the dramatic dialogues of Plato or even of Xenophon; he was a minor Sophist, an inferior Diogenes, yet
a remarkable figure, arresting and disturbing, whose
idiosyncrasies were quite perceptible to the crowd. It
was an original figure, hardly the embodiment of a
turning-point in philosophy, but fruitful of great possi-

bilities, so that we could hardly be surprised if the master of philosophic drama took it over from real life and the stage for his own purposes.

To make clear to myself the possible way — I am far from asserting it was the actual way — in which our legendary Socrates arose, I sometimes think of Chidley. Chidley was an Australian Sophist and Cynic, in the good sense of both these words, and without doubt, it seems to me, the most original and remarkable figure that has ever appeared in Australia, of which, however, he was not a native, though he spent nearly his whole life there. He was always poor, and like most philosophers he was born with a morbid nervous disposition, though he acquired a fine and robust frame. He was liable not only to the shock of outward circumstances but of inward impulses; to these he had in the past often succumbed, and only slowly and painfully gained the complete mastery over as he gained possession of his own philosophy. For all his falls, which he felt acutely, as Augustine and Bunyan as well as Rousseau felt such lapses, there was in him a real nobility, an even ascetic firmness and purity of character. I never met him, but I knew him more intimately, perhaps, than those who came in contact with him. For many years I was in touch with him, and his last letter was written shortly before his death; he always felt I ought to be persuaded of the truth he had to reveal and never quite understood my sympathetic attitude of scepticism. He had devoured all the philosophic literature he could lay hold of, but his philosophy — in the Greek sense, as a way of life, and not in our modern sense as a system of notions — was his own: a new vision of Nature's simplicity and wholeness, only new because it had struck on a new sensibility and sometimes in excessive and fantastic ways, but he held his faith with unbending devotion, and never ceased to believe that all would accept the vision when once they beheld it. So he went about the streets in Sydney, clad (as a concession to public feeling) in bathing drawers, finding anywhere he could the Stoa which might serve for him, to argue and discuss, among all who were willing, with eager faith, keen mind, and pungent speech. A few were won, but most were disturbed and shocked. The police persistently harassed him; they felt bound to interfere with what seemed such an outrage on the prim decency of the streets; and as he quietly persisted in following his own course, and it was hard to bring any serious charge against him, they called in the aid of the doctors, and henceforth he was in and out of the asylum instead of the prison. No one need be blamed; it was nobody's fault; if a man transgresses the ordinary respectable notions of decency, he must be a criminal, and if he is not a criminal, he must be a lunatic; the social organisation takes no account of philosophers; the philosophic Hipparchia and her husband must not nowadays consummate their marriage in public, and our modern philosophers meekly agree that philosophy is to have nothing to do with a life. Every one in the

case seems to have behaved with due conventional
propriety, just as every one behaved around the death-
bed of Tolstoy's Ivan Ilitch. It was Chidley's death-
bed they were preparing, and he knew it, but he un-
flinchingly grasped the cup they held out to him and
drank it to the dregs. He felt he could do no other.
There was no fabled hemlock in it, but it was just as
deadly as though it had been accompanied by all the
dramatic symbolisation of a formal condemnation to
death, such as had really been recorded (Plato well
knew) in old Athenian annals. There was no Plato in
Sydney. But if there had been, it is hard to conceive
any figure more fit for the ends of his transforming art.
Through that inspiring medium the plebeian Sophist
and Cynic, while yet retaining something of the asperity of his original shape, would have taken on a new
glory, his bizarreries would have been spiritualised and
his morbidities become the signs of mystic possession,
his fate would have appeared as consecrated in form as
it genuinely was in substance, he would have been the
mouthpiece, not only of the truths he really uttered,
but of a divine eloquence on the verge of which he had
in real life only trembled, and, like Socrates in the
hands of Plato, he would have passed, as all the finest
philosophy passes at last, into music.[1] So in the end
Chidley would have entered modern history, just as

[1] He had often been bidden in dreams to make music, said the Platonic
Socrates in *Phædo*, and he had imagined that that was meant to encourage him in the pursuit of philosophy, "which is the noblest and best
of music."

Socrates entered ancient history, the Saint and Martyr of Philosophy.[1]

If it should so be that, as we learn to see him truly, the figure of the real Socrates must diminish in magnitude, then — and that is the point which concerns us here — the glory of the artist who made him what he has become for us is immensely enhanced. No longer the merely apt and brilliant disciple of a great master, he becomes himself master and lord, the radiant creator of the chief figure in European philosophy, the most marvellous artist the world has ever known. So that when we look back at the spiritual history of Europe, it may become possible to say that its two supreme figures, the Martyr of Philosophy and the Martyr of Religion, were both — however real the two human persons out of which they were formed — the work of man's imagination. For there, on the one hand, we see the most accomplished of European thinkers, and on the other a little band of barbarians, awkwardly using just the same Greek language, working with an unconscious skill which even transcends all that conscious skill could have achieved, yet both bearing immortal witness to the truth that the human soul only lives truly in art and can only be ruled through art. So it is that in art lies the solution of the conflicts

---

[1] In discussing Socrates I have made some use of Professor Dupréel's remarkable book, *La Légende Socratique* (1922). Dupréel himself, with a little touch of irony, recommends a careful perusal of the beautiful and monumental works erected by Zeller and Grote and Gomperz to the honour of Socrates.

of philosophy. There we see Realism, or the discovery of things, one with Idealism, or the creation of things. Art is the embodied harmony of their conflict. That could not be more exquisitely symbolised than by these two supreme figures in the spiritual life of Europe, the Platonic Socrates and the Gospel Jesus, both alike presented to us, it is so significant to observe, as masters of irony.

There has never again been so great an artist in philosophy, so supreme a dramatist, as Plato. But in later times philosophers themselves have often been willing to admit that even if they were not, like Plato, dramatists, there was poetry and art in their vocation. "One does not see why the sense for Philosophy should be more generally diffused than that for poetry," remarked Schelling, evidently regarding them as on the same plane. F. A. Lange followed with his memorable "History of Materialism," in which the conception of philosophy as a poetic art was clearly set forth. "Philosophy is pure art," says in our own days a distinguished thinker who is in especially close touch with the religious philosophy of the East. "The thinker works with laws of thought and scientific facts in just the same sense as the musical composer with tones. He must find accords, he must think out sequences, he must set the part in a necessary relation to the whole. But for that he needs art."[1] Bergson regards

---

[1] Count Hermann Keyserling, *Philosophie als Kunst* (1920), p. 2. He associates this with the need for a philosophy to possess a subjective

philosophy as an art, and, Croce, the more than rival of Bergson in popular esteem, and with interesting points of contact with the French philosopher, though his standpoint is so different, has repeatedly pointed out — as regards Nietzsche, for instance, and even as regards a philosopher to whom he is so closely related as Hegel — that we may read philosophy for its poetic rather than its historic truth. Croce's position in this matter is not, indeed, easy to state quite simply. He includes æsthetics in philosophy, but he would not regard philosophy as an art. For him art is the first and lowest stratum in the mind, not in rank, but in order, and on it the other strata are laid and combine with it. Or, as he elsewhere says, "art is the root of our whole theoretic life. Without root there can be neither flower nor fruit." [1] But for Croce art is not itself flower or fruit. The "Concept" and other abstractions have to be brought in before Croce is satisfied that he has attained reality. It may, perhaps, indeed, be permitted, even to an admirer of the skill with which Croce spreads out such wide expanses of thought, to suggest that, in spite of his anxiety to keep close to the concrete, he is not therein always successful, and that he tends to move in verbal circles, as may perhaps happen to a philosopher who would reduce the philosophy personal character, without which it can have no value, indeed no content at all.

[1] Croce, *Problemi d' Estetica*, p. 15. I have to admit, for myself, that, while admiring the calm breadth of Croce's wide outlook, it is sometimes my misfortune, in spite of myself, when I go to his works, to play the part of a Balaam à *rebours*. I go forth to bless: and, somehow, I curse.

of art to the philosophy of language. But, however that may be, it is a noteworthy fact that the close relationship of art and philosophy is admitted by the two most conspicuous philosophers of to-day, raised to popular eminence in spite of themselves, the Philosopher of Other-worldliness and the Philosopher of This-worldliness.

If we turn to England, we find that, in an age and a land wherein it was not so easy to make the assertion as it has now more generally become, Sir Leslie Stephen, in harmony, whether or not he knew it, with F. A. Lange, wrote to Lord Morley (as he later became) in the last century: "I think that a philosophy is really made more of poetry than of logic; and the real value of both poetry and philosophy is not the pretended reasoning, but the exposition in one form or other of a certain view of life." It is, we see, just what they have all been saying, and if it is true of men of science and philosophers, who are the typical representatives of human thinking, it is even true of every man on earth who thinks, ever since the day when conscious thinking began. The world is an unrelated mass of impressions, as it first strikes our infant senses, falling at random on the sensory mechanism, and all appearing as it were on the same plane. For an infant the moon is no farther away than his mother's breast, even though he possesses an inherited mental apparatus fitted to coördinate and distinguish the two. It is only when we begin to think, that we can arrange these unrelated impressions into intelligible groups, and thinking is thus of the nature of art.[1]

All such art, moreover, may yet be said to be an invention of fictions. That great and fundamental truth, which underlies so much modern philosophy, has been expounded in the clearest and most detailed manner by Hans Vaihinger in his "Philosophie des Als Ob."

II

HANS VAIHINGER is still little known in England;[2] and that is the more remarkable as he has always been strongly attached to English thought, of which his famous book reveals an intimate knowledge. In early life he had mixed much with English people, for whom he has a deep regard, and learnt to revere, not only Darwin, but Hume and J. S. Mill, who exerted a

[1] James Hinton, a pioneer in so many fields, clearly saw that thinking is really an art fifty years ago. "Thinking is no mere mechanical process," he wrote (*Chapters on the Art of Thinking*, pp. 43 *et seq.*), "it is a great Art, the chief of all the Arts. . . . Those only can be called thinkers who have a native gift, a special endowment for the work, and have been trained, besides, by assiduous culture. And though we continually assume that every one is capable of thinking, do we not all feel that there is somehow a fallacy in this assumption? Do we not feel that what people set up as their 'reasons' for disbelieving or believing are often nothing of the sort?. . . The Art faculty is Imagination, the power of seeing the unseen, the power also of putting ourselves out of the centre, of reducing ourselves to our true proportions, of truly using our own impressions. And is not this in reality the chief element in the work of the thinker?. . . Science *is* poetry."

[2] So far, indeed, as I am aware, I was responsible for the first English account of his work (outside philosophical journals); it appeared in the London *Nation and Athenæum* a few years ago, and is partly embodied in the present chapter.

decisive influence on his own philosophic development. At the beginning of his career he projected a history of English philosophy, but interest in that subject was then so small in Germany that he had regretfully to abandon his scheme, and was drawn instead, through no active effort on his part, to make the study of Kant the by-product of his own more distinctive work, yet it was a fitting study, for in Kant he saw the germs of the doctrine of the "as if," that is to say, the practical significance of fiction in human life, though that is not the idea traditionally associated with Kant, who, indeed, was not himself clear about it, while his insight was further darkened by his reactionary tendencies; yet Vaihinger found that it really played a large part in Kant's work and might even be regarded as his special and personal way of regarding things; he was not so much a metaphysician, Vaihinger remarks, as a metaphorician. Yet even in his Kantian studies the English influence was felt, for Vaihinger's work has here been to take up the Neo-Kantism of F. A. Lange and to develop it in an empirical and positivistic direction.

There was evidently something in Vaihinger's spirit that allied him to the English spirit. We may see that in his portrait; it is not the face of the philosophic dreamer, the scholarly man of the study, but the eager, forceful head of the practical man of action, the daring adventurer, the man who seems made to struggle with the concrete things of the world, the kind of man, that is to say, whom we consider peculiarly English. That, indeed, is the kind of man he would have been; that is the kind of life, a social life full of activity and of sport, that he desired to lead. But it was impossible. An extreme and lifelong short-sightedness proved a handicap of which he has never ceased to be conscious. So it came about that his practical energy was, as it were, sublimated into a philosophy which yet retained the same forceful dynamic quality.

For the rest, his origin, training, and vocation seem all to have been sufficiently German. He came, like many other eminent men, out of a Swabian parsonage, and was himself intended for theology, only branching off into philosophy after his university career was well advanced. At the age of sixteen he was deeply influenced, as so many others have been, by Herder's "Ideen zur Geschichte der Menschheit"; that not only harmonised with his own tendency at the time towards a mixed theism and pantheism, but it first planted within him the conception of evolution in human history, proceeding from an animal origin, which became a fundamental element of his mental constitution. When a year later he came across Darwin's doctrines he felt that he knew them beforehand. These influences were balanced by that of Plato, through whose "Ideas" he caught his first glimpse of an "As-If world." A little later the strenuous training of one of his teachers in the logical analysis of Latin syntax, especially in the use of the conjunctions, furnished the source from which subsequently he drew that now well-known phrase. It was in these years that he reached the view, which he has since definitely advocated, that philosophy should not be made a separate study, but should become a natural part and corollary of every study, since philosophy cannot be fruitfully regarded as a discipline by itself. Without psychology, especially, he finds that philosophy is merely "a methodic abstraction." A weighty influence of these days was constituted by the poems and essays of Schiller, a Swabian like himself, and, indeed, associated with the history of his own family. Schiller was not only an inspiring influence, but it was in Schiller's saying, "Error alone is life, and knowledge is death," that he found (however unjustifiably) the first expression of his own "fictionalism," while Schiller's doctrine of the play impulse as the basis of artistic creation and enjoyment seemed the prophecy of his own later doctrine, for in play he saw later the "as if" as the kernel of æsthetic practice and contemplation.

At the age of eighteen Vaihinger proceeded to the Swabian University of Tübingen and here was free to let his wide-ranging, eager mind follow its own impulses. He revealed a taste for the natural sciences and with this the old Greek nature philosophers, especially Anaximander, for the sake of their anticipations of modern evolutionary doctrines. Aristotle also occupied him, later Spinoza, and, above all, Kant, though it was chiefly the metaphysical antinomies and the practical reason which fascinated him. As ever, it was what made for practice that seemed mostly to concern him. Schelling, Hegel, and Schleiermacher, the official German idealists, said nothing to him. He turned from them to Schopenhauer, and thence he drew the pessimisms, the irrationalism, and the voluntarism which became permanent features of his system of thought. The irrationalism, as he himself points out, was completely opposed to all early influences on him, but it lay in his own personal circumstances. The contrast between his temperamental impulse to energetic practical action in every direction, and the reserve, passivity, and isolation which myopia enforced, seemed to him absolutely irrational and sharpened his vision for all the irrationality of existence. So that a philosophy which, like Schopenhauer's, truthfully recognised and allowed for the irrational element in existence came like a revelation. As to Vaihinger's pessimism, that, as we might expect, is hardly of what would be generally considered a pessimistic character. It is merely a recognition of the fact that most people are over-sanguine and thereby come to grief, whereas a little touch of pessimism would have preserved them from much misery. Long before the Great War, Vaihinger felt that many Germans were over-sanguine regarding the military power of their Empire, and of Germany's place in the world, and that such optimism might easily conduce to war and disaster. In 1911 he even planned to publish anonymously in Switzerland a pamphlet entitled "Finis Germaniæ," with the motto "Quos Deus vult perdere, prius dementat," and was only prevented by a sudden development of the eye-trouble. Vaihinger points out that an unjustified optimism had for a long time past led in the politics of Germany — and also, he might have said, of the countries later opposed to her — to lack of foresight, over-haste, and arrogance; he might have added that a very slight touch of pessimism would also have enabled these countries, on both sides, to discover the not very remote truth that even the victors in such a contest would suffer scarcely less than the conquered. In early life Vaihinger had playfully defined Man as a "species of ape afflicted by megalomania"; he admits that, whatever truth lies behind the definition, the statement is somewhat exaggerated. Yet it is certainly strange to observe, one may comment, how many people seem to feel vain of their own ungratified optimism when the place where optimism most flourishes is the lunatic asylum. They never seem to pause to reflect on the goal that lies ahead of them, though there must be few who on looking back cannot perceive what terrible accidents they might have foreseen and avoided by the aid of a little pessimism. When the gods, to ruin a man, first make him mad, they do it, almost invariably, by making him an optimist. One might hazard the assertion that the chief philosophic distinction between classic antiquity and modern civilisation is the prevalence in the latter of a facile optimism; and the fact that of all ancient writers the most popular in modern times has been the complacently optimistic (or really hedonistic) Horace is hardly due to his technical virtuosity. He who would walk sanely amid the opposing perils in the path of life always needs a little optimism; he also needs a little pessimism.

Reference has been made to Vaihinger's devouring appetite for knowledge. This, indeed, was extraordinary, and of almost universal range. There seem to have been few fields with which he failed to come in touch, either through books or by personal intercourse with experts. He found his way into all the natural sciences, he was drawn to Greek archæology and German philosophy; he began the study of Sanscrit with Roth. Then, realising that he had completely neglected mathematics, he devoted himself with ardour to analytic geometry and infinitesimals, a study which later he found philosophically fruitful. Finally, in 1874, he may be said to have rounded the circle of his self-development by reading the just published enlarged and much improved edition of F. A. Lange's "History of Materialism." Here he realised the presence of a spirit of the noblest order, equipped with the widest culture and the finest lucidity of vision, the keenest religious radicalism combined with largehearted tolerance and lofty moral equilibrium, all manifested in a completed master-work. Moreover, the standpoint of F. A. Lange was precisely that which Vaihinger had been independently struggling towards, for it brought into view that doctrine of the place of fiction in life which he had already seen ahead. It is not surprising that he should generously and enthusiastically acclaim Lange as master and leader, though his subsequent work is his own, and has carried ideas of which Lange held only the seeds to new and fruitful development.[1]

It was in 1876–77 that Vaihinger wrote his book, a marvellous achievement for so youthful a thinker, for he was then only about twenty-five years of age. A final revision it never underwent, and there remain various peculiarities about the form into which it is cast. The serious failure in eyesight seems to have been the main reason for delaying the publication of a work which the author felt to be too revolutionary to put forth in an imperfect form. He preferred to leave it for posthumous publication.

But the world was not standing still, and during the next thirty years many things happened. Vaihinger found the new sect of Pragmatists coming into fashion with ideas resembling his own, though in a cruder shape, which seemed to render philosophy the "meretrix theologorum." Many distinguished thinkers were working towards an attitude more or less like his own,

---

[1] I have based this sketch on an attractive and illuminating account of his own development written by Professor Vaihinger for Dr. Raymund Schmidt's highly valuable series, *Die Deutsche Philosophie der Gegenwart in Selbstdarstellungen* (1921), vol. II.

especially Nietzsche, whom (like many others even to-day) he had long regarded with prejudice and avoided, but now discovered to be "a great liberator" with congenial veins of thought. Vaihinger realised that his conception was being independently put forward from various sides, often in forms that to him seemed imperfect or vicious. It was no longer advisable to hold back his book. In 1911, therefore, "Die Philosophie des Als Ob" appeared.

The problem which Vaihinger set out to solve was this: How comes it about that with consciously false ideas we yet reach conclusions that are in harmony with Nature and appeal to us as Truth? That we do so is obvious, especially in the "exact" branches of science. In mathematics it is notorious that we start from absurdities to reach a realm of law, and our whole conception of the nature of the world is based on a foundation which we believe to have no existence. For even the most sober scientific investigator in science, the most thoroughgoing Positivist, cannot dispense with fiction; he must at least make use of categories, and they are already fictions, analogical fictions, or labels, which give us the same pleasure as children receive when they are told the "name" of a thing. Fiction is, indeed, an indispensable supplement to logic, or even a part of it; whether we are working inductively or deductively, both ways hang closely together with fiction; and axioms, though they seek to be primary verities, are more akin to fiction. If we had realised the nature of axioms, the doctrine of Einstein, which sweeps away axioms so familiar to us that they seem obvious truths, and substitutes others which seem absurd because they are unfamiliar, might not have been so bewildering.

Physics, especially mathematical physics, Vaihinger explains in detail, has been based, and fruitfully based, on fictions. The infinite, infinitely little or infinitely great, while helpful in lightening our mental operations, is a fiction. The Greeks disliked and avoided it, and "the gradual formation of this conception is one of the most charming and instructive themes in the history of science," indeed, one of the most noteworthy spectacles in the history of the human spirit; we see the working of a logical impulse first feeling in the dark, gradually constructing ideas fitted to yield precious service, yet full of hopeless contradictions, without any relation to the real world. That absolute space is a fiction, Vaihinger points out, is no new idea. Hobbes had declared it was only a *phantasma;* Leibnitz, who agreed, added that it was merely "the idolum of a few modern Englishmen," and called time, extension, and movement "*choses idéales.*" Berkeley, in attacking the defective conceptions of the mathematicians, failed to see that it was by means of, and not in spite of, these logically defective conceptions that they attained logically valuable results. All the marks of fiction were set up on the mathematician's pure space; it was impossible and unthinkable; yet it proved useful and fruitful.

The tautological fiction of "Force" — an empty
reduplication of the fact of a succession of relationships — is one that we constantly fall back on with
immense satisfaction and with the feeling of having
achieved something; it has been a highly convenient
fiction which has aided representation and experience.
It is one of the most famous, and also, it must be added,
one of the most fatal of fantasies. For when we talk
of, for instance, a "life-force" and its *élan*, or whatever
other dainty term we like to apply to it, we are not only
summarily mingling together many separate phenomena, but we are running the risk that our conception
may be taken for something that really exists. There
is always temptation, when two processes tend to
follow each other, to call the property of the first to be
followed by the other its "force," and to measure that
force by the magnitude of the result. In reality we
only have succession and coexistence, and the "force"
is something that we imagine.

We must not, therefore, treat our imagination with
contempt as was formerly the fashion, but rather the
reverse. The two great periods of English Philosophy,
Vaihinger remarks, ended with Ockham and with
Hume, who each took up, in effect, the fictional point
of view, but both too much on the merely negative
side, without realising the positive and constructive
value of fictions. English law has above all realised it,
even, he adds, to the point of absurdity. Nothing is so
precious as fiction, provided only one chooses the right

fiction. "Matter" is such a fiction. There are still people who speak with lofty contempt of "Materialism"; they mean well, but they are unhappy in their terms of abuse. When Berkeley demonstrated the impossibility of "matter," he thought he could afford to throw away the conception as useless. He was quite wrong; it is logically contradictory ideas that are the most valuable. Matter is a fiction, just as the fundamental ideas with which the sciences generally operate are mostly fictions, and the scientific materialisation of the world has proved a necessary and useful fiction, only harmful when we regard it as hypothesis and therefore possibly true. The representative world is a system of fictions. It is a symbol by the help of which we orient ourselves. The business of science is to make the symbol ever more adequate, but it remains a symbol, a means of action, for action is the last end of thinking.

The "atom," to which matter is ultimately reduced, is regarded by Vaihinger as equally a fiction, though it was at first viewed as an hypothesis, and it may be added that since he wrote it seems to have returned to the stage of hypothesis.[1] But when with Boscovich the "atom" was regarded as simply the bearer of energy, it became "literally a hypostatised nothing." We have

[1] "Most workers on the problem of atomic constitution," remarks Sir Ernest Rutherford (*Nature*, 5th August, 1922), "take as a working hypothesis that the atoms of matter are purely electrical structures, and that ultimately it is hoped to explain all the properties of atoms as a result of certain combinations of the two fundamental units of positive and negative electricity, the proton and electron."

to realise at the same time that every "thing" is a "summatory fiction," for to say, as is often said, that a "thing" has properties and yet has a real existence apart from its properties is obviously only a convenient manner of speech, a "verbal fiction." The "force of attraction," as Newton himself pointed out, belongs to the same class of summatory fictions.

Vaihinger is throughout careful to distinguish fiction alike from hypothesis and dogma. He regards the distinction as, methodologically, highly important, though not always easy to make. The "dogma" is put forward as an absolute and unquestionable truth; the "hypothesis" is a possible or probable truth, such as Darwin's doctrine of descent; the "fiction" is impossible, but it enables us to reach what for us is relatively truth, and, above all, while hypothesis simply contributes to knowledge, fiction thus used becomes a guide to practical action and indispensable to what we feel to be progress. Thus the mighty and civilising structure of Roman law was built up by the aid of what the Romans themselves recognised as fictions, while in the different and more flexible system of English laws a constant inspiration to action has been furnished by the supposed privileges gained by Magna Carta, though we now recognise them as fictitious. Many of our ideas tend to go through the three stages of Dogma, Hypothesis, and Fiction, sometimes in that order and sometimes in the reverse order. Hypothesis especially presents a state of labile stability which is unpleasant to the mind, so it tends to become either dogma or fiction. The ideas of Christianity, beginning as dogmas, have passed through all three stages in the minds of thinkers during recent centuries: the myths of Plato, beginning as fiction, not only passed through the three stages, but then passed back again, being now again regarded as fiction. The scientifically valuable fiction is a child of modern times, but we have already emerged from the period when the use of fiction was confined to the exact sciences.

Thus we find fiction fruitfully flourishing in the biological and social sciences and even in the highest spheres of human spiritual activity. The Linnæan and similar classificatory systems are fictions, even though put forward as hypotheses, having their value simply as pictures, as forms of representation, but leading to contradictions and liable to be replaced by other systems which present more helpful pictures. There are still people who disdain Adam Smith's "economic man," as though proceeding from a purely selfish view of life, although Buckle, forestalling Vaihinger, long ago explained that Smith was deliberately making use of a "valid artifice," separating facts that he knew to be in nature inseparable — he based his moral theory on a totally different kind of man — because so he could reach results approximately true to the observed phenomena. Bentham also adopted a fiction for his own system, though believing it to be an hypothesis, and Mill criticised it as being "geometrical"; the criticism is correct, comments Vaihinger, but the method was not thereby invalidated, for in complicated fields no other method can be fruitfully used.

The same law holds when we approach our highest and most sacred conceptions. It was recognised by enlightened philosophers and theologians before Vaihinger that the difference between body and soul is not different from that between matter and force, — a provisional and useful distinction, — that light and darkness, life and death, are abstractions, necessary, indeed, but in their application to reality always to be used with precaution. On the threshold of the moral world we meet the idea of Freedom, "one of the weightiest conceptions man has ever formed," once a dogma, in course of time an hypothesis, now in the eyes of many a fiction; yet we cannot do without it, even although we may be firmly convinced that our acts are determined by laws that cannot be broken. Many other great conceptions have tended to follow the same course. God, the Soul, Immortality, the Moral World-Order. The critical hearers understand what is meant when these great words are used, and if the uncritical misunderstand, that, adds Vaihinger, may sometimes be also useful. For these things are Ideals, and all Ideals are, logically speaking, fictions. As Science leads to the Imaginary, so Life leads to the Impossible; without them we cannot reach the heights we are born to scale. "Taken literally, however, our most valuable conceptions are worthless."

When we review the vast field which Vaihinger summarises, we find that thinking and existing must ever be on two different planes. The attempt of Hegel and his followers to transform subjective processes into objective world-processes, Vaihinger maintains, will not work out. The Thing-in-Itself, the Absolute, remains a fiction, though the ultimate and most necessary fiction, for without it representation would be unintelligible. We can only regard reality as a Heraclitean flux of happening — though Vaihinger fails to point out that this "reality" also can only be an image or symbol — and our thinking would itself be fluid if it were not that by fiction we obtain imaginary standpoints and boundaries by which to gain control of the flow of reality. It is the special art and object of thinking to attain existence by quite other methods than that of existence itself. But the wish by so doing to understand the world is both unrealisable and foolish, for we are only trying to comprehend our own fictions. We can never solve the so-called world-riddle because what seem riddles to us are merely the contradictions we have ourselves created. Yet, though the way of thinking cannot be the way of being, since they stand on such different foundations, thinking always has a kind of parallelism with being, and though we make our reckoning with a reality that we falsify, yet the practical result tends to come out right. Just because thinking is different from reality, its forms must also be different in order to correspond with reality. Our conceptions, our conventional signs, have a fictive function to perform; thinking in its lower grades is comparable to paper money, and in its higher forms it is a kind of poetry.

Imagination is thus a constitutive part of all thinking. We may make distinctions between practical scientific thinking and disinterested æsthetic thinking. Yet all thinking is finally a comparison. Scientific fictions are parallel with æsthetic fictions. The poet is the type of all thinkers: there is no sharp boundary between the region of poetry and the region of science. Both alike are not ends in themselves, but means to higher ends.

Vaihinger's doctrine of the "as if" is not immune from criticism on more than one side, and it is fairly obvious that, however sound the general principle, particular "fictions" may alter their status, and have even done so since the book was written. Moreover, the doctrine is not always quite congruous with itself. Nor can it be said that Vaihinger ever really answered the question with which he set out. In philosophy, however, it is not the attainment of the goal that matters, it is the things that are met with by the way. And Vaihinger's philosophy is not only of interest because it presents so clearly and vigorously a prevailing tendency in modern thought. Rightly understood, it supplies a fortifying influence to those who may have seen their cherished spiritual edifice, whatever it may be, fall around them and are tempted to a mood of disillusionment. We make our own world; when we have made it awry, we can remake it, approximately truer, though it cannot be absolutely true, to the facts. It will never be finally made; we are always stretching forth to larger and better fictions which answer more truly to our growing knowledge and experience. Even when we walk, it is only by a series of regulated errors, Vaihinger well points out, a perpetual succession of falls to one side and the other side. Our whole progress through life is of the same nature; all thinking is a regulated error. For we cannot, as Vaihinger insists, choose our errors at random or in accordance with what happens to please us; such fictions are only too likely to turn into deadening dogmas: the old *vis dormitiva* is the type of them, mere husks that are of no vital use and help us not at all. There are good fictions and bad fictions just as there are good poets and bad poets. It is in the choice and regulation of our errors, in our readiness to accept ever-closer approximations to the unattainable reality, that we think rightly and live rightly. We triumph in so far as we succeed in that regulation. "A lost battle," Foch, quoting De Maistre, lays down in his "Principes de Guerre," "is a battle one thinks one has lost"; the battle is won by the fiction that it is won. It is so also in the battle of life, in the whole art of living. Freud regards dreaming as fiction that helps us to sleep; thinking we may regard as fiction that helps us to live. Man lives by imagination.

III

Yet what we consider our highest activities arise out of what we are accustomed to regard as the lowest. That is, indeed, merely a necessary result of evolution; bipeds like ourselves spring out of many-limbed creatures whom we should now regard as little better than vermin, and the adult human creature whose eyes, as he sometimes imagines, are fixed on the stars, was a few years earlier merely a small animal crawling on all fours. The impulse of the philosopher, of the man of science, of any ordinary person who sometimes thinks about seemingly abstract or disinterested questions — we must include the whole range of the play of thought in response to the stimulus of curiosity — may seem at the first glance to be a quite secondary and remote product of the great primary instincts. Yet it is not difficult to bring this secondary impulse into direct relation with the fundamental primary instincts, even, and perhaps indeed chiefly, with the instinct of sex. On the mental side — which is not, of course, its fundamental side — the sexual instinct is mainly, perhaps solely, a reaction to the stimulus of curiosity. Beneath that mental surface the really active force is a physiologically based instinct urgent towards action, but the boy or girl who first becomes conscious of the mental stimulus is unaware of the instinct it springs from, and may even disregard as unimportant its specific physiological manifestations. The child is only conscious of new curiosities, and these it persistently seeks to satisfy at any available or likely source of information, aided by the strenuous efforts of its own restlessly active imagination. It is in exactly the same position as the metaphysician, or the biologist, or any thinker who is faced by complex and yet unsolved problems. And the child is at first baffled by just the same kind of obstacles, due, not like those of the thinker, to the silence of recalcitrant Nature, but to the silence of parents and teachers, or to their deliberate efforts to lead him astray.

Where do babies come from? That is perhaps for many children the earliest scientific problem that is in this way rendered so difficult of solution. No satisfying solution comes from the sources of information to which the child is wont to appeal. He is left to such siight imperfect observations as he can himself make; on such clues his searching intellect works and with the aid of imagination weaves a theory, more or less remote from the truth, which may possibly explain the phenomena. It is a genuine scientific process — the play of intellect and imagination around a few fragments of observed fact — and it is undoubtedly a valuable discipline for the childish mind, though if it is too prolonged it may impede or distort natural development, and if the resulting theory is radically false it may lead, as the theories of scientific adults sometimes lead, if not speedily corrected, to various unfortunate results.

A little later, when he has ceased to be a child and

puberty is approaching, another question is apt to arise in the boy's mind: What is a woman like? There is also, less often and more carefully concealed, the corresponding curiosity in the girl's mind. Earlier this question had seemed of no interest; it had never even occurred to ask it; there was little realisation — sometimes none at all — of any sexual difference. Now it sometimes becomes a question of singular urgency, in the solution of which it is necessary for the boy to concentrate all the scientific apparatus at his command. For there may be no ways of solving it directly, least of all for a well-behaved, self-respecting boy or a shy, modest girl. The youthful intellect is thus held in full tension, and its developing energy directed into all sorts of new channels in order to form an imaginative picture of the unknown reality, fascinating because incompletely known. All the chief recognised mental processes of dogma, hypothesis, and fiction, developed in the history of the race, are to this end instinctively created afresh in the youthful individual mind, endlessly formed and re-formed and tested in order to fill in the picture. The young investigator becomes a diligent student of literature and laboriously examines the relevant passages he finds in the Bible or other ancient primitive naked books. He examines statues and pictures. Perhaps he finds some old elementary manual of anatomy, but here the long list of structures with Latin names proves far more baffling than helpful to the youthful investigator who can in no possible way

fit them all into the smooth surface shown by the statues. Yet the creative and critical habit of thought, the
scientific mind generated by this search, is destined to
be of immense value, and long outlives the time when
the eagerly sought triangular spot, having fulfilled its
intellectual function, has become a familiar region,
viewed with indifference, or at most a homely tenderness.

That was but a brief and passing episode, however
permanently beneficial its results might prove. With
the achievement of puberty, with the coming of adolescence, a larger and higher passion fills the youth's soul.
He forgets the woman's body, his idealism seems to
raise him above the physical: it is the woman's personality — most likely some particular woman's personality — that he desires to know and to grasp.

A twofold development tends to take place at this
age — in those youths, that is to say, who possess the
latent attitude for psychic development — and that in
two diverse directions, both equally away from definite
physical desire, which at this age is sometimes, though
not always, at its least prominent place in consciousness. On the one hand there is an attraction for an
idealised person — perhaps a rather remote person, for
such most easily lend themselves to idealisation — of
the opposite (or occasionally the same) sex, it may
sometimes for a time even be the heroine of a novel.
Such an ideal attraction acts as an imaginative and
emotional ferment. The imagination is stimulated to

construct for the first time, from such material as it has come across, or can derive from within, the coherent picture of a desirable person. The emotions are trained and disciplined to play around the figure thus constructed with a new impersonal and unselfish, even self-sacrificing, devotion. But this process is not enough to use up all the energies of the developing mind, and the less so as such impulses are unlikely by their very nature to receive any considerable degree of gratification, for they are of a nature to which no adequate response is possible.

Thus it happens in adolescence that this new stream of psychic energy, emotional and intellectual, generated from within, concurrently with its primary personal function of moulding the object of love, streams over into another larger and more impersonal channel. It is, indeed, lifted on to a higher plane and transformed, to exercise a fresh function by initiating new objects of ideal desire. The radiant images of religion and of art as well as of science — however true it may be that they have also other adjuvant sources — thus begin to emerge from the depths beneath consciousness. They tend to absorb and to embody the new energy, while its primary personal object may sink into the background, or at this age even fail to be conscious at all.

This process — the process in which all abstract thinking is born as well as all artistic creation — must to some slight extent take place in every person whose mental activity is not entirely confined to the immediate objects of sense. But in persons of more complex psychic organisation it is a process of fundamental importance. In those of the highest complex organisation, indeed, it becomes what we term genius. In the most magnificent achievements of poetry and philosophy, of art and of science, it is no longer forbidden to see the ultimate root in this adolescent development.

To some a glimpse of this great truth has from time to time appeared. Ferrero, who occupied himself with psychology before attaining eminence as a brilliant historian, suggested thirty years ago that the art impulse and its allied manifestations are transformed sexual instinct; the sexual impulse is "the raw material, so to speak, from which art springs"; he connected that transformation with a less development of the sexual emotions in women; but that was much too hasty an assumption, for apart from the fact that such transformation could never be complete, and probably less so in women than in men, we have also to consider the nature of the two organisms through which the transformed emotions would operate, probably unlike in the sexes, for the work done by two machines obviously does not depend entirely upon feeding them with the same amount of fuel, but also on the construction of the two engines. Möbius, a brilliant and original, if not erratic, German psychologist, who was also concerned with the question of difference in the amount of sexual energy, regarded the art impulse as a kind of sexual secondary character. That is to say, no doubt, — if we develop

the suggestion, — that just as the external features of
the male and his external activities, in the ascending
zoölogical series, have been developed out of the impulse of repressed organic sexual desire striving to manifest itself ever more urgently in the struggle to overcome the coyness of the female, so on the psychic side
there has been a parallel impulse, if of later development, to carry on the same task in forms of art which
have afterwards acquired an independent activity and
a yet further growth dissociated from this primary biological function. We think of the natural ornaments
which adorn male animals from far down in the scale
even up to man, of the additions made thereto by tattooing and decoration and garments and jewels, of the
parades and dances and songs and musical serenades
found among lower animals as well as Man, together
with the love-lyrics of savages, furnishing the beginnings of the most exquisite arts of civilisation.

   It is to be noted, however, that these suggestions introduce an assumption of male superiority, or male inferiority — according to our scheme of values — which
unnecessarily prejudices and confuses the issue. We
have to consider the question of the origin of art apart
from any supposed predominance of its manifestations
in one sex or the other. In my own conception — put
forward a quarter of a century ago — of what I called
auto-erotic activities, it was on such a basis that I
sought to place it, since I regarded those auto-erotic
phenomena as arising from the impeded spontaneous

sexual energy of the organism and extending from simple physical processes to the highest psychic manifestations; "it is impossible to say what finest elements in art, in morals, in civilisation generally, may not really be rooted in an auto-erotic impulse," though I was careful to add that the transmutation of sexual energy into other forms of force must not be regarded as itself completely accounting for all the finest human aptitudes of sympathy and art and religion.[1]

It is along this path, it may perhaps be claimed, — as dimly glimpsed by Nietzsche, Hinton, and other earlier thinkers, — that the main explanation of the dynamic process by which the arts, in the widest sense, have come into being, is now chiefly being explored. One thinks of Freud and especially of Dr. Otto Rank, perhaps the most brilliant and clairvoyant of the younger investigators who still stand by the master's side. In 1905 Rank wrote a little essay on the artist[2] in which this mechanism is set forth and the artist placed, in what the psycho-analytic author considers his due place, between the ordinary dreamer at one end and the neurotic subject at the other, the lower forms of art, such as myth-making, standing near to dreams, and the higher forms, such as the drama, philosophy, and the founding of religions, near to psycho-neurosis, but all possessing a sublimated life-force which has its root in some modification of sexual energy.

[1] Havelock Ellis, *Studies in the Psychology of Sex*, vol. I.
[2] Otto Rank, *Der Künstler: Ansätze zu einer Sexual Psychologie.*

It may often seem that, in these attempts to explain the artist, the man of science is passed over or left in the background, and that is true. But art and science, as we now know, have the same roots. The supreme men of science are recognisably artists, and the earliest forms of art, which are very early indeed, — Sir Arthur Evans has suggested that men may have drawn before they talked, — were doubtless associated with magic, which was primitive man's science, or, at all events, his nearest approximation to science. The connection of the scientific instinct with the sexual instinct is not, indeed, a merely recent insight. Many years ago it was clearly stated by a famous Dutch author. "Nature, who must act wisely at the risk of annihilation," wrote Multatuli at the conclusion of his short story, "The Adventures of Little Walter," "has herein acted wisely by turning all her powers in one direction. Moralists and psychologists have long since recognised, without inquiring into the causes, that curiosity is one of the main elements of love. Yet they were only thinking of sexual love, and by raising the two related termini in corresponding wise on to a higher plane I believe that the noble thirst for knowledge springs from the same soil in which noble love grows. To press through, to reveal, to possess, to direct, and to ennoble, that is the task and the longing, alike of the lover and the natural discoverer. So that every Ross or Franklin is a Werther of the Pole, and whoever is in love is a Mungo Park of the spirit."

IV

As soon as we begin to think about the world around us in what we vainly call a disinterested way — for disinterest is, as Leibnitz said, a chimera, and there remains a superior interest — we become youths and lovers and artists, and there is at the same time a significant strain of sexual imagery in our thought.[1] Among ourselves this is not always clear; we have been dulled by the routine of civilisation and the artificial formalities of what is called education. It is clear in the mythopœic creation of comparative primitive thought, but in civilisation it is in the work of men of genius — poets, philosophers, painters, and, as we have to recognise, men of science — that this trait is most conspicuously manifested. To realise this it is sufficient to contemplate the personality and activity of one of the earliest great modern men of science, of Leonardo da Vinci. Until recent times it would have seemed rather strange so to describe Leonardo da Vinci. He still seemed, as he was in his own time, primarily a painter, an artist in the conventionally narrow sense, and as such one of the greatest, fit to paint, as Browning put it, one of the four walls of the New Jerusalem. Yet even his contemporaries who so acclaimed him were a little worried about Leonardo in this capacity. He accomplished so

---

[1] The sexual strain in the symbolism of language is touched on in my *Studies in the Psychology of Sex*, vol. v, and similar traits in primitive legends have been emphasised — many would say over-emphasised — by Freud and Jung.

little, he worked so slowly, he left so much unfinished, he seemed to them so volatile and unstable. He was an enigma to which they never secured the key. They failed to see, though it is clearly to be read even in his face, that no man ever possessed a more piercing concentration of vision, a more fixed power of attention, a more unshakable force of will. All that Leonardo achieved in painting and in sculpture and in architecture, however novel or grandiose, was, as Solmi, the highly competent Vincian scholar has remarked, merely a concession to his age, in reality a violence done to his own nature, and from youth to old age he had directed his whole strength to one end: the knowledge and the mastery of Nature. In our own time, a sensitive, alert, widely informed critic of art, Bernhard Berenson, setting out with the conventional veneration for Leonardo as a painter, slowly, as the years went by and his judgment grew more mature, adopted a more critical attitude, bringing down his achievements in art to moderate dimensions, yet without taking any interest in Leonardo as a stupendous artist in science. We may well understand that vein of contempt for the crowd, even as it almost seems the hatred for human society, the spirit of Timon, which runs across Leonardo's writings, blended, no doubt inevitably blended, with his vein of human sweetness. This stern devotee of knowledge declared, like the author of "The Imitation of Christ," that "Love conquers all things." There is here no discrepancy. The man who poured a contemp-

tuous flood of irony and denunciation over the most
sacred social institutions and their most respectable
representatives was the same man — the Gospels tell
us — who brooded with the wings of a maternal tenderness over the pathos of human things.

When, indeed, our imagination plays with the idea
of a future Overman, it is Leonardo who comes before us as his forerunner. Vasari, who had never seen
Leonardo, but has written so admirable an account of
him, can only describe him as "supernatural" and
"divine." In more recent times Nietzsche remarked
of Leonardo that "there is something super-European
and silent in him, the characteristic of one who has
seen too wide a circle of things good and evil." There
Nietzsche touches, even though vaguely, more nearly
than Vasari could, the distinguishing mark of this endlessly baffling and enchanting figure. Every man of
genius sees the world at a different angle from his fellows, and there is his tragedy. But it is usually a measurable angle. We cannot measure the angle at which
Leonardo stands; he strikes athwart the line of our
conventional human thought in ways that are sometimes a revelation and sometimes an impenetrable
mystery. We are reminded of the saying of Heraclitus:
"Men hold some things wrong and some right; God
holds all things fair." The dispute as to whether he was
above all an artist or a man of science is a foolish and
even unmeaning dispute. In the vast orbit in which
Leonardo moved the distinction had little or no ex-

istence. That was inexplicable to his contemporaries whose opinions Vasari echoes. They could not understand that he was not of the crowd of makers of pretty things who filled the workshops of Florence. They saw a man of beautiful aspect and fine proportions, with a long curled beard and wearing a rose-coloured tunic, and they called him a craftsman, an artist, and thought him rather fantastic. But the medium in which this artist worked was Nature, the medium in which the scientist works; every problem in painting was to Leonardo a problem in science, every problem in physics he approached in the spirit of the artist. "Human ingenuity," he said, "can never devise anything more simple and more beautiful, or more to the purpose, than Nature does." For him, as later for Spinoza, reality and perfection were the same thing. Both aspects of life he treats as part of his task — the extension of the field of human knowledge, the intension of the power of human skill; for art, or, as he called it, practice, without science, he said, is a boat without a rudder. Certainly he occupied himself much with painting, the common medium of self-expression in his day, though he produced so few pictures; he even wrote a treatise on painting; he possessed, indeed, a wider perception of its possibilities than any artist who ever lived. "Here is the creator of modern landscape!" exclaimed Corot before Leonardo's pictures, and a remarkable description he has left of the precise effects of colour and light produced when a woman in white stands on green grass in bright sunshine shows that Leonardo clearly apprehended the *plein-airiste's* problem. Doubtless it will prove possible to show that he foresaw still later methods. He rejected these methods because it seemed to him that the artist could work most freely by moving midway between light and darkness, and, indeed, he, first of painters, succeeded in combining them — just as he said also that Pleasure and Pain should be imaged as twins since they are ever together, yet back to back because ever contrary — and devised the method of *chiaroscuro*, by which light reveals the richness of shade and shade heightens the brightness of light. No invention could be more characteristic of this man whose grasp of the world ever involved the union of opposites, and the opposites both apprehended more intensely than falls to the lot of other men.

Yet it is noteworthy that Leonardo constantly speaks of the artist's function as searching into and imitating Nature, a view which the orthodox artist anathematises. But Leonardo was not the orthodox artist, not even, perhaps, as he is traditionally regarded, one of the world's supreme painters. For one may sympathise with Mr. Berenson's engaging attempt — unconvincing as it has seemed — to "expose" Leonardo. The drawings Mr. Berenson, like every one else, admires whole-heartedly, but, save for the unfinished "Adoration," which he regards as a summit of art, he finds the paintings mostly meaningless and repellent.

He cannot rank Leonardo as an artist higher than
Botticelli, and concludes that he was not so much a
great painter as a great inventor in painting. With
that conclusion it is possible that Leonardo himself
would have agreed. Painting was to him, he said, a
subtle invention whereby philosophical speculation can
be applied to all the qualities of forms. He seemed to
himself to be, here and always, a man standing at the
mouth of the gloomy cavern of Nature with arched
back, one hand resting on his knee and the other shad-
ing his eyes, as he peers intently into the darkness,
possessed by fear and desire, fear of the threatening
gloom of that cavern, desire to discover what miracle
it might hold. We are far here from the traditional
attitude of the painter; we are nearer to the attitude of
that great seeker into the mysteries of Nature, one of
the very few born of women to whom we can ever even
passingly compare Leonardo, who felt in old age that
he had only been a child gathering shells and pebbles
on the shore of the great ocean of truth.

It is almost as plausible to regard Leonardo as primarily an engineer as primarily a painter. He offered
his services as a military engineer and architect to the
Duke of Milan and set forth at length his manifold
claims which include, one may note, the ability to
construct what we should now, without hesitation,
describe as "tanks." At a later period he actually was
appointed architect and engineer-general to Cæsar
Borgia, and in this capacity was engaged on a variety

of works. He has, indeed, been described as the founder of professional engineering. He was the seer of coming steam engines and of steam navigation and transportation. He was, again, the inventor of innumerable varieties of ballistic machines and ordnance, of steam guns and breech-loading arms with screw breech-lock. His science always tended to become applied science. Experience shows the road to practice, he said, science is the guide to art. Thus he saw every problem in the world as in the wide sense a problem in engineering. All nature was a dynamic process of forces beautifully effecting work, and it is this as it were distinctive vision of the world as a whole which seems to give Leonardo that marvellous flair for detecting vital mechanism in every field. It is impossible even to indicate summarily the vast extent of the region in which he was creating a new world, from the statement, which he set down in large letters, "The sun does not move," the earth being, he said, a star, "much like the moon," down to such ingenious original devices as the construction of a diving-bell, a swimming-belt, and a parachute of adequate dimensions, while, as is now well known, Leonardo not only meditated with concentrated attention on the problem of flight, but realised scientifically the difficulties to be encountered, and made ingenious attempts to overcome them in the designing of flying-machines. It is enough — following expert scientific guidance — to enumerate a few points: he studied botany in the bio-

logical spirit; he was a founder of geology, discovering
the significance of fossils and realising the importance
of river erosion; by his studies in the theories of
mechanics and their utilization in peace and war he
made himself the prototype of the modern man of
science. He was in turn biologist in every field of vital
mechanism, and the inaugurator before Vesalius
(who, however, knew nothing of his predecessor's
work) of the minute study of anatomy by direct investigation (after he had found that Galen could not
be relied on) and *post-mortem* dissections; he nearly
anticipated Harvey's conception of the circulation of
the blood by studying the nature of the heart as a
pump. He was hydraulician, hydrographer, geometrician, algebraist, mechanician, optician.[1] These are
but a few of the fields in which Leonardo's marvellous
insight into the nature of the forces that make the
world and his divining art of the methods of employ-
ing them to human use have of late years been revealed. For centuries they were concealed in note-
books scattered through Europe and with difficulty
decipherable. Yet they are not embodied in vague
utterances or casual intuitions, but display a laborious
concentration on the precise details of the difficulties
to be overcome; nor was patient industry in him, as
often happens, the substitute for natural facility, for

[1] Einstein, in conversation with Moszkowski, expressed doubt as to
the reality of Leonardo's previsions of modern science. But it scarcely
appeared that he had investigated the matter, while the definite testimony of the experts in many fields who have done so cannot be put aside.

he was a person of marvellous natural facility, and, like such persons, most eloquent and persuasive in speech. At the same time his more general and reflective conclusions are expressed in a style combining the maximum of clarity with the maximum of concision, — far, indeed, removed from the characteristic florid redundancy of Italian prose, — which makes Leonardo, in addition to all else, a supreme master of language.[1]

Yet the man to whom we must credit these vast intellectual achievements was no abstracted philosopher shut up in a laboratory. He was, even to look upon, one of the most attractive and vivid figures that ever walked the earth. As has sometimes happened with divine and mysterious persons, he was the natural child of his mother, Caterina, of whom we are only told that she was "of good blood," belonging to Vinci like Ser Piero the father, and that a few years after Leonardo's birth she became the reputable wife of a citizen of his native town. Ser Piero da Vinci was a notary, of a race of notaries, but the busiest notary in Florence and evidently a man of robust vigour; he married four times and his youngest child was fifty years the junior of Leonardo. We hear of the extraordinary physical

[1] For the Italian reader of Leonardo the fat little volume of *Frammenti*, edited by Dr. Solmi and published by Barbèra, is a precious and inexhaustible pocket companion. For the English reader Mr. MacCurdy's larger but much less extensive volume of extracts from the *Note-Books*, or the still further abridged *Thoughts*, must suffice. Herbert Horne's annotated version of Vasari's *Life* is excellent for Leonardo's personality and career.

strength of Leonardo himself, of his grace and charm, of his accomplishments in youth, especially in singing and playing on the flute, though he had but an elementary school education. Except for what he learnt in the workshop of the many-sided but then still youthful Verrocchio, he was his own schoolmaster, and was thus enabled to attain that absolute emancipation from authority and tradition which made him indifferent even to the Greeks, to whom he was most akin. He was left-handed; his peculiar method of writing long raised the suspicion that it was deliberately adopted for concealment, but it is to-day recognised as simply the ordinary mirror-writing of a left-handed child without training. This was not the only anomaly in Leonardo's strange nature. We now know that he was repeatedly charged as a youth on suspicion of homosexual offences; the result remains obscure, but there is some reason to think he knew the inside of a prison. Throughout life he loved to surround himself with beautiful youths, though no tradition of license or vice clings to his name. The precise nature of his sexual temperament remains obscure. It mocks us, but haunts us from out of his most famous pictures. There is, for instance, the "John the Baptist" of the Louvre, which we may dismiss with the distinguished art critic of to-day as an impudent blasphemy or brood over long, without being clearly able to determine into what obscure region of the Freudian Unconscious Leonardo had here adventured. Freud himself has devoted one of his most fascinating essays to a psycho-analytic interpretation of Leonardo's enigmatic personality. He admits it is a speculation; we may take it or leave it. But Freud has rightly apprehended that in Leonardo sexual passion was largely sublimated into intellectual passion, in accordance with his own saying, "Nothing can be loved or hated unless first we have knowledge of it," or, as he elsewhere said, "True and great love springs out of great knowledge, and where you know little you can love but little or not at all." So it was that Leonardo became a master of life. Vasari could report of him — almost in the words it was reported of another supreme but widely different figure, the Jesuit saint, Francis Xavier — that "with the splendour of his most beautiful countenance he made serene every broken spirit." To possess by self-mastery the sources of love and hate is to transcend good and evil and so to possess the Overman's power of binding up the hearts that are broken by good and evil.

Every person of genius is in some degree at once man, woman, and child. Leonardo was all three in the extreme degree and yet without any apparent conflict. The infantile strain is unquestioned, and, apart from the problem of his sexual temperament, Leonardo was a child even in his extraordinary delight in devising fantastic toys and contriving disconcerting tricks. His more than feminine tenderness is equally clear, alike in his pictures and in his life. Isabella d'Este, in

asking him to paint the boy Jesus in the Temple,
justly referred to "the gentleness and sweetness which
mark your art." His tenderness was shown not only
towards human beings, but to all living things, animals
and even plants, and it would appear that he was a
vegetarian. Yet at the same time he was emphatically
masculine, altogether free from weakness or softness.
He delighted in ugliness as well as in beauty; he liked
visiting the hospitals to study the sick in his thirst for
knowledge; he pondered over battles and fighting; he
showed no compunction in planning devilish engines
of military destruction. His mind was of a definitely
realistic and positive cast; though there seems no
field of thought he failed to enter, he never touched
metaphysics, and though his worship of Nature has
the emotional tone of religion, even of ecstasy, he was
clearly disdainful of the established religions, and perpetually shocked "the timid friends of God." By precept and by practice he proclaimed the lofty solitude
of the individual soul, and he felt only contempt for the
herd. We see how this temper became impressed on
his face in his own drawing of himself in old age, with
that intent and ruthless gaze wrapped in intellectual
contemplation of the outspread world.

Leonardo comes before us, indeed, in the end, as a
figure for awe rather than for love. Yet, as the noblest
type of the Overman we faintly try to conceive, Leonardo is the foe, not of man, but of the enemies of man.
The great secrets that with clear vision his stern grip

tore from Nature, the new instruments of power that his energy wrought, they were all for the use and delight of mankind. So Leonardo is the everlasting embodiment of that brooding human spirit whose task never dies. Still to-day it stands at the mouth of the gloomy cavern of Nature, even of Human Nature, with bent back and shaded eyes, seeking intently to penetrate the gloom beyond, with the fear of that threatening darkness, with the desire of what redeeming miracle it yet perchance may hold.

V

THAT Leonardo da Vinci was not only supremely great in science, but the incarnation of the spirit of science, the artist and lover of Nature, is a fact it is well to bear in mind. Many mistakes would be avoided if it were more clearly present to consciousness. We should no longer find the artists in design absurdly chafing under what they considered the bondage of the artists in thought. It would no longer be possible, as it was some years ago, and may be still, for a narrow-minded pedagogue like Brunetière, however useful in his own field, to be greeted as a prophet when he fatuously proclaimed what he termed "the bankruptcy of science." Unfortunately so many of the people who masquerade under the name of "men of science" have no sort of title to that name. They may be doing good and honest work by accumulating in little cells the facts which others, more truly inspired by the spirit of sci-

ence, may one day work on; they may be doing more
or less necessary work by the application to practical
life of the discoveries which genuine men of science
have made. But they themselves have just as much,
and no more, claim to use the name of "science" as
the men who make the pots and dishes piled up in a
crockery shop have to use the name of "art." [1] They
have not yet even learnt that "science" is not the ac-
cumulation of knowledge in the sense of piling up isolated facts, but the active organisation of knowledge,
the application to the world of the cutting edge of a
marvellously delicate instrument, and that this task is
impossible without the widest range of vision and the
most restless fertility of imagination.

Of such more genuine men of science — to name one
whom by virtue of several common interests I was
sometimes privileged to come near — was Francis
Galton. He was not a professional man of science; he
was even willing that his love of science should be accounted simply a hobby. From the standpoint of the
ordinary professional scientific man he was probably
an amateur. He was not even, as some have been, a
learned amateur. I doubt whether he had really
mastered the literature of any subject, though I do not
doubt that that mattered little. When he heard of

[1] Morley Roberts, who might be regarded as a pupil in the school of
Leonardo and trained like him in the field of art, has in various places of
his suggestive book, *Warfare in the Human Body*, sprinkled irony over
the examples he has come across of ignorant specialists claiming to be
men of "science."

some famous worker in a field he was exploring, he would look up that man's work; so it was with Weismann in the field of heredity. And, as I would note with a smile in reading his letters, Galton was not able to spell Weismann's name correctly.[1] His attitude in science might be said to be pioneering much like that of the pioneers of museums in the later seventeenth and earlier eighteenth centuries, men like Tradescant and Ashmole and Evelyn and Sloane: an insatiable curiosity in things that were only just beginning, or had not yet begun, to arouse curiosity. So it was that when I made some personal experiments with the Mexican cactus, mescal (*Anhalonium Lewinii*), to explore its vision-producing qualities, then quite unknown in England, Galton was eagerly interested and wanted to experiment on himself, though ultimately dissuaded on account of his advanced age. But, on this basis, Galton's curiosity was not the mere inquisitiveness of the child, it was coördinated with an almost uniquely organised brain as keen as it was well-balanced. So that on the one hand his curiosity was transformed into methods that were endlessly ingenious and inventive, and on the other it was guided and held in check by inflexible caution and good sense. And he knew how to preserve that exquisite balance without

[1] Needless to say, I do not mention this to belittle Galton. A careful attention to words, which in its extreme form becomes pedantry, is by no means necessarily associated with a careful attention to things. Until recent times English writers, even the greatest, were always negligent in spelling; it would be foolish to suppose they were therefore negligent in thinking.

any solemnity or tension or self-assertion, but playfully and graciously, with the most unfailing modesty.
It was this rare combination of qualities — one may
see it all in his "Inquiries into Human Faculty" —
which made him the very type of the man of genius,
operating, not by profession or by deliberate training,
but by natural function, throwing light on the dark
places of the world and creating science in out-of-the-
way fields of human experience which before had been
left to caprice or not even perceived at all. Throughout he was an artist and if, as is reported, he spent the
last year of his life chiefly in writing a novel, that was
of a piece with the whole of his marvellous activity;
he had never been doing anything else. Only his
romances were real.

Galton's yet more famous cousin, Charles Darwin,
presents in equal purity the lover and the artist in the
sphere of Nature and Science. No doubt there were
once many obtuse persons to whom these names
seemed scarcely to fit when applied to Darwin. There
have been people to whom Darwin scarcely seemed a
man of genius, merely a dry laborious pedestrian
student of facts. He himself even — as many people
find it difficult to forget — once lamented his indifference to poetry and art. But Darwin was one of those
elect persons in whose subconscious, if not in their
conscious, nature is implanted the realisation that
"science *is* poetry," and in a field altogether remote
from the poetry and art of convention he was alike

poet and artist. Only a man so endowed could from a suggestion received on reading Malthus have conceived of natural selection as a chief moulding creative force of an infinite succession of living forms; so also of his fantastic theory of pangenesis. Even in trifling matters of experiment, such as setting a musician to play the bassoon in his greenhouse, to ascertain whether music affected plants, he had all the inventive imagination of poet or of artist. He was poet and artist — though I doubt if this has been pointed out — in his whole attitude towards Nature. He worked hard, but to him work was a kind of play, and it may well be that with his fragile health he could not have carried on his work if it had not been play. Again and again in his "Life and Letters" we find the description of his observations or experiments introduced by some such phrase as: "I was infinitely amused." And he remarks of a biological problem that it was like a game of chess. I doubt, indeed, whether any great man of science was more of an artist than Darwin, more consciously aware that he was playing with the world, more deliciously thrilled by the fun of life. That man may well have found "poetry and art" dull who himself had created the theory of sexual selection which made the whole becoming of life art and the secret of it poetry.[1]

[1] Darwin even overestimated the æsthetic element in his theory of sexual selection, and (I have had occasion elsewhere to point out) unnecessarily prejudiced that theory by sometimes unwarily assuming a conscious æsthetic element.

It is not alone among biologists, from whose stand-point it may be judged easier to reach, since they are concerned with living Nature, that we find the attitude of the lover and the artist. We find it just as well marked when the man of genius plays in what some might think the arid field of the physicist. Faraday worked in a laboratory, a simple one, indeed, but the kind of place which might be supposed fatal to the true spirit of science, and without his researches in magnetic electricity we might have missed, with or without a pang, those most practical machines of our modern life, the dynamo and the telephone. Yet Fara-day had no practical ends in view; it has been possible to say of him that he investigated Nature as a poet investigates the emotions. That would not have suf-ficed to make him the supreme man of science he was. His biographer, Dr. Bence Jones, who knew him well, concludes that Faraday's first great characteristic was his trust in facts, and his second his imagination. There we are brought to the roots of his nature. Only, it is important to remember, these two characteristics were not separate and distinct. In themselves they may be opposing traits; it was because in Faraday they were held together in vital tension that he be-came so potent an instrument of research into Nature's secrets. Tyndall, who was his friend and fellow worker, seems to have perceived this. "The force of his imag-ination," wrote Tyndall, "was enormous,"—he "rose from the smallest beginnings to the greatest ends," from "bubbles of oxygen and nitrogen to the atmospheric envelope of the earth itself," — but "he bridled it like a mighty rider." Faraday himself said to the same effect: "Let the imagination go, guarding it by judgment and principles, but holding it in and directing it by experiment." Elsewhere he has remarked that in youth he was, and he might have added that he still remained, "a very lively imaginative person and could believe in the 'Arabian Nights' as easily as in the 'Encyclopædia.'" But he soon acquired almost an instinct for testing facts by experiment, for distrusting such alleged facts as he had not so tested, and for accepting all the conclusions that he had thus reached with a complete indifference to commonly accepted beliefs. (It is true he was a faithful and devout elder in the Sandemanian Church, and that is not the least fascinating trait in this fascinating man.) Tyndall has insisted on both of these aspects of Faraday's mental activity. He had "wonderful vivacity," he was "a man of excitable and fiery nature," and "underneath his sweetness was the heat of a volcano." He himself believed that there was a Celtic strain in his heredity; there was a tradition that the family came from Ireland; I cannot find that there are any Faradays, or people of any name resembling Faraday, now in Ireland, but Tyndall, being himself an Irishman, liked to believe that the tradition was sound. It would only account for the emotionally vivacious side of this nature. There was also the other side, on which Tyndall also insists: the love of order, the extreme tenacity, the high self-discipline able to convert the fire within into a clear concentrated glow. In the fusion of these two qualities "he was a prophet," says Tyndall, "and often wrought by an inspiration to be understood by sympathy alone." His expansive emotional imagination became the servant of truth, and sprang into life at its touch. In carrying out physical experiments he would experience a childlike joy and his eyes sparkled. "Even to his latest days he would almost dance for joy at being shown a new experiment." Silvanus Thompson, in his book on Faraday, insists (as Tyndall had) on the association with this childlike joy in imaginative extravagance of the perpetual impulse to test and to prove, "yet never hesitating to push to their logical conclusions the ideas suggested by experiment, however widely they might seem to lead from the accepted modes of thought." His method was the method of the "Arabian Nights," transferred to the region of facts.

Faraday was not a mathematician. But if we turn to Kepler, who moved in the sphere of abstract calculation, we find precisely the same combination of characteristics. It was to Kepler, rather than to Copernicus, that we owe the establishment of the heliocentric theory of our universe, and Kepler, more than any man, was the precursor of Newton. It has been said that if Kepler had never lived it is difficult to conceive who could have taken his place and achieved his special part in the scientific creation of our universe. For that pioneering part was required a singular blend of seemingly opposed qualities. Only a wildly daring, original, and adventurous spirit could break away from the agelong traditions and rigid preconceptions which had ruled astronomy for thousands of years. Only an endlessly patient, careful, laborious, precise investigator could set up the new revolutionary conceptions needed to replace these traditions and preconceptions. Kepler supplied this rare combination of faculties. He possessed the most absurdly extravagant imagination; he developed a greater regard for accuracy in calculation than the world had ever known. He was willing to believe that the earth was a kind of animal, and would not have been surprised to find that it possessed lungs or gills. At the same time so set was he on securing the precise truth, so patiently laborious, that some of his most elaborate calculations were repeated, and without the help of logarithms, even seventy times. The two essential qualities that make the supreme artist in science have never been so clearly made manifest as in Kepler.

Kepler may well bring us to Einstein, the greatest pioneer in the comprehension of the universe since his day, and, indeed, one who is more than a pioneer, since he already seems to have won a place beside Newton. It is a significant fact that Einstein, though he possesses an extremely cautious, critical mind, and is regarded as conspicuous for his common sense, has a profound admiration for Kepler, whom he frequently quotes. For Einstein also is an imaginative artist.[1]

Einstein is obviously an artist, even in appearance, as has often been noted by those who have met him; "he looks far more the musician than the man of science," one writes, while those who know him well say that he is "essentially as much an artist as a discoverer." As a matter of fact he is an artist in one of the most commonly recognised arts, being an accomplished musician, a good violinist, it is said, while improvisation on the piano, he himself says, is "a necessity of his life." His face, we are told, is illumined when he listens to music; he loves Bach and Haydn and Mozart, Beethoven and Wagner much less, while to Chopin, Schumann, and the so-called romantics in music, as we might anticipate, he is indifferent. His love of music is inborn; it developed when, as a child, he would think out little songs "in praise of God," and sing them by himself; music, Nature, and God began, even

[1] It is probable that the reason why it is often difficult to trace the imaginative artist in great men of supposedly abstract science is the paucity of intimate information about them. Even their scientific friends have rarely had the patience, or even perhaps the intelligence, to observe them reverently and to record their observations. We know almost nothing that is intimately personal about Newton. As regards Einstein, we are fortunate in possessing the book of Moszkowski, *Einstein* (translated into English under the title of *Einstein the Searcher*), which contains many instructive conversations and observations by a highly intelligent and appreciative admirer, who has set them down in a Boswellian spirit that faintly recalls Eckermann's book on Goethe (which, indeed, Moszkowski had in mind), though falling far short of that supreme achievement. The statements in the text are mainly gleaned from Moszkowski.

at that early age, to become a kind of unity to him. "Music," said Leibnitz, "is the pleasure the human soul experiences from counting without being aware that it is counting." It is the most abstract, the most nearly mathematical of the arts — we may recall how music and mathematics had their scientific origin together in the discovery of Pythagoras — and it is not surprising that it should be Einstein's favorite art.[1] It is even more natural that, next to music, he should be attracted to architecture — the art which Goethe called "frozen music" — for here we are actually plunged into mechanics, here statics and dynamics are transformed into visible beauty. To painting he is indifferent, but he is drawn to literature, although no great reader. In literature, indeed, it would seem that it is not so much art that he seeks as emotion; in this field it is no longer the austerely architectonic that draws him; thus he is not attracted to Ibsen; he is greatly attracted to Cervantes as well as Keller and Strindberg; he has a profound admiration for Shakespeare, but is cooler towards Goethe, while it would seem that there is no writer to whom he is more fervently attached than the most highly emotional, the most profoundly disintegrated in nervous organisation of all great writers, Dostoievsky, especially his masterpiece, "The Brothers Karamazov." "Dostoievsky

[1] Spengler holds (*Der Untergang des Abendlandes*, vol. x, p. 329) that the development of music throughout its various stages in our European culture really has been closely related with the stages of the development of mathematics.

gives me more than any scientist, more than Gauss."
All literary analysis or æsthetic subtlety, it seems to
Einstein, fails to penetrate to the heart of a work like
"The Karamazovs," it can only be grasped by the
feelings. His face lights up when he speaks of it and he
can find no word but "ethical satisfaction." For ethics
in the ordinary sense, as a system, means little to
Einstein; he would not even include it in the sciences;
it is the ethical joy embodied in art which satisfies him.
Moreover, it is said, the keynote of Einstein's emotional existence is the cry of Sophocles' Antigone: "I
am not here to hate with you, but to love with you."
The best that life has to offer, he feels, is a face glowing
with happiness. He is an advanced democrat and paci-
fist rather than (as is sometimes supposed) a socialist;
he believes in the internationality of all intellectual
work and sees no reason why this should destroy national characteristics.

Einstein is not — and this is the essential point to
make clear — merely an artist in his moments of leisure and play, as a great statesman may play golf or a
great soldier grow orchids. He retains the same attitude in the whole of his work. He traces science to its
roots in emotion, which is exactly where art also is
rooted. Of Max Planck, the physicist, for whom he has
great admiration, Einstein has said: "The emotional
condition which fits him for his task is akin to that of a
devotee or a lover." We may say the same, it would
seem, of Einstein himself. He is not even to be in-

cluded, as some might have supposed, in that rigid sect which asserts that all real science is precise measurement; he recognises that the biological sciences must be largely independent of mathematics. If mathematics were the only path of science, he once remarked, Nature would have been illegible for Goethe, who had a non-mathematical, even anti-mathematical, mind, and yet possessed a power of intuition greater than that of many an exact investigator.[1] All great achievements in science, he holds, start from intuition. This he constantly repeats, although he adds that the intuition must not stand alone, for invention also is required. He is disposed to regard many scientific discoveries commonly regarded the work of pure thought as really works of art. He would have this view embodied in all education, making education a free and living process, with no drilling of the memory and no examinations, mainly a process of appeal to the senses in order to draw out delicate reactions. With his end, and even for the sake of acquiring ethical personality, he would have every child learn a handicraft, joinery, bookbinding, or other, and, like Élie Faure,[2] he has great faith in

[1] I would here refer to a searching investigation, "Goethe und die mathematische Physik: Eine Erkenntnistheoretische Studie," in Ernst Cassirer's *Idee und Gestalt* (1921). It is here shown that in some respects Goethe pointed the way along which mathematical physics, by following its own paths, has since travelled, and that even when most non-mathematical Goethe's scientific attitude was justifiable.

[2] See the remarkable essay, "De la Cinéplastique," in Élie Faure's *L'Arbre d'Éden* (1922). It is, however, a future and regenerated cinema for which Élie Faure looks, "to become the art of the crowd, the powerful centre of communion in which new symphonic forms will be born in the tumult of passions and utilized for fine and elevating æsthetic ends."

the educational value of the cinema. We see that behind all Einstein's activity lies the conception that
the physicist's work is to attain a picture, "a world-
picture," as he calls it. "I agree with Schopenhauer,"
Einstein said at a celebration in honour of Planck in
1918, "that one of the most powerful motives that attract people to science and art is the longing to escape
from everyday life with its painful coarseness and des-
olating bareness, and to break the fetters of their own
ever-changing desires. It impels those of keener sensibility out of their personal existences into the world of
objective perception and understanding. It is a motive
force of like kind to that which drives the dweller in
noisy confused cities to restful Alpine heights whence
he seems to have an outlook on eternity. Associated
with this negative motive is the positive motive which
impels men to seek a simplified synoptic view of the
world conformable to their own nature, overcoming
the world by replacing it with this picture. The painter,
the poet, the philosopher, the scientist, all do this, each
in his own way." Spengler has elaborately argued that
there is a perfect identity of physics, mathematics, religion, and great art.[1] We might fairly be allowed to
point to Einstein as a lofty embodiment of that identity.

Here, where we reach the sphere of mathematics, we
are among processes which seem to some the most
inhuman of all human activities and the most remote

[1] O. Spengler, *Der Untergang des Abendlandes*, vol. 1, p. 576.

from poetry. Yet it is here that the artist has the fullest scope for his imagination. "Mathematics," says Bertrand Russell in his "Mysticism and Logic," "may be defined as the subject in which we never know what we are talking about, nor whether what we are saying is true." We are in the imaginative sphere of art, and the mathematician is engaged in a work of creation which resembles music in its orderliness, and is yet reproducing on another plane the order of the universe, and so becoming as it were a music of the spheres. It is not surprising that the greatest mathematicians have again and again appealed to the arts in order to find some analogy to their own work. They have indeed found it in the most various arts, in poetry, in painting, in sculpture, although it would certainly seem that it is in music, the most abstract of the arts, the art of number and of time, that we find the closest analogy. "The mathematician's best work is art," said Mittag-Lefler, "a high and perfect art, as daring as the most secret dreams of imagination, clear and limpid. Mathematical genius and artistic genius touch each other." And Sylvester wrote in his "Theory of Reciprocants": "Does it not seem as if Algebra had attained to the dignity of a fine art, in which the workman has a free hand to develop his conceptions, as in a musical theme or a subject for painting? It has reached a point in which every properly developed algebraical composition, like a skilful landscape, is expected to suggest the notion of an infinite distance lying beyond the limits of the canvas." "Mathematics, rightly viewed," says Bertrand Russell again, "possesses not only truth, but supreme beauty—a beauty cold and austere, like that of sculpture. . . . The true spirit of delight, the exaltation, the sense of being more than man, which is the touchstone of the highest excellence, is to be found in mathematics as surely as in poetry."

The mathematician has reached the highest rung on the ladder of human thought. But it is the same ladder which we have all of us been always ascending, alike from the infancy of the individual and the infancy of the race. Molière's Jourdain had been speaking prose for more than forty years without knowing it. Mankind has been thinking poetry throughout its long career and remained equally ignorant.

CHAPTER IV
THE ART OF WRITING

I

FROM time to time we are solemnly warned that in the hands of modern writers language has fallen into a morbid state. It has become degenerate, if not, indeed, the victim of "senile ataxy" or "general paralysis." Certainly it is well that our monitors should seek to arouse in us the wholesome spirit of self-criticism. Whether we write ill or well, we can never be too seriously concerned with what it is that we are attempting to do. We may always be grateful to those who stimulate us to a more wakeful activity in pursuing a task which can never be carried to perfection.

Yet these monitors seldom fail at the same time to arouse a deep revolt in our minds. We are not only impressed by the critic's own inability to write any better than those he criticises. We are moved to question the validity of nearly all the rules he lays down for our guidance. We are inclined to dispute altogether the soundness of the premises from which he starts. Of these three terms of our revolt, covering comprehensively the whole ground, the first may be put aside — since the ancient retort is always ineffective and it helps the patient not at all to bid the physician heal himself — and we may take the last first.

Men are always apt to bow down before the superior might of their ancestors. It has been so always and everywhere. Even the author of the once well-known book of Genesis believed that "there were giants in the earth in those days," the mighty men which were of old, the men of renown, and still to-day among ourselves no plaint is more common than that concerning the physical degeneracy of modern men as compared with our ancestors of a few centuries ago. Now and then, indeed, there comes along a man of science, like Professor Parsons, who has measured the bones from the remains of the ancestors we still see piled up in the crypt at Hythe, and finds that — however fine the occasional exceptions — the average height of those men and women was decidedly less than that of their present-day descendants. Fortunately for the vitality of tradition, we cherish a wholesome distrust of science. And so it is with our average literary stature. The academic critic regards himself as the special depository of the accepted tradition, and far be it from him to condescend to any mere scientific inquiry into the actual facts. He half awakens from slumber to murmur the expected denunciation of his own time, and therewith returns to slumber. He usually seems unaware that even three centuries ago, in the finest period of English prose, Swift, certainly himself a supreme master, was already lamenting "the corruption of our style."

If it is asserted that the average writer of to-day has

not equalled the supreme writer of some earlier age, —
there are but one or two in any age, — we can only
ejaculate: Strange if he had! Yet that is all that the
academic critic usually seems to mean. If he would
take the trouble to compare the average prose writer
of to-day with the average writer of even so great an
age as the Elizabethan, he might easily convince himself that the former, whatever his imperfections, need
not fear the comparison. Whether or not Progress in
general may be described as "the exchange of one
nuisance for another nuisance," it is certainly so with
the progress of style, and the imperfections of our
average everyday writing are balanced by the quite
other imperfections of our forefathers' writing. What,
for instance, need we envy in the literary methods of
that great and miscellaneous band of writers whom
Hakluyt brought together in those admirable volumes
which are truly great and really fascinating only for
reasons that have nothing to do with style? Raleigh
himself here shows no distinction in his narrative of
that discreditable episode, — as he clearly and rightly
felt it to be, — the loss of the *Revenge* by the wilful
Grenville. Most of them are bald, savourless, monotonous, stating the obvious facts in the obvious way,
but hopelessly failing to make clear, when rarely they
attempt it, anything that is not obvious. They have
none of the little unconscious tricks of manner which
worry the critic to-day. But their whole manner is one
commonplace trick from which they never escape.

They are only relieved by its simplicity and by the novelty which comes through age. We have to remember that all mediocrity is impersonal and that when we encourage its manifestations on printed pages we merely make mediocrity more conspicuous. Nor can that be remedied by teaching the mediocre to cultivate tricks of fashion or of vanity. There is more personality in Claude Bernard's "Leçons de Physiologie Expérimentales," a great critic of life and letters has pointed out, Remy de Gourmont, than in Musset's "Confession d'un Enfant du Siècle." For personality is not something that can be sought; it is a radiance that is diffused spontaneously. It may even be most manifest when most avoided, and no writer — the remark has doubtless often been made before — can be more personal than Flaubert who had made almost a gospel of Impersonality. But the absence of research for personality, however meritorious, will not suffice to bring personality out of mediocrity.

Moreover, the obvious fact seems often to be overlooked by the critic that a vastly larger proportion of the population now write, and see their writing printed. We live in what we call a democratic age in which all are compulsorily taught how to make pothooks and hangers on paper. So that every nincompoop — in the attenuated sense of the term — as soon as he puts a pen in ink feels that he has become, like M. Jourdain, a writer of prose. That feeling is justified only in a very limited sense, and if we wish to compare the condition of things to-day with that in an age when people wrote at the bidding of some urgent stimulus from without or from within, we have at the outset to delete certainly over ninety-five per cent of our modern so-called writers before we institute any comparison. The writers thus struck out, it may be added, cannot fail to include many persons of much note in the world. There are all sorts of people to-day who write from all sorts of motives other than a genuine aptitude for writing. To suppose that there can be any comparison at this point of the present with the past and to dodder over the decay of our language would seem a senile proceeding if we do not happen to know that it occurs in all ages, and that, even at the time when our prose speech was as near to perfection as it is ever likely to be, its critics were bemoaning its corruption, lamenting, for instance, the indolent new practice of increasing sibilation by changing "arriveth" into "arrives" and pronouncing "walked" as "walkd," sometimes in their criticisms showing no more knowledge of the history and methods of growth of English than our academic critics show to-day.

For we know what to-day they tell us; it is not hard to know, their exhortations, though few, are repeated in so psittaceous a manner. One thinks, for instance, of that solemn warning against the enormity of the split infinitive which has done so much to aggravate the Pharisaism of the bad writers who scrupulously avoid it. This superstition seems to have had its origin in a false analogy with Latin in which the infinitive is never split for the good reason that it is impossible to split. In the greater freedom of English it is possible and has been done for at least the last five hundred years by the greatest masters of English; only the good writer never uses this form helplessly and involuntarily, but with a definite object; and that is the only rule to observe. An absolute prohibition in this matter is the mark of those who are too ignorant, or else too unintelligent, to recognise a usage which is of the essence of English speech.[1]

One may perhaps refer, again, to those who lay down that every sentence must end on a significant word, never on a preposition, and who reprobate what has been technically termed the post-habited prefix. They are the same worthy and would-be old-fashioned people who think that a piece of music must always end monotonously on a banging chord. Only here they have not, any more than in music, even the virtue — if such it be — of old fashion, for the final so-called preposition is in the genius of the English language and associated with the Scandinavian — in the wider ancient sense Danish — strain of English, one of the finest strains it owns, imparting much of the plastic force which renders it flexible, the element which helped to save it from the straitlaced tendency

[1] It may be as well to point that it is the amateur literary grammarian and not the expert who is at fault in these matters. The attitude of the expert (as in C. T. Onions, *Advanced English Syntax*) is entirely reasonable.

of Anglo-Saxon and the awkward formality of Latin and French influence. The foolish prejudice we are here concerned with seems to date from a period when the example of French, in which the final preposition is impossible, happened to be dominant. Its use in English is associated with the informal grace and simplicity, the variety of tender cadence, which our tongue admits.

In such matters as the "split infinitive" and the "post-habited preposition," there should never have been any doubt as to the complete validity and authority of the questioned usages. But there are other points at which some even good critics may be tempted to accept the condemnation of the literary grammarians. It is sufficient to mention one: the nominative use of the pronoun "me." Yet, surely, any one who considers social practice as well as psychological necessity should not fail to see that we must recognise a double use of "me" in English. The French, who in such matters seem to have possessed a finer social and psychological tact, have realised that *je* cannot be the sole nominative of the first person and have supplemented it by *moi* (*mi* from *mihi*). The Frenchman, when asked who is there, does not reply "Je!" But the would-be English purist is supposed to be reduced to replying "I!" Royal Cleopatra asks the Messenger: "Is she as tall as me?" The would-be purist no doubt transmutes this as he reads into: "Is she as tall as I?" We need not envy him.

Such an example indicates how independent the free and wholesome life of language is of grammatical rules. This is not to diminish the importance of the grammarian's task, but simply to define it, as the formulator, and not the lawgiver, of usage. His rules are useful, not merely in order to know how best to keep them, but in order to know how best to break them. Without them freedom might become licence. Yet even licence, we have to recognise, is the necessary offscouring of speech in its supreme manifestations of vitality and force. English speech was never more syntactically licentious than in the sixteenth century, but it was never more alive, never more fitly the material for a great artist to mould. So it is that in the sixteenth century we find Shakespeare. In post-Dryden days (though Dryden was an excellent writer and engaged on an admirable task) a supreme artist in English speech became impossible, and if a Shakespeare had appeared all his strength would have been wasted in a vain struggle with the grammarians. French speech has run a similar and almost synchronous course with English. There was a magnificently natural force and wealth in sixteenth-century French: in Rabelais it had been even extravagantly exuberant; in Montaigne it is still flexible and various — *ondoyant et divers* — and still full of natural delight and freedom. But after Malherbe and his fellows French speech acquired orderliness, precision, and formality; they were excellent qualities, no doubt, but had to be paid for by some degree of thinness and primness, even some stiffening of the joints. Rousseau came and poured fresh blood from Switzerland into the language and a new ineffable grace that was all his own; so that if we now hesitate to say, with Landor, that he excels all the moderns for harmony, it is only because they have learnt what he taught; and the later Romantics, under the banner of Hugo, imparted colour and brilliance. Yet all the great artists who have wrestled with French speech for a century have never been able to restore the scent and the savour and the substance which Villon and Montaigne without visible effort could once find within its borders. In this as in other matters what we call Progress means the discovery of new desirable qualities, and therewith the loss of other qualities that were at least equally desirable.

Then there is yet another warning which, especially in recent times, is issued at frequent intervals, and that is against the use of verbal counters, of worn or even worn-out phrases, of what we commonly fall back on modern French to call *clichés*. We mean thereby the use of old stereotyped phrases — Goethe called them "stamped" or *gestempelt* — to save the trouble of making a new living phrase to suit our meaning. The word *cliché* is thus typographic, though, it so happens, it is derived from an old French word of phonetic meaning, *cliqueter* or *cliquer* (related to the German *klatschen*), which we already have in English as to "click" or to "clack," in a sense which well supplements its more modern technical sense for this literary end. Yet the warning against *clichés* is vain. The good writer, by the very fact that he is alive and craves speech that is vivid, as *clichés* never are, instinctively avoids their excessive use, while the nervous and bad writer, in his tremulous anxiety to avoid these tabooed *clichés*, falls into the most deplorable habits, like the late Mr. Robert Ross, who at one time was so anxious to avoid *clichés* that he acquired the habit of using them in an inverted form and wrote a prose that made one feel like walking on sharp flints; for, though a macadamized road may not be so good to walk in as a flowered meadow, it is better than a macadamized road with each stone turned upside down and the sharp edge uppermost. As a matter of fact it is impossible to avoid the use of *clichés* and counters in speech, and if it were possible the results would be in the highest degree tedious and painful. The word "*cliché*" itself, we have seen, is a *cliché*, a worn counter of a word, with its original meaning all effaced, and even its secondary meaning now only just visible. That, if those folk who condemn *clichés* only had the intelligence to perceive it, is a significant fact. You cannot avoid using *clichés*, not even in the very act of condemning them. They include, if we only look keenly enough, nearly the whole of language, almost every separate word. If one could avoid them one would be unintelligible. Even those common phrases which it is peculiarly meet to call counters are not to be absolutely condemned.

They have become so common to use because so fit to use, as Baudelaire understood when he spoke of "the immense depth of thought in vulgar locutions." [1] There is only one rule to follow here, — and it is simply the rule in every part of art, — to know what one is doing, not to go sheeplike with the flock, ignorantly, unthinkingly, heedlessly, but to mould speech to expression the most truly one knows how. If, indeed, we are seeking clarity and the precise expression of thought, there is nothing we may not do if only we know how to do it — but that "if" might well be in capitals. One who has spent the best part of his life in trying to write things that had not been written before, and that were very difficult to write, may perhaps be allowed to confess the hardness of this task.

To write is thus an arduous intellectual task, a process which calls for the highest tension of the muscles in the escalade of a heaven which the strongest and bravest and alertest can never hope to take by violence. He has to be true, — whether it is in the external world he is working or in his own internal world, — and as truth can only be seen through his own temperament, he is engaged in moulding the

[1] It is interesting to note that another aristocratic master of speech had also made just the same observation. Landor puts into the mouth of Horne Tooke the words: "No expression can become a vulgarism which has not a broad foundation. The language of the vulgar hath its source in physics: in known, comprehended, and operative things." At the same time Landor was as stern a judge as Baudelaire of the random use of *clichés*.

expression of a combination which has never been seen in the world before.

It is sometimes said that the great writer seldom quotes, and that in the main is true, for he finds it difficult to mix an alien music of thought and speech with his own. Montaigne, it is also said, is an exception, but that is scarcely true. What Montaigne quoted he often translated and so moulded to the pattern of his own mind. The same may be said of Robert Burton. If it had not been so these writers (almost certainly Burton) could scarcely have attained to the rank of great authors. The significant fact to note, however, is not that the great writer rarely quotes, but that he knows how to quote. Schopenhauer was here a master. He possessed a marvellous flair for fine sayings in remote books, and these he would now and again let fall like jewels on his page, with so happy a skill that they seem to be created for the spot on which they fell. It is the little writer rather than the great writer who seems never to quote, and the reason is that he is really never doing anything else.[1]

---

[1] Speaking as a writer who has been much quoted, — it ought to be a satisfaction, but I have had my doubts, — I may say that I have observed that those who quote belong mostly to two classes, one consisting of good, or at all events indifferent, writers, and the other of bad writers. Those of the first class quote with fair precision and due acknowledgement, those of the second with no precision, and only the vaguest intimation, or none at all, that they are quoting. This would seem to indicate that the good writer is more honest than the bad writer, but that conclusion may be unjust to the bad writer. The fact is that, having little thought or knowledge of his own, he is not fully conscious of what he is doing. He is like a greedy child who, seeing food in front of him, snatches it at random, without being able to recognise whether or

It is not in writing only, in all art, in all science, the task before each is that defined by Bacon: *man added to Nature*. It is so also in painting, as a great artist of modern time, Cézanne, recognised even in those same words: "He who wishes to make art," he once said to Vollard, "must follow Bacon, who defined the artist as 'Homo additus Naturæ.'" So it is that the artist, if he has succeeded in being true to his function, is necessarily one who makes all things new.[1] That remarkable artist who wrote the Book of the Revelation has expressed this in his allegorical, perhaps unconscious, Oriental way, for he represents the artist as hearing the divine spirit from the throne within him uttering the command: "Behold, I make all things new. Write!" The command is similar whatever the art may be, though it is here the privilege of the writer to find his own art set forth as the inspired ensample of all art.

Thus it is that to write is a strenuous intellectual task not to be achieved without the exercise of the best

not it is his own. There is, however, a third class of those who cannot resist the temptation of deliberately putting forth the painfully achieved thought or knowledge of others as their own, sometimes, perhaps, seeking to gloss over the lapse with: "As every one knows — "

[1] Croce, who is no doubt the most instructive literary critic of our time, has, in his own way, insisted on this essential fact. As he would put it, there are no objective standards of judgment; we cannot approach a work of art with our laws and categories. We have to comprehend the artist's own values, and only then are we fit to pronounce any judgment on his work. The task of the literary critic is thus immensely more difficult than it is vulgarly supposed to be. The same holds good, I would add, of criticism in the fields of art, not including the art of love and the arts of living in general.

trained and most deliberate rational faculties. That is the outcome of the whole argument up to this point. There is so much bad writing in the world because writing has been dominated by ignorance and habit and prudery, and not least by the academic teachers and critics who have known nothing of what they claim to teach and were often themselves singular examples of how not to write. There has, on the other hand, been a little good writing here and there in the world, through the ages, because a few possessed not only courage and passion and patience, but knowledge and the concentrated intellectual attention, and the resolution to seek truth, and the conviction that, as they imagined, the genius they sought consisted in taking pains.

Yet, if that were all, many people would become great writers who, as we well know, will never become writers; if that were all, writing could scarcely even be regarded as an art. For art, or one side of it, transcends conscious knowledge; a poet, as Landor remarked, "is not aware of all that he knows, and seems at last to know as little about it as a silkworm knows about the fineness of her thread." Yet the same great writer has also said of good poetry, and with equal truth, that "the ignorant and inexpert lose half its pleasures." We always move on two feet, as Élie Faure remarks in his "L'Arbre d'Éden," the two poles of knowledge and of desire, the one a matter of deliberate acquirement and the other of profound instinct, and all our move-

ments are a perpetual leap from one to the other, seeking a centre of gravity we never attain.[1] So the achievement of style in writing, as in all human intercourse, is
something more than an infinite capacity for taking
pains. It is also defined — and, sometimes I think,
supremely well defined — as "grace seasoned with
salt." Beyond all that can be achieved by knowledge
and effort, there must be the spontaneous grace that
springs up like a fountain from the depth of a beautifully harmonious nature, and there must be also the
quality which the Spaniards call "sal," and so rightly
admire in the speech of the women of the people of
their own land, the salt quality which gives savour and
point and antiseptic virtue.[2]

The best literary prose speech is simply the idealisation in the heaven of art of the finest common speech
of earth, simply, yet never reached for more than a
moment in a nation's long history. In Greece it was
immortally and radiantly achieved by Plato; in England it was attained for a few years during the last
years of the seventeenth and the first years of the

[1] "This search is the art of all great thinkers, of all great artists, indeed
of all those who, even without attaining expression, desire to live deeply.
If the dance brings us so near to God, it is, I believe, because it symbol-
izes for us the movement of this gesture." (Élie Faure, L'Arbre d'Éden,
p. 318.)

[2] This is that "divine malice" which Nietzsche, in Ecce Homo, speaking of Heine ("one day Heine and I will be regarded as by far the greatest artists of the German language," he says rather egotistically, but perhaps truly) considered essential to perfection. "I estimate the value of
men and of races," he added, "by their need to identify their God with a
satyr," a hard saying, no doubt, to the modern man, but it has its meaning.

eighteenth centuries, lingering on, indeed, here and there to the end of that century until crushed between the pedantry of Johnson and the poetic licence of the Romantics. But for the rest only the most happily endowed genius can even attain for a rare moment the perfection of the Pauline ideal of "grace seasoned with salt."

It is fortunate, no doubt, that an age of machinery is well content with machine-made writing. It would be in bad taste — too physiological, too sentimental, altogether too antiquated — to refer to the symbolical significance of the highly relevant fact that the heart, while undoubtedly a machine, is at the same time a sensitively pulsating organ with fleshy strings stretched from ventricle to valves, a harp on which the great artist may play until our hearts also throb in unison. Yet there are some to whom it still seems that, beyond mechanical skill, the cadences of the artist's speech are the cadences of his heart, and the footfalls of his rhythm the footfalls of his spirit, in a great adventure across the universe.

II

THUS we do not always realise that learning to write is partly a matter of individual instinct. This is so even of that writing which, as children, we learnt in copybooks with engraved maxims at the head of the page. There are some, indeed, probably the majority, who quickly achieve the ability to present a passable imitation of the irreproachable model presented to them. There are some who cannot. I speak as one who knows, for I recall how my first schoolmaster, a sarcastic little Frenchman, irritated by my unchastenable hand, would sometimes demand if I wrote with the kitchen poker, or again assert that I kept a tame spider to run over the page, while a later teacher, who was an individualist and more tolerant, yet sometimes felt called upon to murmur, in a tone of dubious optimism: "You will have a hand of your own, my boy." It is not lack of docility that is in question, but an imperative demand of the nervous system which the efforts of the will may indeed bend but cannot crush.

Yet the writers who cheerfully lay down the laws of style seldom realise this complexity and mystery en- wrapping even so simple a matter as handwriting. No one can say how much atavistic recurrence from remote ancestors, how much family nervous habit, how much wayward yet deep-rooted personal idiosyn- crasy deflect the child's patient efforts to imitate the copperplate model which is set before him. The son often writes like the father, even though he may seldom or never see his father's handwriting; brothers may write singularly alike, though taught by different teachers and even in different continents. It has been noted of the ancient and distinguished family of the Tyrrells that their handwriting in the parish books of Stowmarket remained the same throughout many generations. I have noticed, in a relation of my own, peculiarities of handwriting identical with those of an ancestor two centuries ago whose writing he certainly never saw. The resemblance is often not that of exact formation, but of general air or underlying structure.[1] One is tempted to think that often, in this as in other matters, the possibilities are limited, and that when the child is formed in his mother's womb Nature cast the same old dice and the same old combinations inevitably tend to recur. But that notion scarcely fits all the facts, and our growing knowledge of the infinite subtlety of heredity, of its presence even in the most seemingly elusive psychic characters, indicates that the dice may be loaded and fall in accord with harmonies we fail to perceive. The development of Mendelian analysis may in time help us to understand them.

The part in style which belongs to atavism, to heredity, to unconscious instinct, is probably very large. It eludes us to an even greater extent than the corresponding part in handwriting because the man of letters may have none among his ancestors who sought expression in style, so that only one Milton speaks for a mute inglorious family, and how far he speaks truly remains a matter of doubt. We only divine the truth when we know the character and deeds of the family. There could be no more instructive revelation of

[1] Since this was written I have found that Laycock, whose subtle observation pioneered so many later ideas, long ago noted ("Some Organic Laws of Memory," *Journal of Mental Science*, July, 1875) reversion to ancestral modes of handwriting.

family history in style than is furnished by Carlyle. There had never been any writer in the Carlyle family, and if there had, Carlyle at the time when his manner of writing was formed, would scarcely have sought to imitate them. Yet we could not conceive this stern, laborious, plebeian family of Lowland Scots — with its remote Teutonic affinities, its coarseness, its narrowness, its assertive inarticulative force — in any more fitting verbal translation than was given it by this its last son, the pathetic little figure with the face of a lost child, who wrote in a padded room and turned the rough muscular and reproductive activity of his fathers into more than half a century of eloquent chatter concerning Work and Silence, so writing his name in letters of gold on the dome of the British Museum.[1]

---

[1] This was written fifteen years ago, and as Carlyle has of late been unduly depreciated I would add that, while strictly to the present point, it is not put forward as an estimate of Carlyle's genius. That I seem to have attempted twenty-five years earlier in a private letter (to my friend the late Reverend Angus Mackay) I may here perhaps be allowed to quote. It was in 1883, soon after the publication of Carlyle's *Reminiscences:* "This is not Carlylese, but it is finer. The popular judgment is hopelessly wrong. We can never understand Carlyle till we get rid of the 'great prophet' notion. Carlyle is not (as we were once taught) a 'great moral teacher,' but, in the high sense, a great *comedian*. His books are wonderful comedies. He is the Scotch Aristophanes, as Rabelais is the French and Heine the German Aristophanes — of course, with the intense northern imagination, more clumsy, more imperfect, more profound than the Greek. But, at a long distance, there is a close resemblance to Aristophanes with the same mixture of audacity in method and conservatism in spirit. Cariyle's account of Lamb seems in the true sense Aristophanic. His humour is, too, as broad as he dares (some curious resemblances there, too). In his lyrical outbursts, again, he follows Aristophanes, and again at a distance. Of course he cannot be

When we consider the characteristics, not of the family, but of the race, it is easier to find examples of the force of ancestry, even remote ancestry, overcoming environment and dominating style. Shakespeare and Bacon were both Elizabethans who both lived from youth upwards in London, and even moved to some extent almost in the same circles. Yet all the influences of tradition and environment, which sometimes seem to us so strong, scarcely sufficed to spread even the faintest veneer of similarity over their style, and we could seldom mistake a sentence of one for a sentence of the other. We always know that Shakespeare — with his gay extravagance and redundancy, his essential idealism — came of a people that had been changed in character from the surrounding stock by a Celtic infolding of the receding British to Wales.[1] We never fail to realise that Bacon — with his instinctive gravity and temperance, the suppressed ardour of his aspiring intellectual passion, his temperamental naturalism — was rooted deep in that East Anglian soil which he had never so much as visited. In Shakespeare's veins there dances the blood of the men who made the "Mabinogion"; we recognise Bacon as a man of the same countryside which pro-

compared as an artist. He has not, like Rabelais, created a world to play with, but, like Aristophanes generally, he sports with the things that are." That youthful estimate was alien to popular opinion then because Carlyle was idolised; it is now, no doubt, equally alien for an opposite reason. It is only on extremes that the indolent popular mind can rest.

[1] J. Beddoe, *The Races of Britain*, p. 254.

duced the forefathers of Emerson. Or we may consider the mingled Breton and Gascon ancestry of Renan, in whose brain, in the very contour and melody of his style, the ancient bards of Brittany have joined hands with the tribe of Montaigne and Brantôme and the rest. Or, to take one more example, we can scarcely fail to recognise in the style of Sir Thomas Browne — as later, may be, in that of Hawthorne — the glamour of which the latent aptitude had been handed on by ancestors who dwelt on the borders of Wales.

In these examples hereditary influence can be clearly distinguished from merely external and traditional influences. Not that we need imply a disparagement of tradition: it is the foundation of civilised progress. Speech itself is a tradition, a naturally developed convention, and in that indeed it has its universal applicability and use. It is the crude amorphous material of art, of music and poetry. But on its formal side, whatever its supreme significance as the instrument and medium of expression, speech is a natural convention, an accumulated tradition.

Even tradition, however, is often simply the corporeal embodiment, as it were, of heredity. Behind many a great writer's personality there stands tradition, and behind tradition the race. That is well illustrated in the style of Addison. This style — with a resilient fibre underneath its delicacy and yet a certain freedom as of conversational familiarity — has as its most easily marked structural signature a tendency to a usage it has already been necessary to mention: the tendency to allow the preposition to lag to the end of the sentence rather than to come tautly before the pronoun with which in Latin it is combined. In a century in which the Latin-French elements of English were to become developed, as in Gibbon and Johnson, to the utmost, the totally different physiognomy of Addison's prose remained conspicuous, — though really far from novel, — and to the sciolists of a bygone age it seemed marked by carelessness, if not licence, at the best by personal idiosyncrasy. Yet, as a matter of fact, we know it was nothing of the kind. Addison, as his name indicates, was of the stock of the Scandinavian English, and the Cumberland district he belonged to is largely Scandinavian; the adjoining peninsula of Furness, which swarms with similar patronymics, is indeed one of the most purely Scandinavian spots in England. Now in the Scandinavian languages, as we know, and in the English dialects based upon them, the preposition comes usually at the end of the sentence, and Scandinavian structural elements form an integral part of English, even more than Latin-French, for it has been the part of the latter rather to enrich the vocabulary than to mould the structure of our tongue. So that, instead of introducing a personal idiosyncrasy or perpetrating a questionable licence, Addison was continuing his own ancestral traditions and at the same time asserting an organic prerogative of English speech. It may be added that Addison reveals his Scandinavian affinities not merely in the material structure, but in the spiritual quality, of his work. This delicate sympathetic observation, the vein of gentle melancholy, the quiet restrained humour, meet us again in modern Norwegian authors like Jonas Lie.

When we put aside these ancestral and traditional influences, there is still much in the writer's art which, even if personal, we can only term instinctive. This may be said of that music which at their finest moments belongs to all the great writers of prose. Every writer has his own music, though there are few in whom it becomes audible save at rare and precious intervals. The prose of the writer who can deliberately make his own personal cadences monotonously audible all the time grows wearisome; it affects us as a tedious mannerism. This is a kind of machine-made prose which indeed it requires a clever artisan to produce; but, as Landor said, "he must be a bad writer to whom there are no inequalities." The great writers, though they are always themselves, attain the perfect music of their style under the stress of a stimulus adequate to arouse it. Their music is the audible translation of emotion, and only arises when the waves of emotion are stirred. It is not properly speaking a voluntary effect. We can but say that the winds of the spirit are breathed upon the surface of style, and they lift it into rhythmic movement. And for each writer these waves have their own special rate of vibration, their peculiar shape and interval. The rich deep slow tones of Bacon have nothing in common with the haunting, long-drawn melody, faint and tremulous, of Newman; the high metallic falsetto ring of De Quincey's rhetoric is far away from the pensive low-toned music of Pater.

Imitation, as psychologists have taught us to realise, is a part of instinct. When we begin to learn to write, it rarely happens that we are not imitators, and, for the most part, unconsciously. The verse of every young poet, however original he may afterwards grow, usually has plainly written across it the rhythmic signature of some great master whose work chances to be abroad in the world; once it was usually Tennyson, then Swinburne, now various later poets; the same thing happens with prose, but the rhythm of the signature is less easy to hear.

As a writer slowly finds his own centre of gravity, the influence of the rhythm of other writers ceases to be perceptible except in so far as it coincides with his own natural movement and *tempo*. That is a familiar fact. We less easily realise, perhaps, that not only the tunes but the notes that they are formed of are, in every great writer, his own. In other words, he creates even his vocabulary. That is so not only in the more obvious sense that out of the mass of words that make up a language every writer uses only a limited number and even among these has his words of predilection.[1] It is

[1] I once studied, as an example, colour-words in various writers, finding that every poet has his own colour formula. Variations in length of sentence and peculiarities of usage in metre have often been studied. Reference is made to some of these studies by A. Niceforo, "Metodo Statistico e Documenti Litterari," *Revista d'Italia*, August, 1917.

in the meanings he gives to words, to names, that a writer creates his vocabulary. All language, we know, is imagery and metaphor; even the simplest names of the elementary things are metaphors based on resemblances that suggested themselves to the primitive men who made language. It is not otherwise with the aboriginal man of genius who uses language to express his new vision of the world. He sees things charged with energy, or brilliant with colour, or breathing out perfume, that the writers who came before him had overlooked, and to designate these things he must use names which convey the qualities he has perceived. Guided by his own new personal sensations and perceptions, he creates his metaphorical vocabulary. If we examine the style of Montaigne, so fresh and personal and inventive, we see that its originality lies largely in its vocabulary, which is not, like that of Rabelais, manufactured afresh, but has its novelty in its metaphorical values, such new values being tried and tempered at every step, to the measure of the highly individual person behind them, who thereby exerts his creative force. In later days Huysmans, who indeed saw the world at a more eccentric angle than Montaigne, yet with unflinching veracity and absolute devotion, set himself to the task of creating his own vocabulary, and at first the unfamiliarity of its beauty estranges us.

To think of Huysmans is to be led towards an aspect of style not to be passed over. To say that the artist

in words is expressing a new vision of the world and
seeking the designations for things as he sees them, is a
large part of the truth, and, I would say, perhaps the
most important part of it. For most of us, I suppose
(as I know it has been for me), our vision of Nature has
been largely, though by no means entirely, constituted
by pictures we have seen, by poems we have read, that
left an abiding memory. That is to say that Nature
comes to us through an atmosphere which is the
emanation of supreme artists who once thrilled us.
But we are here concerned with the process of the
artist's work and not with his æsthetic influence. The
artist finds that words have a rich content of their
own, they are alive and they flourish or decay. They
send out connecting threads in every direction, they
throb with meaning that ever changes and reverber-
ates afar. The writer is not always, or often, merely
preparing a *catalogue raisonné* of things, he is an artist
and his pigments are words. Often he merely takes his
suggestions from the things of the world and makes his
own pictures without any real resemblance to the
scene it is supposed to depict. Dujardin tells us that he
once took Huysmans to a Wagner concert; he scarcely
listened to the music, but he was fascinated by the
programme the attendant handed to him; he went
home to write a brilliant page on "Tannhäuser."
Mallarmé, on the other hand, was soaked in music; to
him music was the voice of the world, and it was the
aim of poetry to express the world by itself becoming

music; he stood on a height like a pioneer and looked towards the Promised Land, trying to catch intimations of a new sensibility and a future art, but a great master of language, like Huysmans, he never was. Huysmans has written superb pages about Gustave Moreau and Félicien Rops, thinking, no doubt, that he was revealing supreme artists (though we need not follow too closely the fashion of depreciating either of those artists), but he was really only attracted to their programmes and therein experiencing a stimulus that chanced to be peculiarly fitted for drawing out his own special art. Baudelaire would have written less gorgeously, but he would have produced a more final critical estimate.

Yet even the greatest writers are affected by the intoxication of mere words in the artistry of language. Shakespeare is, constantly, and, not content with "making the green one red," he must needs at the same time "the multitudinous seas incarnadine." It is conspicuous in Keats (as Leigh Hunt, perhaps his first sensitively acute critic, clearly explained), and often, as in "The Eve of St. Agnes," where he seemed to be concerned with beautiful things, he was really concerned with beautiful words. In that way he is sometimes rather misleading for the too youthful reader; "porphyry" seemed to me a marvellous substance when as a boy of twelve I read of it in Keats, and I imagine that Keats himself would have been surprised, had he lived long enough to walk to St. Thomas's

Hospital over the new London Bridge, when told that he was treading a granite that was porphyritic. I recall how Verlaine would sometimes repeat in varying tones some rather unfamiliar word, rolling it round and round in his mouth, sucking it like a sweetmeat, licking the sound into the shape that pleased him; some people may perhaps have found a little bizarre the single words ("Green," for example) which he sometimes made the title of a song, but if they adopt the preliminary Verlainian process they may understand how he had fitted such words to music and meaning.

The most obviously beautiful things in the world of Nature are birds and flowers and the stones we call precious. But the attitude of the poet in the presence of Nature is precisely that of Huysmans in the presence of art: it is the programme that interests him. Of birds the knowledge of poets generally is of the most generalised and elementary kind; they are the laughing-stock of the ornithologist; they are only a stage removed from the standpoint of the painter who was introducing a tree into his landscape and when asked what tree, replied, "Oh, just the ordinary tree." Even Goethe mistook the finches by the roadside for larks. The poet, one may be sure, even to-day seldom carries in his pocket the little "Führer durch unsere Vogelwelt" of Bernhard Hoffmann, and has probably never so much as heard of it. Of flowers his knowledge seems to be limited by the quality of the flower's name. I have long cherished an exquisite and quite common

English wild-flower, but have never come across a poem about it, for its unattractive name is the stitch-wort, and it is only lately that even in prose it has met (from Mr. Salt) with due appreciation. As regards precious stones the same may be said, and in the galleries of the Geological Museum it has hardly seemed to me that, among the few visitors, there were poets (unless I chanced to bring one myself) to brood over all that beauty. It is the word and its inner reverberation with which the poet is really concerned, even sometimes perhaps deliberately. When Milton misused the word "eglantine" one realises the uncon-scious appeal to him of the name and one cannot feel quite sure that it was altogether unconscious. Cole-ridge has been solemnly reproved for speaking of the "loud" bassoon. But it was to the timbre of the word, not of the instrument, that Coleridge was responding, and had he been informed that the bassoon is not loud, I doubt not he would have replied: "Well, if it is not loud it ought to be." On the plane on which Coleridge moved "the loud bassoon" was absolutely right. We see that the artist in speech moves among words rather than among things. Originally, it is true, words are closely related to things, but in their far reverberation they have become enriched by many associations, saturated with many colours; they have acquired a life of their own, moving on another plane than that of things, and it is on that plane that the artist in words is, as an artist, concerned with them.

It thus comes about that the artist in words, like the artist in pigments, is perpetually passing between two planes — the plane of new vision and the plane of new creation. He is sometimes remoulding the external world and sometimes the internal world; sometimes, by predilection, lingering more on one plane than on the other plane. The artist in words is not irresistibly drawn to the exact study of things or moved by the strong love of Nature. The poets who describe Nature most minutely and most faithfully are not usually the great poets. That is intelligible because the poet — even the poet in the wide sense who also uses prose — is primarily the instrument of human emotion and not of scientific observation. Yet that poet possesses immense resources of strength who in early life has stored within him the minute knowledge of some field of the actual external world.[1] One may doubt, indeed, whether there has been any supreme poet, from Homer on, who has not had this inner reservoir of sensitive impressions to draw from. The youthful Shakespeare who wrote the poems, with their minute descriptions, was not a great poet, as the youthful Marlowe was, but he was storing up the material which, when he had

[1] "The Muses are the daughters of Memory," Paul Morand tells us that Proust would say; "there is no art without recollection," and certainly it is supremely true of Proust's art. It is that element of art which imparts at once both atmosphere and poignant intimacy, external fairness with internal nearness. The lyrics of Thomas Hardy owe their intimacy of appeal to the dominance in them of recollection (in *Late Lyrics and Earlier* one might say it is never absent), and that is why they can scarcely be fully appreciated save by those who are no longer very young.

developed into a great poet, he could draw on at need with a careless and assured hand. Without such reservoirs, the novelists also would never attain to that touch of the poet which, beyond their story-telling power, can stir our hearts. "À la Recherche du Temps Perdu" is the name of a great modern book, but every novelist during part of his time has been a Ulysses on a perilous voyage of adventure for that far home. One thinks of George Eliot and her early intimacy with the life of country people, of Hardy who had acquired so acute a sensitivity to the sounds of Nature, of Conrad who had caught the flashes of penetrating vision which came to the sailor on deck; and in so far as they move away into scenes where they cannot draw from those ancient reservoirs, the adventures of these artists, however brilliant they may become, lose their power of intimate appeal. The most extravagant example of this to-day is the Spanish novelist Blasco Ibañez, who wrote of the Valencian *huerta* that had saturated his youth in novels that were penetrating and poignant, and then turned to writing for the cosmopolitan crowd novels about anything, that were completely negligible.

We grow familiar in time with the style of the great writers, and when we read them we translate them easily and unconsciously, as we translate a foreign language we are familiar with; we understand the vocabulary because we have learnt to know the special seal of the creative person who moulded the vocabulary. But at the outset the great writer may be almost as unintelligible to us as though he were writing in a language we had never learnt. In the now remote days when "Leaves of Grass" was a new book in the world, few who looked into it for the first time, however honestly, but were repelled and perhaps even violently repelled, and it is hard to realise now that once those who fell on Swinburne's "Poems and Ballads" saw at first only picturesque hieroglyphics to which they had no key. But even to-day how many there are who find Proust unreadable and Joyce unintelligible. Until we find the door and the clue the new writer remains obscure. Therein lies the truth of Landor's saying that the poet must himself create the beings who are to enjoy his Paradise.

For most of those who deliberately seek to learn to write, words seem generally to be felt as of less importance than the art of arranging them. It is thus that the learner in writing tends to become the devoted student of grammar and syntax whom we came across at the outset. That is indeed a tendency which always increases. Civilisation develops with a conscious adhesion to formal order, and the writer — writing by fashion or by ambition and not by divine right of creative instinct — follows the course of civilisation. It is an unfortunate tendency, for those whom it affects conquer by their number. As we know, writing that is real is not learnt that way. Just as the solar system was not made in accordance with the astronomer's laws, so writing is not made by the laws of grammar. Astronomer and grammarian alike can only come in at the end, to give a generalised description of what usually happens in the respective fields it pleases them to explore. When a new comet, cosmic or literary, enters their sky, it is their descriptions which have to be readjusted, and not the comet. There seems to be no more pronounced mark of the decadence of a people and its literature than a servile and rigid subserviency to rule. It can only make for ossification, for anchylosis, for petrification, all the milestones on the road of death. In every age of democratic plebeianism, where each man thinks he is as good a writer as the others, and takes his laws from the others, having no laws of his own nature, it is down this steep path that men, in a flock, inevitably run.

We may find an illustration of the plebeian anchylosis of advancing civilisation in the minor matter of spelling. We cannot, it is true, overlook the fact that writing is read and that its appearance cannot be quite disregarded. Yet, ultimately, it appeals to the ear, and spelling can have little to do with style. The laws of spelling, properly speaking, are few or none, and in the great ages men have understood this and boldly acted accordingly. They exercised a fine personal discretion in the matter and permitted without question a wide range of variation. Shakespeare, as we know, even spelt his own name in several different ways, all equally correct. When that great old Elizabethan mariner, Sir Martin Frobisher, entered on one

of his rare and hazardous adventures with the pen, he
created spelling absolutely afresh, in the spirit of
simple heroism with which he was always ready to sail
out into strange seas. His epistolary adventures are,
certainly, more interesting than admirable, but we
have no reason to suppose that the distinguished
persons to whom these letters were addressed viewed
them with any disdain. More anæmic ages cannot
endure creative vitality even in spelling, and so it
comes about that in periods when everything beautiful
and handmade gives place to manufactured articles
made wholesale, uniform, and cheap, the same principles are applied to words, and spelling becomes a
mechanic trade. We must have our spelling uniform,
even if uniformly bad.[1]   Just as the man who, having
out of sheer ignorance eaten the wrong end of his
asparagus, was thenceforth compelled to declare that
he preferred that end, so it is with our race in the matter of spelling; our ancestors, by chance or by igno-

[1] The Oxford University Press publishes a little volume of *Rules for
Compositors and Readers* in which this uniform is set forth. It is a useful
and interesting manual, but one wonders how many unnecessary and
even undesirable usages — including that morbid desire to cling to the
ize termination (charming as an eccentricity but hideous as a rule) when
ise would suffice — are hereby fostered. Even when we leave out of consideration the great historical tradition of variety in this matter, it is
doubtful, when we consider them comprehensively, whether the advantages of encouraging every one to spell like his fellows overbalances the
advantages of encouraging every one to spell unlike his fellows. When I
was a teacher in the Australian bush I derived far less enjoyment from
the more or less "correctly" spelt exercises of my pupils than from the
occasional notes I received from their parents who, never having been
taught to spell, were able to spell in the grand manner. We are wilfully
throwing away an endless source of delight.

rance, tended to adopt certain forms of spelling and we, their children, are forced to declare that we prefer those forms. Thus we have not only lost all individuality in spelling, but we pride ourselves on our loss and magnify our anchylosis. In England it has become almost impossible to flex our stiffened mental joints sufficiently to press out a single letter, in America it is almost impossible to extend them enough to admit that letter. It is convenient, we say, to be rigid and formal in these things, and therewith we are content; it matters little to us that we have thereby killed the life of our words and only gained the conveniency of death. It would be likewise convenient, no doubt, if men and women could be turned into rigid geometrical diagrams, — as indeed our legislators sometimes seem to think that they already are, — but we should pay by yielding up all the infinite variations, the beautiful sinuosities, that had once made up life.

There can be no doubt that in the much greater matter of style we have paid heavily for the attainment of our slavish adherence to mechanical rules, however convenient, however inevitable. The beautiful incorrection, as we are now compelled to regard it, that so often marked the great and even the small writers of the seventeenth century, has been lost, for all can now write what any find it easy to read, what none have any consuming desire to read. But when Sir Thomas Browne wrote his "Religio Medici" it was with an art made up of obedience to personal law and abandonment to free inspiration which still ravishes us. It is extraordinary how far indifference or incorrection of style may be carried and yet remain completely adequate even to complex and subtle ends. Pepys wrote his "Diary," at the outset of a life full of strenuous work and not a little pleasure, with a rare devotion indeed, but with a concision and carelessness, a single eye on the fact itself, and an extraordinary absence of self-consciousness which rob it of all claim to possess what we conventionally term style. Yet in this vehicle he has perfectly conveyed not merely the most vividly realised and delightfully detailed picture of a past age ever achieved in any language, but he has, moreover, painted a psychological portrait of himself which for its serenely impartial justice, its subtle gradations, its bold juxtapositions of colours, has all the qualities of the finest Velasquez. There is no style here, we say, merely the diarist, writing with careless poignant vitality for his own eye, and yet no style that we could conceive would be better fitted, or so well fitted, for the miracle that has here been effected.

The personal freedom of Browne led up to splendour, and that of Pepys to clarity. But while splendour is not the whole of writing, neither, although one returns to it again and again, is clarity. Here we come from another side on to a point we had already reached. Bergson, in reply to the question: "Comment doivent écrire les Philosophes?" lets fall some observations, which, as he himself remarks, concern other writers beside philosophers. A technical word, he remarks, even a word invented for the occasion or used in a special sense, is always in its place provided the instructed reader — though the difficulty, as he fails to point out, is to be sure of possessing this instructed reader — accepts it so easily as not even to notice it, and he proceeds to say that in philosophic prose, and in all prose, and indeed in all the arts, "the perfect expression is that which has come so naturally, or rather so necessarily, by virtue of so imperious a predestination, that we do not pause before it, but go straight on to what it seeks to express, as though it were blended with the idea; it became invisible by force of being transparent."[1] That is well said. Bergson also is on the side of clarity. Yet I do not feel that that is all there is to say. Style is not a sheet of glass in which the only thing that matters is the absence of flaws. Bergson's own style is not so diaphanous that one never pauses to admire its quality, nor, as a hostile critic (Edouard Dujardin) has shown, is it always so clear as to be transparent. The dancer in prose as well as in verse — philosopher or whatever he may be — must reveal all his limbs through the garment he wears; yet the garment must have its own proper beauty, and there is a failure of art, a failure of revelation, if it possesses no beauty. Style indeed is not really a mere invisible transparent medium, it is not really a garment, but, as Gourmont said, the very thought itself.

[1] *Le Monde Nouveau*, 15th December, 1922.

It is the miraculous transubstantiation of a spiritual body, given to us in the only form in which we may receive and absorb that body, and unless its clarity is balanced by its beauty it is not adequate to sustain that most high function. No doubt, if we lean on one side more than the other, it is clarity rather than beauty which we should choose, for on the other side we may have, indeed, a Sir Thomas Browne, and there we are conscious not so much of a transubstantiation as of a garment, with thick embroidery, indeed, and glistening jewels, but we are not always sure that much is hidden beneath. A step further and we reach D'Annunzio, a splendid mask with nothing beneath, just as in the streets of Rome one may sometimes meet a Franciscan friar with a head superb as a Roman Emperor's and yet, one divines, it means nothing. The Italian writer, it is significant to note, chose so ostentatiously magnificent a name as Gabriele D'Annunzio to conceal a real name which was nothing. The great angels of annunciation create the beauty of their own real names. Who now finds Shakespeare ridiculous? And how lovely a name is Keats!

As a part of the harmony of art, which is necessarily made out of conflict, we have to view that perpetual seeming alternation between the two planes—the plane of vision and the plane of creation, the form within and the garment that clothes it — which may sometimes distract the artist himself. The prophet Jeremiah once said (and modern prophets have doubtless had occasion to recognise the truth of his remark) that he seemed to the people round him only as "one that hath a pleasant voice and can play well on an instrument." But he failed to understand that it was only through this quality of voice and instrument that his lamentations had any vital force or even any being, and that if the poem goes the message goes. Indeed, that is true of all his fellow prophets of the Old Testament and the New who have fascinated mankind with the sound of those harps that they had once hung by the waters of Babylon. The whole Bible, we may be very sure, would have long ago been forgotten by all but a few intelligent archæologists, if men had not heard in it, again and again and again, "one that hath a pleasant voice and can play well on an instrument." Socrates said that philosophy was simply music. But the same might be said of religion. The divine dance of satyrs and nymphs to the sound of pipes — it is the symbol of life which in one form or another has floated before human eyes from the days of the sculptors of Greek bas-reliefs to the men of our own day who catch the glimpse of new harmonies in the pages of "L'Esprit Nouveau." We cannot but follow the piper that knows how to play, even to our own destruction. There may be much that is objectionable about Man. But he has that engaging trait. And the world will end when he has lost it.

One asks one's self how it was that the old way of writing, as a personal art, gave place to the new way of

writing, as a mere impersonal pseudo-science, rigidly
bound by formal and artificial rules. The answer, no
doubt, is to be found in the existence of a great new
current of thought which began mightily to stir in
men's minds towards the end of the seventeenth
century. It will be remembered that it was at that
time, both in England and France, that the new devitalised, though more flexible, prose appeared, with
its precision and accuracy, its conscious orderliness, its
deliberate method. But only a few years before, over
France and England alike, a great intellectual wave
had swept, imparting to the mathematical and geometrical sciences, to astronomy, physics, and allied
studies, an impetus that they had never received before on so great a scale. Descartes in France and Newton in England stand out as the typical representatives
of the movement. If that movement had to exert any
influence on language — and we know how sensitively
language reacts to thought — it could have been manifested in no other way than by the change which actually took place. And there was every opportunity for
that influence to be exerted.[1] This sudden expansion
of the mathematical and geometrical sciences was so
great and novel that interest in it was not confined to

[1] Ferris Greenslet (in his study of *Joseph Glanvill*, p. 183), referring to
the Cartesian influence on English prose style, quotes from Sprat's
History of the Royal Society that the Society "exacted from its members
a close, naked, natural way of speaking, positive expressions, a native
easiness, bringing all things as near the mathematic plainness as they
can." The Society passed a resolution to reject "all amplifications, di-
gressions, and swellings of style."

a small band of men of science: it excited the man in the street, the woman in the drawing-room; it was indeed a woman, a bright and gay woman of the world, who translated Newton's profound book into French. Thus it was that the new qualities of style were invented, not merely to express new qualities of thought, but because new scientific ideals were moving within the minds of men. A similar reaction of thought on language took place at the beginning of the nineteenth century, when an attempt was made to vitalise language once more, and to break the rigid and formal moulds the previous century had constructed. The attempt was immediately preceded by the awakening of a new group of sciences, but this time the sciences of life, the biological studies associated with Cuvier and Lamarck, with John Hunter and Erasmus Darwin. With the twentieth century we see the temporary exhaustion of the biological spirit with its historical form in science and its romantic form in art, and we have a neo-classic spirit which has involved a renaissance of the mathematical sciences and, even before that, was beginning to affect speech.

To admire the old writers, because for them writing was an art to be exercised freely and not a vain attempt to follow after the ideals of the abstract sciences, thus by no means implies a contempt for that decorum and orderliness without which all written speech must be ineffective and obscure. The great writers in the great ages, standing above classicism and above romanticism, have always observed this decorum and orderliness. In their hands such observance was not a servile and rigid adherence to external rules, but a beautiful convention, an instinctive fine breeding, such as is naturally observed in human intercourse when it is not broken down by intimacy or by any great crisis of life or of death.

The freedom of art by no means involves the easiness of art. It may rather, indeed, be said the difficulty increases with freedom, for to make things in accordance with patterns is ever the easiest task. The problem is equally arduous for those who, so far as their craft is conscious, seek an impersonal and for those who seek a personal ideal of style. Flaubert sought — in vain, it is true — to be the most objective of artists and to mould speech with heroic energy in shapes of abstract perfection. Nietzsche, one of the most personal artists in style, sought likewise, in his own words, to work at a page of prose as a sculptor works at a statue. Though the result is not perhaps fundamentally different, whichever ideal it is that, consciously or instinctively, is followed, the personal road of style is doubtless theoretically — though not necessarily in practice — the sounder, usually also that which moves most of us more profoundly. The great prose writers of the Second Empire in France made an unparalleled effort to carve or paint impersonal prose, but its final beauty and effectiveness seem scarcely equal to the splendid energy it embodies. Jules de Goncourt, his brother thought,

literally died from the mental exhaustion of his un-
ceasing struggle to attain an objective style adequate
to express the subtle texture of the world as he saw it.
But, while the Goncourts are great figures in literary
history, they have pioneered no new road, nor are they
of the writers whom men continuously love to read;
for it is as a document that the "Journal" remains of
enduring value.

Yet the great writers of any school bear witness,
each in his own way, that, deeper than these conventions and decorums of style, there is a law which no
writer can escape from, a law which must needs be
learnt, but can never be taught. That is the law of the
logic of thought. All the conventional rules of the
construction of speech may be put aside if a writer is
thereby enabled to follow more closely and lucidly the
form and process of his thought. It is the law of that
logic that he must for ever follow and in attaining it
alone find rest. He may say of it as devoutly as Dante:
"In la sua voluntade è nostra pace." All progress in
literary style lies in the heroic resolve to cast aside
accretions and exuberances, all the conventions of a
past age that were once beautiful because alive and are
now false because dead. The simple and naked beauty
of Swift's style, sometimes so keen and poignant, rests
absolutely on this truth to the logic of his thought.
The twin qualities of flexibility and intimacy are of
the essence of all progress in the art of language, and
in their progressive achievement lies the attainment of

great literature. If we compare Shakespeare with his predecessors and contemporaries, we can scarcely say that in imaginative force he is vastly superior to Marlowe, or in intellectual grip to Jonson, but he immeasurably surpasses them in flexibility and in intimacy. He was able with an incomparable art to weave a garment of speech so flexible in its strength, so intimate in its transparence, that it lent itself to every shade of emotion and the quickest turns of thought. When we compare the heavy and formal letters of Bacon, even to his closest friends, with the "Familiar Letters" of the vivacious Welshman Howell, we can scarcely believe the two men were contemporaries, so incomparably more expressive, so flexible and so intimate, is the style of Howell. All the writers who influence those who come after them have done so by the same method. They have thrown aside the awkward and outworn garments of speech, they have woven a simpler and more familiar speech, able to express subtleties or audacities that before seemed inexpressible. That was once done in English verse by Cowper and Wordsworth, in English prose by Addison and Lamb. That has been done in French to-day by Proust and in English by Joyce. When a great writer, like Carlyle or Browning, creates a speech of his own which is too clumsy to be flexible and too heavy to be intimate, he may arouse the admiration of his fellows, but he leaves no traces on the speech of the men who come after him. It is not easy

to believe that such will be Joyce's fate. His "Ulysses"
— carrying to a much further point qualities that began to appear in his earlier work — has been hailed
as epoch-making in English literature, though a distinguished critic holds that it is this rather by closing
than by opening an epoch. It would still be preparing
a new road, and as thus operative we may accept it
without necessarily judging it to be at the same time a
master-work, provided we understand what it is that
has been here attempted. This huge Odyssey is an
ordinary day's history in the ordinary life of one
ordinary man and the persons of his immediate environment. It is here sought to reproduce as Art the
whole of the man's physical and psychic activity during that period, omitting nothing, not even the actions
which the most naturalistic of novelists had hitherto
thought too trivial or too indelicate to mention. Not
only the thoughts and impulses that result in action,
but also the thoughts and emotions that drift aimlessly
across the field of his consciousness, are here; and, in
the presentation of this combined inner and outer life,
Joyce has sometimes placed both on the same plane,
achieving a new simplicity of style, though we may at
first sometimes find it hard to divine what is outer and
what inner. Moreover, he never hesitates, when he
pleases, to change the tone of his style and even to
adopt without notice, in a deliberately ironical and
chameleon-like fashion, the manner of other writers.
In these ways Joyce has here achieved that new

intimacy of vision, that new flexibility of expression, which are of the essence of all great literature at its vitally moving point of advance. He has succeeded in realising and making manifest in art what others had passed over or failed to see. If in that difficult and dangerous task he has failed, as some of us may believe, to reach either complete clarity or complete beauty, he has at all events made it possible for those who come after to reach a new height which, without the help of the road he had constructed, they might have missed, or even failed to conceive, and that is enough for any writer's fame.

When we turn to Proust we are in the presence of a writer about whom, no doubt, there is no violent dispute. There may be much about his work that is disturbing to many, but he was not concerned, like Joyce, to affront so many prejudices, and in France it is not even necessary, for the road has already been prepared by heroic pioneers of old during a thousand years. But the writer who brings a new revelation is not necessarily called upon to invite the execration of the herd. That is a risk he must be called upon to face, it is not an inevitable fate. When the mob yell: "Crucify him! Crucify him!" the artist, in whatever medium, hears a voice from Heaven: "This is my beloved son." Yet it is conceivable that the more perfectly a new revelation is achieved the less antagonism it arouses. Proust has undoubtedly been the master of a new intimacy of vision, a new flexibility of expression, even though the style through which the revelation has been made, perhaps necessarily on account of the complexity involved, has remained a little difficult and also, it must be said, a little negligent. But it has achieved a considerable degree of clarity and a high degree of beauty. So there is less difficulty in recognising a great masterpiece in "À la Recherche du Temps Perdu" than if it were more conspicuously the work of a daring pioneer. It is seen as the revelation of a new æsthetic sensibility embodied in a new and fitting style. Marcel Proust has experienced clearly what others have felt dimly or not at all. The significance of his work is thus altogether apart from the power of its dramatic incidents or its qualities as a novel. To the critic of defective intelligence, craving for scenes of sensation, it has sometimes seemed that "À l'Ombre des Jeunes Filles en Fleur" is the least important section of Proust's work. Yet it is on that quiet and uneventful tract of his narrative that Proust has most surely set the stamp of his genius, a genius, I should like to add, which is peculiarly congenial to the English mind because it was in the English tradition, rather than in the French tradition, that Proust was moving.[1]

[1] If it is asked why I take examples of a quality in art that is universal from literary personalities that to many are questionable, even morbid or perverse, rather than from some more normal and unquestioned figure, Thomas Hardy, for example, I would reply that I have always regarded it as more helpful and instructive to take examples that are still questionable rather than to fall back on the unquestionable that all will accept tamely without thought. Forty years ago, when Hardy's genius

No doubt it is possible for a writer to go far by the exercise of a finely attentive docility. By a dutiful study of what other people have said, by a refined cleverness in catching their tricks, and avoiding their subtleties, their profundities, their audacities, by, in short, a patient perseverance in writing out copper-plate maxims in elegant copybooks, he can become at last, like Stevenson, the idol of the crowd. But the great writer can only learn out of himself. He learns to write as a child learns to walk. For the laws of the logic of thought are not other than those of physical movement. There is stumbling, awkwardness, hesita-tion, experiment — before at last the learner attains the perfect command of that divine rhythm and peril-ous poise in which he asserts his supreme human privi-lege. But the process of his learning rests ultimately on his own structure and function and not on others' example. "Style must be founded upon models"; it is the rule set up by the pedant who knows nothing of what style means. For the style that is founded on a model is the negation of style.

The ardour and heroism of great achievement in style never grow less as the ages pass, but rather tend to grow more. That is so, not merely because the hardest tasks are left for the last, but because of the ever increasing impediments placed in the path of

was scarcely at all recognised, it seemed worth while to me to set forth the quality of his genius. To-day, when that quality is unquestioned, and Hardy receives general love and reverence, it would seem idle and unprofitable to do so.

style by the piling up of mechanical rules and rigid conventions. It is doubtful whether on the whole the forces of life really gain on the surrounding inertia of death. The greatest writers must spend the blood and sweat of their souls, amid the execration and disdain of their contemporaries, in breaking the old moulds of style and pouring their fresh life into new moulds. From Dante to Carducci, from Rabelais to Proust, from Chaucer to Whitman, the giants of letters have been engaged in this life-giving task, and behind them the forces of death swiftly gather again. Here there is always room for the hero. No man, indeed, can write anything that matters who is not a hero at heart, even though to the people who pass him in the street or know him in the house he may seem as gentle as any dove. If all progress lies in an ever greater flexibility and intimacy of speech, a finer adaptation to the heights and depths of the mobile human soul, the task can never be finally completed. Every writer is called afresh to reveal new strata of life. By digging in his own soul he becomes the discoverer of the soul of his family, of his nation, of the race, of the heart of humanity. For the great writer finds style as the mystic finds God, in his own soul. It is the final utterance of a sigh, which none could utter before him, and which all can who follow.

In the end, it will be seen we return at last to the point from which we start. We have completed the cycle of an art's evolution, — and it might, indeed, be any other art as much as writing, — reaching in the final sweep of ever wider flights the fact from which we started, but seeing it anew, with a fresh universal significance. Writing is an arduous spiritual and intellectual task, only to be achieved by patient and deliberate labour and much daring. Yet therewith we are only at the beginning. Writing is also the expression of individual personality, which springs up spontaneously, or is slowly drawn up from within, out of a well of inner emotions which none may command. But even with these two opposite factors we have not attained the complete synthesis. For style in the full sense is more than the deliberate and designed creation, more even than the unconscious and involuntary creation, of the individual man who therein expresses himself. The self that he thus expresses is a bundle of inherited tendencies that came the man himself can never entirely know whence. It is by the instinctive stress of a highly sensitive, or slightly abnormal constitution, that he is impelled to instil these tendencies into the alien magic of words. The stylum wherewith he strives to write himself on the yet blank pages of the world may have the obstinate vigour of the metal rod or the wild and quavering waywardness of an insect's wing, but behind it lie forces that extend into infinity. It moves us because it is itself moved by pulses which in varying measure we also have inherited, and because its primary source is in the heart of a cosmos from which we ourselves spring.

CHAPTER V
THE ART OF RELIGION

I

RELIGION is a large word, of good import and of evil import, and with the general discussion of religion we are not in this place concerned. Its quintessential core — which is the art of finding our emotional relationship to the world conceived as a whole — is all that here matters, and it is best termed "Mysticism." No doubt it needs some courage to use that word. It is the common label of abuse applied to every pseudo-spiritual thing that is held up for contempt. Yet it would be foolish to allow ourselves to be deflected from the right use of a word by the accident of its abuse. "Mysticism," however often misused, will here be used, because it is the correct term for the relationship of the Self to the Not-Self, of the individual to a Whole, when, going beyond his own personal ends, he discovers his adjustment to larger ends, in harmony or devotion or love.

It has become a commonplace among the unthinking, or those who think badly, to assume an opposition of hostility between mysticism and science.[1] If

[1] It is scarcely necessary to remark that if we choose to give to "mysticism" a definition incompatible with "science," the opposition cannot be removed. This is, for example, done by Croce, who yet recognises as highly important a process of "conversion" which is nothing else but mysticism as here understood. (See, e.g., Piccoli, *Benedetto Croce*, p. 184.) Only he has left himself no name to apply to it.

"science" is, as we have some reason to believe, an art, if "mysticism" also is an art, the opposition can scarcely be radical since they must both spring from the same root in natural human activity.

II

IF, indeed, by "science" we mean the organisation of an intellectual relationship to the world we live in adequate to give us some degree of power over that world, and if by "mysticism" we mean the joyful organisation of an emotional relationship to the world conceived as a whole,[1] the opposition which we usually assume to exist between them is of comparatively modern origin.

Among savage peoples such an opposition can scarcely be said to have any existence. The very fact that science, in the strict sense, seems often to begin with the stars might itself have suggested that the basis of science is mystical contemplation. Not only is there usually no opposition between the "scientific" and the "mystical" attitude among peoples we may fairly call primitive, but the two attitudes may be combined in the same person. The "medicine-man" is not more an embryonic man of science than he is an embryonic mystic; he is both equally. He cultivates not only

1 "The endeavour of the human mind to enjoy the blessedness of actual communion with the highest," which is Pringle Pattison's widely accepted definition of mysticism, I prefer not to use because it is ambiguous. The "endeavour," while it indicates that we are concerned with an art, also suggests its strained pathological forms, while "actual communion" lends itself to ontological interpretations.

magic but holiness, he achieves the conquest of his own
soul, he enters into harmony with the universe; and in
doing this, and partly, indeed, through doing this, his
knowledge is increased, his sensations and power of
observation are rendered acute, and he is enabled so
to gain organised knowledge of natural processes that
he can to some extent foresee or even control those
processes. He is the ancestor alike of the hermit following after sanctity and of the inventor crystallising
discoveries into profitable patents. Such is the medicine-man wherever we may find him in his typical
shape — which he cannot always adequately achieve
— all over the world, around Torres Straits just as
much as around Behring's Straits. Yet we have failed
to grasp the significance of this fact.

It is the business of the *Shaman*, as on the mystical
side we may conveniently term the medicine-man,
to place himself under the conditions — and even in
primitive life those conditions are varied and subtle —
which bring his will into harmony with the essence of
the world, so that he grows one with that essence,
that its will becomes his will, and, reversely, that, in a
sense, his will becomes its. Herewith, in this unity
with the spirit of the world, the possibility of magic
and the power to control the operation of Nature are
introduced into human thought, with its core of
reality and its endless trail of absurdity, persisting
even into advanced civilisation.

But this harmony with the essence of the universe,

this control of Nature through oneness with Nature, is not only at the heart of religion; it is also at the heart of science. It is only by the possession of an acquired or inborn temperament attuned to the temperament of Nature that a Faraday or an Edison, that any scientific discoverer or inventor, can achieve his results. And the primitive medicine-man, who on the religious side has attained harmony of the self with the Not-Self, and by obeying learnt to command, cannot fail on the scientific side also, under the special conditions of his isolated life, to acquire an insight into natural methods, a practical power over human activities and over the treatment of disease, such as on the imaginative and emotional side he already possesses. If we are able to see this essential and double attitude of the *Shaman* — medicine-man — if we are able to eliminate all the extraneous absurdities and the extravagancies which conceal the real nature of his function in the primitive world, the problem of science and mysticism, and their relationship to each other, ceases to have difficulties for us.

It is as well to point out, before passing on, that the investigators of primitive thought are not altogether in agreement with one another on this question of the relation of science to magic, and have complicated the question by drawing a distinction between magic (understood as man's claim to control Nature) and religion (understood as man's submission to Nature). The difficulties seem due to an attempt to introduce

clear-cut definitions at a stage of thought where none
such existed. That medicine-men and priests cultivated science, while wrapping it up in occult and
magical forms, seems indicated by the earliest historical traditions of the Near East. Herbert Spencer long
ago brought together much of the evidence on this
point. McDougall to-day in his "Social Psychology"
(Chapter XIII) accepts magic as the origin of science,
and Frazer in the early edition of his "Golden Bough"
regarded magic as "the savage equivalent of our
natural science." Marett [1] "profoundly doubts" this,
and declares that if we can use the word "science"
at all in such a contest, magic is occult science and the
very antithesis of natural science. While all that
Marett states is admirably true on the basis of his own
definitions, he scarcely seems to realise the virtue of
the word "equivalent," while at the same time, it may
be, his definition of magic is too narrow. Silberer,
from the psycho-analytic standpoint, accepting the
development of exact science from one branch of magic,
points out that science is, on the one hand, the recognition of concealed natural laws and, on the other,
the dynamisation of psychic power,[2] and thus falls
into two great classes, according as its operation is
external or internal. This seems a true and subtle distinction which Marett has overlooked. In the latest
edition of his work,[3] Frazer has not insisted on the

[1] *The Threshold of Religion* (1914), p. 48.
[2] *Zentralblatt für Psychoanalyse* (1911), p. 272.
[3] *Golden Bough*, "Balder the Beautiful," vol. II, pp. 304-05.

relation or analogy of science to magic, but has been
content to point out that Man has passed through the
three stages of magic, religion, and science. "In magic
Man depends on his own strength to meet the difficulties and dangers that beset him on every side. He
believes in a certain established order of Nature on
which he can surely count, and which he can manipu-
late for his own ends." Then he finds he has overestimated his own powers and he humbly takes the
road of religion, leaving the universe to the more or less
capricious will of a higher power. But he finds this
view inadequate and he proceeds to revert in a measure to the older standpoint of magic by postulating
explicitly what in magic had only been implicitly assumed, "to wit, an inflexible regularity in the order of
natural events which, if carefully observed, enables us
to foresee their course with certainty, and to act accordingly." So that science, in Frazer's view, is not so
much directly derived from magic as itself in its
original shape one with magic, and Man has proceeded, not in a straight line, but in a spiral.

The profound significance of this early personage is,
however, surely clear. If science and mysticism are
alike based on fundamental natural instincts, appearing spontaneously all over the world; if, moreover,
they naturally tend to be embodied in the same individual, in such a way that each impulse would seem to
be dependent on the other for its full development;
then there can be no ground for accepting any dis-

harmony between them. The course of human evolution involves a division of labour, a specialisation of science and of mysticism along special lines and in separate individuals.[1] But a fundamental antagonism of the two, it becomes evident, is not to be thought of; it is unthinkable, even absurd. If at some period in the course of civilisation we seriously find that our science and our religion are antagonistic, then there must be something wrong either with our science or with our religion. Perhaps not seldom there may be something wrong with both. For if the natural impulses which normally work best together are separated and specialised in different persons, we may expect to find a concomitant state of atrophy and hypertrophy, both alike morbid. The scientific person will become atrophied on the mystical side, the mystical person will become atrophied on the scientific side. Each will become morbidly hypertrophied on his own side. But the assumption that, because there is a lack of harmony between opposing pathological states, there must also be a similar lack of harmony in the normal state, is unreasonable. We must severely put out of count alike the hypertrophied scientific people with atrophied religious instincts, and the hypertrophied religious

[1] Farnell even asserts (in his *Greek Hero Cults*) that "it is impossible to quote a single example of any one of the higher world-religions working in harmony with the development of physical science." He finds a "special and unique" exception in the cult of Asclepios at Cos and Epidauros and Pergamon, where, after the fourth century B.C., were physicians, practising a rational medical science, who were also official priests of the Asclepios temples.

people with atrophied scientific instincts. Neither group can help us here; they only introduce confusion. We have to examine the matter critically, to go back to the beginning, to take so wide a survey of the phenomena that their seemingly conflicting elements fall into harmony.

The fact, in the first place, that the person with an overdeveloped religious sense combined with an under-developed scientific sense necessarily conflicts with a person in whom the reverse state of affairs exists, cannot be doubted, nor is the reason of it obscure. It is difficult to conceive a Darwin and a St. Theresa entering with full and genuine sympathy into each other's point of view. And that is so by no means because the two attitudes, stripped of all but their essentials, are irreconcilable. If we strip St. Theresa of her atrophied pseudo-science, which in her case was mostly theological "science," there was nothing in her attitude which would not have seemed to harmonise and to exalt that absolute adoration and service to natural truth which inspired Darwin. If we strip Darwin of that atrophied sense of poetry and the arts which he deplored, and that anæmic secular conception of the universe as a whole which he seems to have accepted without deploring, there was nothing in his attitude which would not have served to fertilise and enrich the spiritual exaltation of Theresa and even to have removed far from her that temptation to *acedia* or slothfulness which all the mystics who are mystics only have recognised as their besetting sin, minimised as it was, in Theresa, by her practical activities. Yet, being as they were persons of supreme genius developed on opposite sides of their common human nature, an impassable gulf lies between them. It lies equally between much more ordinary people who yet show the same common character of being undergrown on one side, overgrown on the other.

This difficulty is not diminished when the person who is thus hypertrophied on one side and atrophied on the other suddenly wakes up to his one-sided state and hastily attempts to remedy it. The very fact that such a one-sided development has come about indicates that there has probably been a congenital basis for it, an innate disharmony which must require infinite patience and special personal experience to overcome. But the heroic and ostentatious manner in which these ill-balanced people hastily attempt the athletic feat of restoring their spiritual balance has frequently aroused the interest, and too often the amusement, of the spectator. Sir Isaac Newton, one of the most quintessentially scientific persons the world has seen, a searcher who made the most stupendous effort to picture the universe intelligently on its purely intelligible side, seems to have realised in old age, when he was, indeed, approaching senility, that the vast hypertrophy of his faculties on that side had not been compensated by any development on the religious side. He forthwith set himself to the interpretation of the Book of Daniel and puzzled over the prophecies of the Book of Revelation, with the same scientifically serious air as though he were analysing the spectrum. In reality he had not reached the sphere of religion at all; he had merely exchanged good science for bad science. Such senile efforts to penetrate, ere yet life is quite over, the mystery of religion recall, and, indeed, have a real analogy to, that final effort of the emotionally starved to grasp at love which has been called "old maid's insanity"; and just as in this aberration the woman who has all her life put love into the subconscious background of her mind is overcome by an eruption of the suppressed emotions and driven to create baseless legends of which she is herself the heroine, so the scientific man who has put religion into the subconscious and scarcely known that there is such a thing may become in the end the victim of an imaginary religion. In our own time we may have witnessed attempts of the scientific mind to become religious, which, without amounting to mental aberration, are yet highly instructive. It would be a double-edged compliment, in this connection, to compare Sir Oliver Lodge to Sir Isaac Newton. But after devoting himself for many years to purely physical research, Lodge also, as he has confessed, found that he had overlooked the religious side of life, and therefore set himself with characteristic energy to the task — the stages of which are described in a long series of books — of developing this atrophied side of his nature.

Unlike Newton, who was worried about the future, Lodge became worried about the past. Just as Newton found what he was contented to regard as religious peace in speculating on the meaning of the Books of Daniel and Revelation, so Lodge found a similar satisfaction in speculations concerning the origin of the soul and in hunting out tags from the poets to support his speculations. So fascinating was this occupation that it seemed to him to constitute a great "message" to the world. "My message is that there is some great truth in the idea of preëxistence, not an obvious truth, nor one easy to formulate — a truth difficult to express — not to be identified with the guesses of reincarnation and transmigration, which may be fanciful. We may not have been individuals before, but we are chips or fragments of a great mass of mind, of spirit, and of life — drops, as it were, taken out of a germinal reservoir of life, and incubated until incarnate in a material body." [1] The genuine mystic would smile if asked to accept as a divine message these phraseological gropings in the darkness, with their culmination in the gospel of "incubated drops." They certainly represent an attempt to get at a real fact. But the mystic is not troubled by speculations about the origin of the individual, or theories of preëxistence, fantastic myths which belong to the earlier Plato's stage of thought. It is abundantly evident that when the hypertrophied man of science seeks to cultivate his atrophied religious

[1] Sir Oliver Lodge, *Reason and Belief*, p. 19.

instincts it is with the utmost difficulty that he escapes from science. His conversion to religion merely means, for the most part, that he has exchanged sound science for pseudo-science.

Similarly, when the man with hypertrophied religious instincts seeks to cultivate his atrophied scientific instincts, the results are scarcely satisfactory. Here, indeed, we are concerned with a phenomenon that is rarer than the reverse process. The reason may not be far to seek. The instinct of religion develops earlier in the history of a race than the instinct of science. The man who has found the massive satisfaction of his religious cravings is seldom at any stage conscious of scientific cravings; he is apt to feel that he already possesses the supreme knowledge. The religious doubters who vaguely feel that their faith is at variance with science are merely the creatures of creeds, the product of Churches; they are not the genuine mystics. The genuine mystics who have exercised their scientific instincts have generally found scope for such exercise within an enlarged theological scheme which they regarded as part of their religion. So it was that St. Augustine found scope for his full and vivid, if capricious, intellectual impulses; so also Aquinas, in whom there was doubtless less of the mystic and more of the scientist, found scope for the rational and orderly development of a keen intelligence which has made him an authority and even a pioneer for many who are absolutely indifferent to his theology.

Again we see that to understand the real relations of science and mysticism, we must return to ages when, on neither side, had any accumulated mass of dead traditions effected an artificial divorce between two great natural instincts. It has already been pointed out that if we go outside civilisation the divorce is not found; the savage mystic is also the savage man of science, the priest and the doctor are one.[1] It is so also for the most part in barbarism, among the ancient Hebrews for instance, and not only among their priests, but even among their prophets. It appears that the most usual Hebrew word for what we term the "prophet" signified "one who bursts forth," presumably into the utterance of spiritual verities, and the less usual words signify "seer." That is to say, the prophet was primarily a man of religion, secondarily a man of science. And that predictive element in the prophet's function, which to persons lacking in religious instinct seems the whole of his function, has no relationship at all to religion; it is a function of science. It is an insight into cause and effect, a conception of sequences based on extended observation and enabling the

[1] It is scarcely necessary to point out that a differentiation of function has to be made sooner or later, and sometimes it is made soon. This was so among the Todas of India. "Certain Todas," says Dr. Rivers (*The Todas*, 1906, p. 249), "have the power of divination, others are sorcerers, and others again have the power of curing diseases by means of spells and rites, while all three functions are quite separate from those of the priest or sharman. The Todas have advanced some way towards civilisation of function in this respect, and have as separate members of the community their prophets, their magicians, and their medicine-men in addition to their priests."

"prophet" to assert that certain lines of action will probably lead to the degeneration of a stock, or to the decay of a nation. It is a sort of applied history. "Prophecy" has no more to do with religion than have the forecasts of the Meteorological Bureau, which also are a kind of applied science in earlier stages associated with religion.

If, keeping within the sphere of civilisation, we go back as far as we can, the conclusion we reach is not greatly different. The earliest of the great mystics in historical times is Lao-tze. He lived six hundred years earlier than Jesus, a hundred years earlier than Sakya-Muni, and he was more quintessentially a mystic than either. He was, moreover, incomparably nearer than either to the point of view of science. Even his occupation in life was, in relation to his age and land, of a scientific character; he was, if we may trust uncertain tradition, keeper of the archives. In the substance of his work this harmony of religion and science is throughout traceable, the very word "Tao," which to Lao-tze is the symbol of all that to which religion may mystically unite us, is susceptible of being translated "Reason," although that word remains inadequate to its full meaning. There are no theological or metaphysical speculations here concerning God (the very word only occurs once and may be a later interpolation), the soul, or immortality. The delicate and profound art of Lao-tze largely lies in the skill with which he expresses spiritual verities in the form of natural truths. His-affirmations not only go to the core of religion, but they express the essential methods of science. This man has the mystic's heart, but he has also the physicist's touch and the biologist's eye. He moves in a sphere in which religion and science are one.

If we pass to more modern times and the little European corner of the world, around the Mediterranean shores, which is the cradle of our latter-day civilisation, again and again we find traces of this fundamental unity of mysticism and science. It may well be that we never again find it in quite so pure a form as in Laotze, quite so free from all admixture alike of bad religion and bad science. The exuberant unbalanced activity of our race, the restless acquisitiveness—already manifested in the sphere of ideas and traditions before it led to the production of millionaires — soon became an ever-growing impediment to such unity of spiritual impulses. Among the supple and yet ferocious Greeks, indeed, versatility and recklessness seem at a first glance always to have stood in the way of approach to the essential terms of this problem. It was only when the Greeks began to absorb Oriental influences, we are inclined to say, that they became genuine mystics, and as they approached mysticism they left science behind.

Yet there was a vein of mysticism in the Greeks from the first, not alone due to seeds from the East flung to germinate fruitfully in Greek soil, though perhaps to that Ionian element of the Near East which was an essential part of the Greek spirit. All that Karl Joël of

Basel has sought to work out concerning the evolution
of the Greek philosophic spirit has a bearing on this
point. We are wrong, he believes, to look on the early
Greek philosophers of Nature as mainly physicists,
treating the religious and poetic mystic elements in
them as mere archaisms, concessions, or contradictions. Hellas needed, and possessed, an early Romantic
spirit, if we understand the Romantic spirit, not
merely through its reactionary offshoots, but as a deep
mystico-lyrical expression; it was comparable in early
Greece to the Romantic spirit of the great creative
men of the early Renaissance or the early nineteenth
century, and the Apollinian classic spirit was developed out of an ordered discipline and formulation of
the Dionysian spirit more mystically near to Nature.[1]
If we bear this in mind we are helped to understand
much in the religious life of Greece which seems not to
harmonise with what we conventionally call "classic."

In the dim figure of Pythagoras we perhaps see not
only a great leader of physical science, but also a great
initiator in spiritual mystery. It is, at any rate, fairly
clear that he established religious brotherhoods of carefully selected candidates, women as well as men being
eligible, and living on so lofty and aristocratic a level
that the populace of Magna Grecia, who could not
understand them, decided out of resentment to burn

[1] Joël, *Ursprung der Naturphilosophie aus dem Geiste der Romantik*
(1903); *Nietzsche und die Romantik* (1905). But I am here quoting from
Professor Joël's account of his own philosophical development in *Die
Deutsche Philosophie der Gegenwart*, vol. I (1921).

them alive, and the whole order was annihilated about B.C. 500. But exactly how far these early Pythagoreans, whose community has been compared to the mediæval orders of chivalry, were mystics, we may imagine as we list, in the light of the Pythagorean echoes we find here and there in Plato. On the whole we scarcely go to the Greeks for a clear exposition of what we now term "mysticism." We see more of it in Lucretius than we can divine in his master Epicurus. And we see it still more clearly in the Stoics. We can, indeed, nowhere find a more pure and concise statement than in Marcus Aurelius of the mystical core of religion as the union in love and harmony and devotion of the self with the Not-Self.

If Lucretius may be accounted the first of moderns in the identification of mysticism and science, he has been followed by many, even though, one sometimes thinks, with an ever-increasing difficulty, a drooping of the wings of mystical aspiration, a limping of the feet of scientific progress. Leonardo and Giordano Bruno and Spinoza and Goethe, each with a little imperfection on one side or the other, if not on both sides, have moved in a sphere in which the impulses of religion are felt to spring from the same centre as the impulses of science. Einstein, whose attitude in many ways is so interesting, closely associates the longing for pure knowledge with religious feeling, and he has remarked that "in every true searcher of Nature there is a kind of religious reverence." He is inclined to attach significance to the fact that so many great men of science — Newton, Descartes, Gauss, Helmholtz — have been in one way or another religious. If we cannot altogether include such men as Swedenborg and Faraday in the same group, it is because we cannot feel that in them the two impulses, however highly developed, really spring from the same centre or really make a true harmony. We suspect that these men and their like kept their mysticism in a science-proof compartment of their minds, and their science in a mysticism-proof compartment; we tremble for the explosive result, should the wall of partition ever be broken down.

The difficulty, we see again, has been that, on each hand, there has been a growth of non-essential traditions around the pure and vital impulse, and the obvious disharmony of these two sets of accretions conceals the underlying harmony of the impulses themselves. The possibility of reaching the natural harmony is thus not necessarily by virtue of any rare degree of intellectual attainment, nor by any rare gift of inborn spiritual temperament, — though either of these may in some cases be operative, — but rather by the happy chance that the burden of tradition on each side has fallen and that the mystical impulse is free to play without a dead metaphysical theology, the scientific impulse without a dead metaphysical formalism. It is a happy chance that may befall the simple more easily than the wise and learned.

III

THE foregoing considerations have perhaps cleared the way to a realisation that when we look broadly at the matter, when we clear away all the accumulated superstitions, the unreasoned prepossessions, on either side, and so reach firm ground, not only is there no opposition between science and mysticism, but in their essence, and at the outset, they are closely related. The seeming divorce between them is due to a false and unbalanced development on either side, if not on both sides.

Yet all such considerations cannot suffice to make present to us this unity of apparent opposites. There is, indeed, it has often seemed to me, a certain futility in all discussion of the relative claims of science and religion. This is a matter which, in the last resort, lies beyond the sphere of argument. It depends not only on a man's entire psychic equipment, brought with him at birth and never to be fundamentally changed, but it is the outcome of his own intimate experience during life. It cannot be profitably discussed because it is experiential.

It seems to me, therefore, that, having gone so far, and stated what I consider to be the relations of mysticism and science as revealed in human history, I am bound to go further and to state my personal grounds for believing that the harmonious satisfaction alike of the religious impulse and the scientific impulse may be

attained to-day by an ordinarily balanced person in
whom both impulses crave for satisfaction. There is,
indeed, a serious difficulty. To set forth a personal religious experience for the first time requires considerable resolution, and not least to one who is inclined to
suspect that the experiences usually so set forth can be
of no profound or significant nature; that if the underlying motives of a man's life can be brought to the surface and put into words their vital motive power is
gone. Even the fact that more than forty years have
passed since the experience took place scarcely suffices
to make the confession of it easy. But I recall to mind
that the first original book I ever planned (and in fact
began to write) was a book, impersonal though suggested by personal experience, on the foundations of religion.[1] I put it aside, saying to myself I would complete it in old age, because it seemed to me that the
problem of religion will always be fresh, while there
were other problems more pressingly in need of speedy
investigation. Now, it may be, I begin to feel the time
has come to carry that early project a stage further.

Like many of the generation to which I belonged, I
was brought up far from the Sunday-school atmosphere
of conventional religiosity. I received little religious
instruction outside the home, but there I was made to
feel, from my earliest years, that religion is a very vital

[1] In connection with this scheme, it may be interesting to note, I prepared, in 1879, a *questionnaire* on "conversion," on the lines of the inves-
tigations which some years later began to be so fruitfully carried out by
the psychologists of religion in America.

and personal matter with which the world and the fashion of it had nothing to do. To that teaching, while still scarcely more than a child, I responded in a wholehearted way. Necessarily the exercise of this early impulse followed the paths prescribed for it by my environment. I accepted the creed set before me; I privately studied the New Testament for my own satisfaction; I honestly endeavoured, strictly in private, to mould my actions and impulses on what seemed to be Christian lines. There was no obtrusive outward evidence of this; outside the home, moreover, I moved in a world which might be indifferent but was not actively hostile to my inner aspirations, and, if the need for any external affirmation had become inevitable, I should, I am certain, have invoked other than religious grounds for my protest. Religion, as I instinctively felt then and as I consciously believe now, is a private matter, as love is. This was my mental state at the age of twelve.

Then came the period of emotional and intellectual expansion, when the scientific and critical instincts began to germinate. These were completely spontaneous and not stimulated by any influences of the environment. To inquire, to question, to investigate the qualities of the things around us and to search out their causes, is as native an impulse as the religious impulse would be found to be if only we would refrain from exciting it artificially. In the first place, this scientific impulse was not greatly concerned with the traditional body of beliefs which were then inextricably entwined

in my mind with the exercise of the religious instinct.
In so far, indeed, as it touched them it took up their defence. Thus I read Renan's "Life of Jesus," and the
facile sentiment of this book, the attitude of artistic reconstruction, aroused a criticism which led me to overlook any underlying sounder qualities. Yet all the time
the inquiring and critical impulse was a slowly permeat-
ing and invading influence, and its application to
religion was from time to time stimulated by books,
although such application was in no slightest degree
favoured by the social environment. When, too, at the
age of fifteen, I came to read Swinburne's "Songs before Sunrise," — although the book made no very personal appeal to me, — I realised that it was possible to
present in an attractively modern emotional light religious beliefs which were incompatible with Christianity, and even actively hostile to its creed. The process of
disintegration took place in slow stages that were not
perceived until the process was complete. Then at last I
realised that I no longer possessed any religious faith.
All the Christian dogmas I had been brought up to accept unquestioned had slipped away, and they had
dragged with them what I had experienced of religion,
for I could not then so far analyse all that is roughly
lumped together as "religion" as to disentangle the
essential from the accidental. Such analysis, to be
effectively convincing, demanded personal experiences
I was not possessed of.

I was now seventeen years of age. The loss of religious faith had produced no change in conduct, save that religious observances, which had never been ostentatiously performed, were dropped, so far as they might be without hurting the feelings of others. The revolution was so gradual and so natural that even inwardly the shock was not great, while various activities, the growth of mental aptitudes, sufficiently served to occupy the mind. It was only during periods of depression that the absence of faith as a satisfaction of the religious impulse became at all acutely felt. Possibly it might have been felt less acutely if I could have realised that there was even a real benefit in the cutting down and clearing away of traditional and non-vital beliefs. Not only was it a wholesome and strenuous effort to obey at all costs the call of what was felt as "truth," and therefore having in it a spirit of religion even though directed against religion, but it was evidently favourable to the training of intelligence. The man who has never wrestled with his early faith, the faith that he was brought up with and that yet is not truly his own, — for no faith is our own that we have not arduously won, — has missed not only a moral but an intellectual discipline. The absence of that discipline may mark a man for life and render all his work in the world ineffective. He has missed a training in criticism, in analysis, in open-mindedness, in the resolutely impersonal treatment of personal problems, which no other training can compensate. He is, for the most part, condemned to live in a mental jungle where his arm will soon be too feeble to clear away the growths that enclose him and his eyes too weak to find the light.

While, however, I had adopted, without knowing it, the best course to steel the power of thinking and to render possible a patient, humble, self-forgetful attitude towards Nature, there were times when I became painfully, almost despairingly, conscious of the unsatisfied cravings of the religious impulse. These moods were emphasised even by the books I read which argued that religion, in the only sense in which I understood religion, was unnecessary, and that science, whether or not formulated into a creed, furnished all that we need to ask in this direction. I well remember the painful feelings with which I read at this time D. F. Strauss's "The Old Faith and the New." It is a scientific creed set down in old age, with much comfortable complacency, by a man who found considerable satisfaction in the evening of life in the enjoyment of Haydn's quartets and Munich brown beer. They are both excellent things, as I am now willing to grant, but they are a sorry source of inspiration when one is seventeen and consumed by a thirst for impossibly remote ideals. Moreover, the philosophic horizon of this man was as limited and as prosaic as the æsthetic atmosphere in which he lived. I had to acknowledge to myself that the scientific principles of the universe as Strauss laid them down presented, so far as I knew, the utmost scope in which the human spirit could move.

But what a poor scope! I knew nothing of the way that Nietzsche, about that time, had demolished Strauss. But I had the feeling that the universe was represented as a sort of factory filled by an inextricable web of wheels and looms and flying shuttles, in a deafening din. That, it seemed, was the world as the most competent scientific authorities declared it to be made. It was a world I was prepared to accept, and yet a world in which, I felt, I could only wander restlessly, an ignorant and homeless child. Sometimes, no doubt, there were other visions of the universe a little less disheartening, such as that presented by Herbert Spencer's "First Principles." But the dominant feeling always was that while the scientific outlook, by which I mainly meant the outlook of Darwin and Huxley, commended itself to me as presenting a sound view of the world, on the emotional side I was a stranger to that world, if, indeed, I would not, with Omar, "shatter it to bits."

At the same time, it must be noted, there was no fault to find with the general trend of my life and activities. I was fully occupied, with daily duties as well as with the actively interested contemplation of an ever-enlarging intellectual horizon. This was very notably the case at the age of nineteen, three years after all vestiges of religious faith had disappeared from the psychic surface.

I was still interested in religious and philosophic questions, and it so chanced that at this time I read the "Life in Nature" of James Hinton, who had already attracted my attention as a genuine man of science with yet an original and personal grasp of religion. I had read the book six months before and it had not greatly impressed me. Now, I no longer know why, I read it again, and the effect was very different. Evidently by this time my mind had reached a stage of saturated solution which needed but the shock of the right contact to recrystallise in forms that were a revelation to me. Here evidently the right contact was applied. Hinton in this book showed himself a scientific biologist who carried the mechanistic explanation of life even further than was then usual.[1] But he was a man of highly passionate type of intellect, and what might otherwise be formal and abstract was for him soaked in emotion. Thus, while he saw the world as an orderly mechanism, he was not content, like Strauss, to stop there and see in it nothing else. As he viewed it, the mechanism was not the mechanism of a factory, it was vital, with all the glow and warmth and beauty of life; it was, therefore, something which not only the intellect might accept, but the heart might cling to. The

[1] It must be remembered that for science the mechanistic assumption always remains; it is, as Vaihinger would say, a necessary fiction. To abandon it is to abandon science. Driesch, the most prominent vitalist of our time, has realised this, and in his account of his own mental development (*Die Deutsche Philosophie der Gegenwart*, vol. 1, 1921) he shows how, beginning as a pupil of Haeckel and working at zoölogy for many years, after adopting the theory of vitalism he abandoned all zoölogical work and became a professor of philosophy. When the religious spectator, or the æsthetic spectator (as is well illustrated in the French review *L'Esprit Nouveau*), sees the "machinery" as something else than machinery he is legitimately going outside the sphere of science, but he is not thereby destroying the basic assumption of science.

bearing of this conception on my state of mind is obvious. It acted with the swiftness of an electric contact; the dull aching tension was removed; the two opposing psychic tendencies were fused in delicious harmony, and my whole attitude towards the universe was changed. It was no longer an attitude of hostility and dread, but of confidence and love. My self was one with the Not-Self, my will one with the universal will. I seemed to walk in light; my feet scarcely touched the ground; I had entered a new world.

The effect of that swift revolution was permanent. At first there was a moment or two of wavering, and then the primary exaltation subsided into an attitude of calm serenity towards all those questions that had once seemed so torturing. In regard to all these matters I had become permanently satisfied and at rest, yet absolutely unfettered and free. I was not troubled about the origin of the "soul" or about its destiny; I was entirely prepared to accept any analysis of the "soul" which might commend itself as reasonable. Neither was I troubled about the existence of any superior being or beings, and I was ready to see that all the words and forms by which men try to picture spiritual realities are mere metaphors and images of an inward experience. There was not a single clause in my religious creed because I held no creed. I had found that dogmas were — not, as I had once imagined, true, not, as I had afterwards supposed, false, — but the mere empty shadows of intimate personal experience. I had become indifferent to shadows, for I held the substance. I had sacrificed what I held dearest at the call of what seemed to be Truth, and now I was repaid a thousand-fold. Henceforth I could face life with confidence and joy, for my heart was at one with the world and whatever might prove to be in harmony with the world could not be out of harmony with me.[1]

Thus, it might seem to many, nothing whatever had happened; I had not gained one single definite belief that could be expressed in a scientific formula or hardened into a religious creed. That, indeed, is the essence of such a process. A "conversion" is not, as is often assumed, a turning towards a belief. More strictly, it is a turning round, a revolution; it has no primary reference to any external object. As the greater mystics have often understood, "the Kingdom of Heaven is within." To put the matter a little more precisely, the change is fundamentally a readjustment of psychic elements to each other, enabling the whole machine to work harmoniously. There is no necessary introduction of new ideas; there is much more likely to be a casting out of dead ideas which have clogged the vital process. The psychic organism — which in conven-

[1] Long ago Edith Simcox (in a passage of her *Natural Law* which chanced to strike my attention very soon after the episode above narrated) well described "conversion" as a "spiritual revolution," not based on any single rational consideration, but due to the "cumulative evidence of cognate impressions" resulting, at a particular moment, not in a change of belief, but in a total rearrangement and recolouring of beliefs and impressions, with the supreme result that the order of the universe is apprehended no longer as hostile, but as friendly. This is the fundamental fact of "conversion," which is the gate of mysticism.

tional religion is called the "soul" — had not been in harmony with itself; now it is revolving truly on its own axis, and in doing so it simultaneously finds its true orbit in the cosmic system. In becoming one with itself, it becomes one with the universe.[1]

The process, it will be seen, is thus really rather analogous to that which on the physical plane takes place in a person whose jaw or arm is dislocated, whether by some inordinate effort or some sudden shock with the external world. The miserable man with a dislocated jaw is out of harmony with himself and with the universe. All his efforts cannot reduce the dislocation, nor can his friends help him; he may even come to think there is no cure. But a surgeon comes along, and with a

[1] How we are to analyse the conception of "universe" — apart from its personal emotional tone, which is what mainly concerns us — is, of course, a matter that must be left altogether open and free. Sir James Frazer at the end of his *Golden Bough* ("Balder the Beautiful," vol. II, p. 306) finds that the "universe" is an "ever-shifting phantasmagoria of thought," or, he adds, suddenly shifting to a less idealistic and more realistic standpoint, "shadows on the screen." That is a literary artist's metaphysical way of describing the matter and could not occur to any one who was not familiar with the magic lantern which has now developed into the cinema, beloved of philosophers for its symbolic significance. Mr. Bertrand Russell, a more abstract artist, who would reject any such "imaginative admixture" as he would find in Frazer's view, once severely refused to recognise any such thing as a "universe," but has since less austerely admitted that there is, after all, a "set of appearances," which may fairly be labelled "reality," so long as we do not assume "a mysterious Thing-in-Itself behind the appearances." (*Nation*, 6th January, 1923.) But there are always some people who think that an "appearance" must be an appearance of *Something*, and that when a "shadow" is cast on the screen of our sensory apparatus it must be cast by *Something*. So every one defines the "universe" in his own way, and no two people — not even the same person long — can define it in the same way. We have to recognise that even the humblest of us is entitled to his own "universe."

slight pressure of his two thumbs, applied at the right spot, downwards and backwards, the jaw springs into place, the man is restored to harmony — and the universe is transformed. If he is ignorant enough, he will be ready to fall on his knees before his deliverer as a divine being. We are concerned with what is called a "spiritual" process, — for it is an accepted and necessary convention to distinguish between the "spiritual" and the "physical," — but this crude and imperfect analogy may help some minds to understand what is meant.

Thus may be explained what may seem to some the curious fact that I never for a moment thought of accepting as a gospel the book which had brought me a stimulus of such inestimable value. The person in whom "conversion" takes place is too often told that the process is connected in some magical manner with a supernatural influence of some kind, a book, a creed, a church, or what not. I had read this book before and it had left me unmoved; I knew that the book was merely the surgeon's touch, that the change had its source in me and not in the book. I never looked into the book again; I cannot tell where or how my copy of it disappeared; for all that I know, having accomplished its mission, it was drawn up again to Heaven in a sheet. As regards James Hinton, I was interested in him before the date of the episode here narrated; I am interested in him still.[1]

¹ The simple and essential outlines of "conversion" have been ob-

It may further be noted that this process of "conversion" cannot be regarded as the outcome of despair or as a protective regression towards childhood. The unfortunate individual, we sometimes imagine, who is bereft of religious faith sinks deeper and deeper into despondency, until finally he unconsciously seeks the relief of his woes by plunging into an abyss of emotions, thereby committing intellectual suicide. On the contrary, the period in which this event occurred was not a period of dejection either mental or physical. I was fully occupied; I lived a healthy, open-air life, in a fine climate, amid beautiful scenery; I was revelling

---

scured because chiefly studied in the Churches among people whose prepossessions and superstitions have rendered it a highly complex process, and mixed up with questions of right and wrong living which, important as they are, properly form no part of religion. The man who waits to lead a decent life until he has "saved his soul" is not likely to possess a soul that is worth saving. How much ignorance prevails in regard to "conversion," even among the leaders of religious opinion, and what violent contrasts of opinion — in which sometimes both the opposing parties are mistaken — was well illustrated by a discussion on the subject at the Church Congress at Sheffield in 1922. A distinguished Churchman well defined "conversion" as a unification of character, involving the whole man, — will, intellect, and emotion, — by which a "new self" was achieved; but he also thought that this great revolutionary process consisted usually in giving up some "definite bad habit," very much doubted whether sudden conversion was a normal phenomenon at all, and made no attempt to distinguish between that kind of "conversion" which is merely the result of suggestion and auto-suggestion, after a kind of hysterical attack produced by feverish emotional appeals, and that which is spontaneous and of lifelong effect. Another speaker went to the opposite extreme by asserting that "conversion" is an absolutely necessary process, and an Archbishop finally swept away "conversion" altogether by declaring that the whole of the religious life (and the whole of the irreligious life?) is a process of conversion. (*The Times*, 12th October, 1922.) It may be a satisfaction to some to realise that this is a matter on which it is vain to go to the Churches for light.

in new studies and the growing consciousness of new
powers. Instead of being the ultimate stage in a process of descent, or a return to childhood, such psychic
revolution may much more fittingly be regarded as the
climax of an ascensional movement. It is the final
casting off of childish things, the initiation into complete manhood.

There is nothing ascetic in such a process. One is
sometimes tempted to think that to approve mysticism is to preach asceticism. Certainly many mystics
have been ascetic. But that has been the accident of
their philosophy, and not the essence of their religion.
Asceticism has, indeed, nothing to do with normal
religion. It is, at the best, the outcome of a set of
philosophical dogmas concerning the relationship of
the body to the soul and the existence of a transcendental spiritual world. That is philosophy, of a sort, not
religion. Plotinus, who has been so immensely influential in our Western world because he was the main
channel by which Greek spiritual tendencies reached
us, to become later embodied in Christianity, is usually
regarded as a typical mystic, though he was primarily
a philosopher, and he was inclined to be ascetic.
Therein we may not consider him typically Greek,
but the early philosophical doctrine of Plato concerning the transcendental world of "Ideas" easily lent
itself to developments favourable to an ascetic life.
Plotinus, indeed, was not disposed to any extreme
ascetic position. The purification of the soul meant

for him "to detach it from the body, and to elevate it to a spiritual world." But he would not have sympathised with the harsh dualism of flesh and spirit which often flourished among Christian ascetics. He lived celibate, but he was willing to regard sex desire as beautiful, though a delusion.[1] When we put aside the philosophic doctrines with which it may be associated, it is seen that asceticism is merely an adjuvant discipline to what we must regard as pathological forms of mysticism.

People who come in contact with the phenomenon of "conversion" are obsessed by the notion that it must have something to do with morality. They seem to fancy that it is something that happens to a person leading a bad life whereby he suddenly leads a good life. That is a delusion. Whatever virtue morality may possess, it is outside the mystic's sphere. No doubt a person who has been initiated into this mystery is likely to be moral because he is henceforth in harmony with himself, and such a man is usually, by a natural impulse, in harmony also with others. Like Leonardo, who through the glow of his adoration of Nature was as truly a mystic as St. Francis, even by contact with him "every broken heart is made serene." But a religious man is not necessarily a moral man. That is to say that we must by no means expect to find that the religious man, even when he is in harmony

---

[1] Dean Inge (*Philosophy of Plotinus*, vol. II, p. 165) has some remarks on Plotinus in relation to asceticism.

with his fellows, is necessarily in harmony with the
moral laws of his age. We fall into sad confusion if we
take for granted that a mystic is what we conventionally term a "moral" man. Jesus, as we know, was
almost as immoral from the standpoint of the society
in which he moved as he would be in our society. That,
no doubt, is an extreme example, yet the same holds
good, in a minor degree, of many other mystics, even
in very recent times. The satyrs and the fauns were
minor divinities in antiquity, and in later times we
have been apt to misunderstand their holy functions
and abuse their sacred names.

Not only is there no necessary moral change in such
a process, still less is there any necessary intellectual
change. Religion need not involve intellectual suicide.
On the intellectual side there may be no obvious
change whatever. No new creed or dogma had been
adopted.[1] It might rather be said that, on the contrary, some prepossessions, hitherto unconscious, had
been realised and cast out. The operations of reason,
so far from being fettered, can be effected with greater
freedom and on a larger scale. Under favourable
conditions the religious process, indeed, throughout
directly contributes to strengthen the scientific atti-

[1] Jules de Gaultier (*La Philosophie officielle et la Philosophie*, p. 150)
refers to those Buddhist monks the symbol of whose faith was contained
in one syllable: *Om*. But those monks, he adds, belonged to "the only
philosophic race that ever existed" and by the aid of their pure faith,
placed on a foundation which no argumentation can upset, all the religious philosophies of the Judeo-Helleno-Christian tradition are but
as fairy-tales told to children.

tude. The mere fact that one has been impelled by the sincerity of one's religious faith to question, to analyse, and finally to destroy one's religious creed, is itself an incomparable training for the intelligence. In this task reason is submitted to the hardest tests; it has every temptation to allow itself to be lulled into sleepy repose or cajoled into specious reconciliations. If it is true to itself here it is steeled for every other task in the world, for no other task can ever demand so complete a self-sacrifice at the call of Truth. Indeed, the final restoration of the religious impulse on a higher plane may itself be said to reënforce the scientific impulse, for it removes that sense of psychic disharmony which is a subconscious fetter on the rational activity. The new inward harmony, proceeding from a psychic centre that is at one alike with itself and with the Not-Self, imparts confidence to every operation of the intellect. All the metaphysical images of faith in the unseen — too familiar in the mystical experiences of men of all religions to need specification — are now on the side of science. For he who is thus held in his path can pursue that path with serenity and trust, however daring its course may sometimes seem.

It appears to me, therefore, on the basis of personal experience, that the process thus outlined is a natural process. The harmony of the religious impulse and of the scientific impulse is not merely a conclusion to be deduced from the history of the past. It is a living fact to-day. However obscured it may sometimes be,

the process lies in human nature and is still open to all
to experience.

IV

IF the development of the religious instinct and the
development of the scientific instinct are alike natural,
and if the possibility of the harmony of the two instincts is a verifiable fact of experience, how is it, one
may ask, that there has ever been any dispute on the
matter? Why has not this natural experience been the
experience of all?

Various considerations may help to make clear to
us how it has happened that a process which might
reasonably be supposed to be intimate and sacred
should have become so obscured and so deformed
that it has been fiercely bandied about by opposing
factions. At the outset, as we have seen, among comparatively primitive peoples, it really is a simple
and natural process carried out harmoniously with
no sense of conflict. A man, it would seem, was not
then overburdened by the still unwritten traditions
of the race. He was comparatively free to exercise
his own impulses unfettered by the chains forged
out of the dead impulses of those who had gone
before him.

It is the same still among uncultivated persons of
our own race in civilisation. I well remember how once,
during a long ride through the Australian bush with a
settler, a quiet, uncommunicative man with whom I

had long been acquainted, he suddenly told me how at times he would ascend to the top of a hill and become lost to himself and to everything as he stood in contemplation of the scene around him. Those moments of ecstasy, of self-forgetful union with the divine beauty of Nature, were entirely compatible with the rational outlook of a simple, hard-working man who never went to church, for there was no church of any kind to go to, but at such moments had in his own humble way, like Moses, met God in a mountain. There can be no doubt that such an experience is not uncommon among simple folk unencumbered by tradition, even when of civilised race.

The burden of traditions, of conventions, of castes has too often proved fatal alike to the manifestation of the religious impulse and the scientific impulse. It is unnecessary to point out how easily this happens in the case of the religious impulse. It is only too familiar a fact how, when the impulse of religion first germinates in the young soul, the ghouls of the Churches rush out of their caverns, seize on the unhappy victim of the divine effluence and proceed to assure him that his rapture is, not a natural manifestation, as free as the sunlight and as gracious as the unfolding of a rose, but the manifest sign that he has been branded by a supernatural force and fettered for ever to a dead theological creed. Too often he is thus caught by the bait of his own rapture; the hook is firmly fixed in his jaw and he is drawn whither his blind guides will; his wings droop and fall away; so far as the finer issues of life are concerned, he is done for and damned.[1]

But the process is not so very different on the scientific side, though here it is more subtly concealed. The youth in whom the natural impulse of science arises is sternly told that the spontaneous movement of his intelligence towards Nature and truth is nothing, for the one thing needful is that he shall be put to discipline, and trained in the scientific traditions of the ages. The desirability of such training for the effective questioning of Nature is so clear that both teacher and pupil are apt to overlook the fact that it involves much that is not science at all: all sorts of dead traditions, unrealised fragments of ancient metaphysical systems, prepossessions and limitations, conscious or unconscious, the obedience to arbitrary authorities. It is never made clear to him that science also is an art. So that the actual outcome may be that the finally accomplished man of science has as little of the scientific impulse as the fully fledged religious man need have of the religious impulse; he becomes the victim of another kind of ecclesiastical sectarianism.

There is one special piece of ancient metaphysics which until recently scientific and religious sects have

[1] We must always remember that "Church" and "religion," though often confused, are far from being interchangeable terms. "Religion" is a natural impulse, "Church" is a social institution. The confusion is unfortunate. Thus Freud (*Group Psychology*, p. 51) speaks of the probability of religion disappearing and Socialism taking its place. He means, not "religion," but a "Church." We cannot speak of a natural impulse disappearing; an institution easily may.

alike combined to support: the fiction of "matter,"
which we passingly came upon when considering the
art of thinking. It is a fiction that has much to answer
for in distorting the scientific spirit and in creating an
artificial opposition between science and religion. All
sorts of antique metaphysical peculiarities, inherited
from the decadence of Greek philosophy, were attributed to "matter" and they were mostly of a bad character; all the good qualities were attributed to "spirit";
"matter" played the Devil's part to this more divine
"spirit." Thus it was that "materialistic" came to be
a term signifying all that is most heavy, opaque, de-
pressing, soul-destroying, and diabolical in the universe. The party of traditionalised religion fostered
this fiction and the party of traditionalised science
frequently adopted it, cheerily proposing to find infinite potentialities in this despised metaphysical substance. So that "matter" which was on one side
trodden underfoot was on the other side brandished
overhead as a glorious banner.

Yet "matter," as psychologically minded philosophers at last began to point out, is merely a substance
we have ourselves invented to account for our sensations. We see, we touch, we hear, we smell, and by a
brilliant synthetic effort of imagination we put together all those sensations and picture to ourselves
"matter" as being the source of them. Science itself
is now purging "matter" of its complicated metaphysical properties. That "matter," the nature of

which Dr. Johnson, as Boswell tells us, thought he had settled by "striking his foot with mighty force against a large stone," is coming to be regarded as merely an electrical emanation. We now accept even that transmutation of the elements of which the alchemists dreamed. It is true that we still think of "matter" as having weight. But so cautious a physicist as Sir Joseph Thomson long ago pointed out that weight is only an "apparently" invariable property of matter. So that "matter" becomes almost as "ethereal" as "spirit," and, indeed, scarcely distinguishable from "spirit." The spontaneous affirmation of the mystic that he lives in the spiritual world here and now will then be, in other words, merely the same affirmation which the man of science has more laboriously reached. The man, therefore, who is terrified by "materialism" has reached the final outpost of absurdity. He is a simple-minded person who places his own hand before his eyes and cries out in horror: The Universe has disappeared!

We have not only to realise how our own prepossessions and the metaphysical figments of our own creation have obscured the simple realities of religion and science alike; we have also to see that our timid dread lest religion should kill our science, or science kill our religion, is equally fatal here. He who would gain his life must be willing to lose it, and it is by being honest to one's self and to the facts by applying courageously the measuring rod of Truth, that in the end salvation is found. Here, it is true, there are those who smilingly assure us that by adopting such a method we shall merely put ourselves in the wrong and endure much unnecessary suffering. There is no such thing as "Truth," they declare, regarded as an objective impersonal reality; we do not "discover" truth, we invent it. Therefore your business is to invent a truth which shall harmoniously satisfy the needs of your nature and aid your efficiency in practical life. That we are justified in being dishonest towards truth has even been argued from the doctrine of relativity by some who failed to realise that that doctrine is here hardly relative. Certainly the philosophers of recent times, from Nietzsche to Croce, have loved to analyse the idea of "truth" and to show that it by no means signifies what we used to suppose it signified. But to show that truth is fluid, or even the creation of the individual mind, is by no means to show that we can at will play fast and loose with it to suit our own momentary convenience. If we do we merely find ourselves, at the end, in a pool where we must tramp round and round in intellectual slush out of which there is no issue. One may well doubt whether any Pragmatist has ever really invented his truth that way. Practically, just as the best result is attained by the man who acts as though free-will were a reality and who exerts it, so in this matter, also, practically, in the end the best result is attained by assuming that truth is an objective reality which we must patiently seek, and in accordance

Neo-Platonists in whom the whole movement of modern mysticism began, of their glorious pupils in the Moslem world, of Ramon Lull and Francis of Assisi and François Xavier and John of the Cross and George Fox and the "De Imitatione Christi" and "Towards Democracy"? There is no end to that list of glorious names, and they are all passed by.

To write of the mystics, whether Pagan or Christian or Islamic, is a most delightful task. It has been done, and often very well done. The mystics are not only themselves an incarnation of beauty, but they reflect beauty on all who with understanding approach them.

Moreover, in the phenomena of religious mysticism we have a key — if we only knew it — to many of the most precious human things which on the surface may seem to have nothing in them of religion. For this is an art which instinctively reveals to us the secrets of other arts. It presents to us in the most naked and essential way the inward experience which has inspired men to find modes of expression which are transmutations of the art of religion and yet have on the surface nothing to indicate that this is so. It has often been seen in poetry and in music and in painting. One might say that it is scarcely possible to understand completely the poetry of Shelley or the music of César Franck or the pictures of Van Gogh unless there is somewhere within an intimation of the secret of mysticism. This is so not because of any imperfection in the achieved work of such men in poetry and in

music and in painting, — for work that fails to contain
its own justification is always bad work, — but because we shall not be in possession of the clue to explain
the existence of that work. We may even go beyond
the sphere of the recognised arts altogether, and say
that the whole love of Nature and landscape, which in
modern times has been so greatly developed, largely
through Rousseau, the chief creator of our modern
spiritual world, is not intelligible if we are altogether
ignorant of what religion means.

But we are not so much concerned here with the
rich and variegated garments the impulse of religion
puts on, or with its possible transmutations, as with
the simple and naked shape of those impulses when
bared of all garments. It was peculiarly important to
present the impulse of mysticism naked because, of all
the fundamental human impulses, that is the one most
often so richly wrapped round with gorgeous and
fantastic garments that, alike to the eye of the ordinary
man and the acute philosopher, there has seemed to be
no living thing inside at all. It was necessary to strip
off all these garments, to appeal to simple personal
direct experience for the actual core of fact, and to
show that that core, so far from being soluble by
analysis into what science counts as nothing, is itself,
like every other natural organic function, a fact of
science.

It is enough here, where we are concerned only with
the primary stuff of art, the bare simple technique of

the human dance, to have brought into as clear a light as may be the altogether natural mechanism which lies behind all the most magnificent fantasies of the mystic impulse, and would still subsist and operate even though they were all cast into the flames. That is why it has seemed necessary to dwell all the time on the deep-lying harmony of the mystic's attitude with the scientific man's attitude. It is a harmony which rests on the faith that they are eternally separate, however close, however intimately coöperative. When the mystic professes that, as such, he has knowledge of the same order as the man of science, or when the scientist claims that, as such, he has emotion which is like that of the man of religion, each of them deceives himself. He has introduced a confusion where no confusion need be; perhaps, indeed, he has even committed that sin against the Holy Ghost of his own spiritual integrity for which there is no forgiveness. The function of intellectual thought — which is that of the art of science — may, certainly, be invaluable for religion; it makes possible the purgation of all that pseudo-science, all that philosophy, good or bad, which has poisoned and encrusted the simple spontaneous impulse of mysticism in the open air of Nature and in the face of the sun. The man of science may be a mystic, but cannot be a true mystic unless he is so relentless a man of science that he can tolerate no alien science in his mysticism. The mystic may be a man of science, but he will not be a good man of science unless he understands that science must be kept for ever bright and pure from all admixture of mystical emotion; the fountain of his emotion must never rust the keenness of his analytic scalpel. It is useless to pretend that any such rustiness can ever convert the scalpel into a mystical implement, though it can be an admirable aid in cutting towards the mystical core of things, and perhaps if there were more relentless scientific men there would be more men of pure mystic vision. Science by itself, good or bad, can never be religion, any more than religion by itself can ever be science, or even philosophy.

It is by looking back into the past that we see the facts in an essential simplicity less easy to reach in more sophisticated ages. We need not again go so far back as the medicine-men of Africa and Siberia. Mysticism in pagan antiquity, however less intimate to us and less seductive than that of later times, is perhaps better fitted to reveal to us its true nature. The Greeks believed in the spiritual value of "conversion" as devoutly as our Christian sects and they went beyond most such sects in their elaborately systematic methods for obtaining it, no doubt for the most part as superficially as has been common among Christians. It is supposed that almost the whole population of Athens must have experienced the Eleusinian initiation. These methods, as we know, were embodied in the Mysteries associated with Dionysus and Demeter and Orpheus and the rest, the most famous and

typical being those of Attic Eleusis.[1] We too often see
those ancient Greek Mysteries through a concealing
mist, partly because it was rightly felt that matters of
spiritual experience were not things to talk about, so
that precise information is lacking, partly because the
early Christians, having their own very similar Mysteries to uphold, were careful to speak evil of Pagan
Mysteries, and partly because the Pagan Mysteries no
doubt really tended to degenerate with the general
decay of classic culture. But in their large simple
essential outlines they seem to be fairly clear. For just
as there was nothing "orgiastic" in our sense in the
Greek "orgies," which were simply ritual acts, so
there was nothing, in our sense, "mysterious" in the
Mysteries. We are not to suppose, as is sometimes
supposed, that their essence was a secret doctrine, or
even that the exhibition of a secret rite was the sole
object, although it came in as part of the method. A
mystery meant a spiritual process of initiation, which
was, indeed, necessarily a secret to those who had not
yet experienced it, but had nothing in itself "mysterious" beyond what inheres to-day to the process in any
Christian "revival," which is the nearest analogue to

[1] The modern literature of the Mysteries, especially of Eleusis, is very
extensive and elaborate in many languages. I will only mention here a
small and not very recent book, Cheetham's Hulsean Lectures on *The
Mysteries Pagan and Christian* (1897) as for ordinary readers sufficiently
indicating the general significance of the Mysteries. There is, yet
briefer, a more modern discussion of the matter in the Chapter on "Religion" by Dr. W. R. Inge in R. W. Livingstone's useful collection of
essays, *The Legacy of Greece* (1921).

the Greek Mystery. It is only "mysterious" in the sense that it cannot be expressed, any more than the sexual embrace can be expressed, in words, but can only be known by experience. A preliminary process of purification, the influence of suggestion, a certain religious faith, a solemn and dramatic ritual carried out under the most impressive circumstances, having a real analogy to the Catholic's Mass, which also is a function, at once dramatic and sacred, which culminates in a spiritual communion with the Divine — all this may contribute to the end which was, as it always must be in religion, simply a change of inner attitude, a sudden exalting realisation of a new relationship to eternal things. The philosophers understood this; Aristotle was careful to point out, in an extant fragment, that what was gained in the Mysteries was not instruction but impressions and emotions, and Plato had not hesitated to regard the illumination which came to the initiate in philosophy as of the nature of that acquired in the Mysteries. So it was natural that when Christianity took the place of Paganism the same process went on with only a change in external circumstances. Baptism in the early Church — before it sank to the mere magical sort of rite it later became — was of the nature of initiation into a Mystery, preceded by careful preparation, and the baptised initiate was sometimes crowned with a garland as the initiated were at Eleusis.

When we go out of Athens along the beautiful road

that leads to the wretched village of Eleusis and linger among the vast and complicated ruins of the chief shrine of mysticism in our Western world, rich in associations that seem to stretch back to the Neolithic Age and suggest a time when the mystery of the blossoming of the soul was one with the mystery of the upspringing of the corn, it may be that our thoughts by no unnatural transition pass from the myth of Demeter and Kore to the remembrance of what we may have heard or know of the manifestations of the spirit among barbarian northerners of other faiths or of no faith in far Britain and America and even of their meetings of so-called "revival." For it is always the same thing that Man is doing, however various and fantastic the disguises he adopts. And sometimes the revelation of the new life, springing up from within, comes amid the crowd in the feverish atmosphere of artificial shrines, maybe soon to shrivel up, and sometimes the blossoming forth takes place, perhaps more favourably, in the open air and under the light of the sun and amid the flowers, as it were to a happy faun among the hills. But when all disguises have been stripped away, it is always and everywhere the same simple process, a spiritual function which is almost a physiological function, an art which Nature makes. That is all.

CHAPTER VI
THE ART OF MORALS

I

No man has ever counted the books that have been written about morals. No subject seems so fascinating to the human mind. It may well be, indeed, that nothing imports us so much as to know how to live. Yet it can scarcely be that on any subject are the books that have been written more unprofitable, one might even say unnecessary.

For when we look at the matter objectively it is, after all, fairly simple. If we turn our attention to any collective community, at any time and place, in its moral aspect, we may regard it as an army on the march along a road of life more or less encompassed by danger. That, indeed, is scarcely a metaphor; that is what life, viewed in its moral aspect, may really be considered. When thus considered, we see that it consists of an extremely small advance guard in front, formed of persons with a limited freedom of moral action and able to act as patrols in various directions, of a larger body in the rear, in ancient military language called the blackguard and not without its uses, and in the main of a great compact majority with which we must always be chiefly concerned since they really are the army; they are the community. What we call "morals" is simply blind obedience to words of command — whether or not issued by leaders the army believes it has itself chosen — of which the significance is hidden, and beyond this the duty of keeping in step with the others, or of trying to keep in step, or of pretending to do so.[1] It is an automatic, almost unconscious process and only becomes acutely conscious when the individual is hopelessly out of step; then he may be relegated to the rear blackguard. But that happens seldom. So there is little need to be concerned about it. Even if it happened very often, nothing overwhelming would have taken place; it would merely be that what we called the blackguard had now become the main army, though with a different discipline. We are, indeed, simply concerned with a discipline or routine which in this field is properly described as *custom*, and the word *morals* essentially means *custom*. That is what morals must always be for the mass, and, indeed, to some extent for all, a discipline, and, as we have already seen, a discipline cannot properly be regarded as a science or an art. The innumerable books on morals, since they have usually confused and befogged this simple and central

[1] What we call crime is, at the beginning, usually an effort to get, or to pretend to get, into step, but, being a violent or miscalculated effort. it is liable to fail, and the criminal falls to the rear of the social army. "I believe that most murders are really committed by Mrs. Grundy," a woman writes to me, and, with the due qualification, the saying is worthy of meditation. That is why justice is impotent to prevent or even to punish murder, for Mrs. Grundy is within all of us, being a part of the social discipline, and cannot be hanged.

fact, cannot fail to be rather unprofitable. That, it would seem, is what the writers thought — at all events about those the others had written — or else they would not have considered it necessary for themselves to add to the number. It was not only an unprofitable task, it was also — except in so far as an objectively scientific attitude has been assumed — aimless. For, although the morals of a community at one time and place is never the same as that of another or even the same community at another time and place, it is a complex web of conditions that produces the difference, and it must have been evident that to attempt to affect it was idle.[1] There is no occasion for any one who is told that he has written a "moral" book to be unduly elated, or when he is told that his book is "immoral" to be unduly cast down. The significance of these adjectives is strictly limited. Neither the one book nor the other can have more than the faintest effect on the march of the great compact majority of the social army.

Yet, while all this is so, there is still some interest in the question of morals. For, after all, there is the small body of individuals ahead, alertly eager to find the road, with a sensitive flair for all the possibilities the future may hold. When the compact majority, blind

[1] Herbert Spencer, writing to a correspondent, once well expressed the harmlessness — if we choose so to regard it — of moral teaching: "After nearly two thousand years' preaching of the religion of amity, the religion of enmity remains predominant, and Europe is peopled by two hundred million pagans, masquerading as Christians, who revile those who wish them to act on the principles they profess."

and automatic and unconscious, follows after, to tramp along the road these pioneers have discovered, it may seem but a dull road. But before they reached it that road was interesting, even passionately interesting.

The reason is that, for those who, in any age, are thus situated, life is not merely a discipline. It is, or it may become, really an art.

II

THAT living is or may be an art, and the moralist the critic of that art, is a very ancient belief. It was especially widespread among the Greeks. To the Greeks, indeed, this belief was so ingrained and instinctive that it became an implicitly assumed attitude rather than a definitely expressed faith. It was natural to them to speak of a virtuous person as we should speak of a beautiful person. The "good" was the "beautiful"; the sphere of ethics for the Greeks was not distinguished from the sphere of æsthetics. In Sophocles, above all poets, we gather the idea of a natural agreement between duty and inclination which is at once both beauty and moral order. But it is the beautiful that seems to be most fundamental in τὸ καλόν, which was the noble, the honourable, but fundamentally the beautiful. "Beauty is the first of all things," said Isocrates, the famous orator; "nothing that is devoid of beauty is prized. . . . The admiration for virtue comes to this, that of all manifestation of

life, virtue is the most beautiful." The supremely
beautiful was, for the finer sort of Greeks, instinctively
if not always consciously, the supremely divine, and
the Argive Hera, it has been said, "has more divinity
in her countenance than any Madonna of them all."
That is how it came to pass that we have no word in
our speech to apply to the Greek conception; æsthetics
for us is apart from all the serious business of life, and
the attempt to introduce it there seems merely comic.
But the Greeks spoke of life itself as a craft or a fine
art. Protagoras, who appears to-day as a pioneer of
modern science, was yet mainly concerned to regard
living as an art, or as the sum of many crafts, and the
Platonic Socrates, his opponent, still always assumed
that the moralist's position is that of a critic of a craft.
So influential a moralist as Aristotle remarks in a
matter-of-fact way, in his "Poetics," that if we wish to
ascertain whether an act is, or is not, morally right we
must consider not merely the intrinsic quality of the
act, but the person who does it, the person to whom it
is done, the time, the means, the motive. Such an attitude towards life puts out of court any appeal to rigid
moral laws; it meant that an act must befit its particular relationships at a particular moment, and that its
moral value could, therefore, only be judged by the
standard of the spectator's instinctive feeling for proportion and harmony. That is the attitude we adopt
towards a work of art.

It may well appear strange to those who cherish the

modern idea of "æstheticism" that the most complete statement of the Greek attitude has come down to us in the writings of a philosopher, an Alexandrian Greek who lived and taught in Rome in the third century of our Christian Era, when the Greek world had vanished, a religious mystic, moreover, whose life and teaching were penetrated by an austere ascetic severity which some would count mediæval rather than Greek.[1] It is in Plotinus, a thinker whose inspiring influence still lives to-day, that we probably find the Greek attitude, in its loftiest aspect, best mirrored, and it was probably through channels that came from Plotinus — though their source was usually unrecognised — that the Greek moral spirit has chiefly reached modern times. Many great thinkers and moralists of the eighteenth and nineteenth centuries, it has been claimed, were ultimately indebted to Plotinus, who represented the only genuinely creative effort of the Greek spirit in the third century.[2]

[1] But later asceticism was strictly the outcome of a Greek tendency, to be traced in Plato, developed through Antisthenes, through Zeno, through Epictetus, who all desired to liberate the soul from the bonds of matter. The Neo-Platonists carried this tendency further, for in their time the prevailing anarchy and confusion rendered the world and society less than ever a fitting haven for the soul. It was not Christianity that made the world ascetic (and there were elements of hedonism in the teaching of Jesus), but the world that made Christianity ascetic, and it was easy for a Christian to become a Neo-Platonist, for they were both being moulded by the same forces.

[2] Maurice Croiset devotes a few luminous critical pages to Plotinus in the Croisets' *Histoire de la Littérature Grecque*, vol. v, pp. 820–31. As an extended account of Plotinus, from a more enthusiastically sympathetic standpoint, there are Dr. Inge's well-known Gifford Lectures, *The Philosophy of Plotinus* (1918); I may also mention a careful scholastic

THE DANCE OF LIFE

Plotinus seems to have had little interest in art, as
commonly understood, and he was an impatient, rapid,
and disorderly writer, not even troubling to spell correctly. All his art was in the spiritual sphere. It is
impossible to separate æsthetics, as he understood it,
from ethics and religion. In the beautiful discourse on
Beauty, which forms one of the chapters of his first
"Ennead," it is mainly with spiritual beauty that he is
concerned. But he insists that it *is* beauty, beauty of
the same quality as that of the physical world, which
inheres in goodness, "nor may those tell of the splendour of Virtue who have never known the face of
Justice and of Wisdom beautiful beyond the beauty of
Evening and of Dawn." It is a beauty, he further
states, — though here he seems to be passing out of the
purely æsthetic sphere, — that arouses emotions of
love. "This is the spirit that Beauty must ever induce,
wonderment and a delicious trouble, longing and love,
and a trembling that is also delight. For the unseen all
this may be felt as for the seen, and this souls feel for it,
every soul in some degree, but those the more deeply
who are the more truly apt to this higher love — just
as all take delight in the beauty of the body, but all
are not strung as sharply, and those only that feel the
keener wound are known as Lovers." Goodness and
Truth were on the same plane for Plotinus as Beauty.
It may even be said that Beauty was the most funda-

study, *L'Esthétique de Plotin* (1913), by Cochez, of Louvain, who regards Plotinus as the climax of the objective æsthetics of antiquity and
the beginning of the road to modern subjective æsthetics.

mental of all, to be identified ultimately as the Absolute, as Reality itself. So it was natural that in the sphere of morals he should speak indifferently either of "extirpating evil and implanting goodness" or of "introducing order and beauty to replace goodness" — in either case "we talk of real things." "Virtue is a natural concordance among the phenomena of the soul, vice a discord." But Plotinus definitely rejects the notion that beauty is only symmetry, and so he avoids the narrow conception of some more modern æsthetic moralists, notably Hutcheson. How, then, he asks, could the sun be beautiful, or gold, or light, or night, or the stars? "Beauty is something more than symmetry, and symmetry owes its beauty to a remoter principle" — its affinity, in the opinion of Plotinus, with the "Ideal Form," immediately recognised and confirmed by the soul.

It may seem to some that Plotinus reduces to absurdity the conception of morality as æsthetics, and it may well be that the Greeks of the great period were wiser when they left the nature of morals less explicit. Yet Plotinus had in him the root of the matter. He had risen to the conception that the moral life of the soul is a dance; "Consider the performers in a choral dance: they sing together, though each one has his own particular part, and sometimes one voice is heard while the others are silent; and each brings to the chorus something of his own; it is not enough that all lift their voices together; each must sing, choicely, his own part

in the music set for him. So it is with the Soul."[1] The
Hellenic extension of the æsthetic emotion, as Benn
pointed out, involved no weakening of the moral fibre.
That is so, we see, and even emphatically so, when it
becomes definitely explicit as in Plotinus, and revolu-
tionarily hostile to all those ideals of the moral life
which most people have been accustomed to consider
modern.

As usually among the Greeks, it is only implicitly,
also, that we detect this attitude among the Romans,
the pupils of the Greeks. For the most part, the
Romans, whose impulses of art were very limited,
whose practical mind craved precision and definition,
proved rebellious to the idea that living is an art; yet it
may well be that they still retained that idea at the
core of their morality. It is interesting to note that St.
Augustine, who stood on the threshold between the
old Roman and new Christian worlds was able to
write: "The art of living well and rightly is the definition that the ancients give of 'virtue.'" For the
Latins believed that *ars* was derived from the Greek
word for virtue, ἀρετή.[2] Yet there really remained
a difference between the Greek and the Roman views
of morals. The Greek view, it is universally admitted,
was æsthetic, in the most definite sense; the Roman
was not, and when Cicero wishes to translate a Greek
reference to a "beautiful" action it becomes an

[1] *Ennead*, bk. III, chap. VI. I have mostly followed the translation of
Stephen McKenna.
[2] St. Augustine, *De Civitate Dei*, bk. IV, chap. XXI.

ised and even ritualistic, but the motive forces of living lay in life itself and had all the binding sanction of instincts; the penalty of every failure in living, it was felt, would be swiftly and automatically experienced. To apply reason here was to introduce a powerful solvent into morals. Objectively it made morality clearer but subjectively it destroyed the existing motives for morality; it deprived man, to use the fashionable phraseology of the present day, of a vital illusion.

Thus we have morality in the fundamental sense, the actual practices of the main army of the population, while in front a variegated procession of prancing philosophers gaily flaunt their moral theories before the world. Kant, whose personal moral problems were concerned with eating sweetmeats,[1] and other philosophers of varyingly inferior calibre, were regarded as the lawgivers of morality, though they carried little enough weight with the world at large.

---

[1] Kant was habitually cold and calm. But he was very fond of dried fruits and used to have them specially imported for him by his friend Motherby. "At one time he was eagerly expecting a vessel with French fruits which he had ordered, and he had already invited some friends to a dinner at which they were to be served. The vessel was, however, delayed a number of days by a storm. When it arrived, Kant was informed that the provisions had become short on account of the delay, and that the crew had eaten his fruit. Kant was so angry that he declared they ought rather to have starved than to have touched it. Surprised at this irritation, Motherby said, 'Professor, you cannot be in earnest.' Kant answered, 'I am really in earnest,' and went away. Afterwards he was sorry." (Quoted by Stuckenberg, *The Life of Kant*, p. 138.) But still it was quite in accordance with Kantian morality that the sailors should have starved.

Thus it comes about that abstract moral speculations, culminating in rigid maxims, are necessarily sterile and vain. They move in the sphere of reason, and that is the sphere of comprehension, but not of vital action. In this way there arises a moral dualism in civilised man. Objectively he has become like the gods and able to distinguish the ends of life; he has eaten of the fruit of the tree and has knowledge of good and evil. Subjectively he is still not far removed from the savage, oftenest stirred to action by a confused web of emotional motives, among which the interwoven strands of civilised reason are as likely to produce discord or paralysis as to furnish efficient guides, a state of mind first, and perhaps best, set forth in its extreme form by Shakespeare in Hamlet. On the one hand he cannot return to the primitive state in which all the motives for living flowed harmoniously in the same channel; he cannot divest himself of his illuminating reason; he cannot recede from his hardly acquired personal individuality. On the other hand he can never expect, he can never even reasonably hope, that reason will ever hold in leash the emotions. It is clear that along neither path separately can the civilised man pursue his way in harmonious balance with himself. We begin to realise that what we need is not a code of beautifully cut-and-dried maxims — whether emanating from sacred mountains or from philosophers' studies — but a happy combination of two different ways of living. We need, that is, a traditional and instinctive way of living, based on real motor instincts, which will blend with reason and the manifold needs of personality, instead of being destroyed by their solvent actions, as rigid rules inevitably are. Our only valid rule is a creative impulse that is one with the illuminative power of intelligence.

IV

At the beginning of the eighteenth century, the seed-time of our modern ideas, as it has so often seemed to be, the English people, having in art at length brought their language to a fine degree of clarity and precision, and having just passed through a highly stimulating period of dominant Puritanism in life, became much interested in philosophy, psychology, and ethics. Their interest was, indeed, often superficial and amateurish, though they were soon to produce some of the most notable figures in the whole history of thought. The third Earl of Shaftesbury, one of the earliest of the group, himself illustrated this unsystematic method of thinking. He was an amateur, an aristocratic amateur, careless of consistency, and not by any means concerned to erect a philosophic system. Not that he was a worse thinker on that account. The world's greatest thinkers have often been amateurs; for high thinking is the outcome of fine and independent living, and for that a professorial chair offers no special opportunities. Shaftesbury was, moreover, a man of fragile physical constitution, as

Kant was; but, unlike Kant, he was not a childish hypochondriac in seclusion, but a man in the world, heroically seeking to live a complete and harmonious life. By temperament he was a Stoic, and he wrote a characteristic book of "Exercises," as he proposed to call what his modern editor calls the "Philosophical Regimen," in which he consciously seeks to discipline himself in fine thinking and right living, plainly acknowledging that he is the disciple of Epictetus and Marcus Aurelius. But Shaftesbury was also a man of genius, and as such it was his good fortune to throw afresh into the stream of thought a fruitful conception, in part absorbed, indeed, from Greece, and long implicit in men's minds, but never before made clearly recognisable as a moral theory and an ethical temper, susceptible of being labelled by the philosophic historian, as it since has been under the name, passable no doubt as any other, of "Æsthetic Intuitionism."

Greek morality, it has been well said, is not a conflict of light and darkness, of good and evil, the clear choice between the broad road that leads to destruction and the narrow path of salvation: it is "an artistic balance of light and shade." Gizycki, remarking that Shaftesbury has more affinity to the Greeks than perhaps any other modern moralist, says that "the key lay not only in his head, but in his heart, for like can only be recognised by like." [1] We have to remember at the same time that Shaftesbury was really something of a

[1] Georg von Gizycki, *Die Ethik David Hume's*, p. II.

classical scholar, even from childhood. Born in 1671, the grandson of the foremost English statesman of his time, the first Earl, Anthony Cooper, he had the advantage of the wise oversight of his grandfather, who placed with him as a companion in childhood a lady who knew both Greek and Latin so well that she could converse fluently in both languages. So it was that by the age of eleven he was familiar with the two classic tongues and literatures. That doubtless was also a key to his intimate feeling for the classic spirit, though it would not have sufficed without a native affinity. He became the pupil of Locke, and at fifteen he went to Italy, to spend a considerable time there. He knew France also, and the French tongue, so well that he was often taken for a native. He lived for some time in Holland, and there formed a friendship with Bayle, which began before the latter was aware of his friend's rank and lasted till Bayle's death. In Holland he may have been slightly influenced by Grotius.[1] Shaftesbury was not of robust constitution; he suffered from asthma, and his health was further affected by his zeal in public affairs as well as his enthusiasm in study, for his morality was not that of a recluse, but of a man who played an active part in life, not only in social benevolence, like his descendant the enlightened philanthropic Earl of the nineteenth century, but in the establishment of civil freedom and toleration. Locke wrote of his pupil (who was not, however, in agreement with his

[1] F. C. Sharp, *Mind* (1912), p. 388.

tutor's philosophic standpoint,[1] though he always treated him with consideration) that "the sword was too sharp for the scabbard."

"He seems," wrote of Shaftesbury his unfriendly contemporary Mandeville, "to require and expect goodness in his species as we do a sweet taste in grapes and China oranges, of which, if any of them are sour, we boldly pronounce that they are not come to that perfection their nature is capable of." In a certain sense this was correct. Shaftesbury, it has been said, was the father of that new ethics which recognises that Nature is not a mere impulse of self-preservation, as Hobbes thought, but also a racial impulse, having regard to others; there are social inclinations in the individual, he realised, that go beyond individual ends. (Referring to the famous dictum of Hobbes, *Homo homini lupus*, he observes: "To say in disparagement of Man 'that he is to Man a wolf' appears somewhat absurd when one considers that wolves are to wolves very kind and loving creatures.") Therewith "goodness" was seen, virtually for the first time in the modern period, to be as "natural" as the sweetness of ripe fruit.

There was another reason, a fundamental physiological and psychological reason, why "goodness" of actions and the "sweetness" of fruits are equally

---

[1] Shaftesbury held that Locke swept away too much and failed to allow for inborn instincts (or "senses," as he sometimes called them) developing naturally. We now see that he was right.

natural, a reason that would, no doubt, have been found strange both by Mandeville and Shaftesbury. Morality, Shaftesbury describes as "the taste of beauty and the relish of what is decent," and the "sense of beauty" is ultimately the same as the "moral sense." "My first endeavour," wrote Shaftesbury, "must be to distinguish the true taste of fruits, refine my palate, and establish a just relish in the kind." He thought, evidently, that he was merely using a metaphor. But he was speaking essentially in the direct, straightforward way of natural and primitive Man. At the foundation, "sweetness" and "goodness" are the same thing. That can still be detected in the very structure of language, not only of primitive languages, but those of the most civilised peoples. That morality is, in the strict sense, a matter of taste, of æsthetics, of what the Greeks called αἴσθησις, is conclusively shown by the fact that in the most widely separated tongues — possibly wherever the matter has been carefully investigated — moral goodness is, at the outset, expressed in terms of *taste*. What is *good* is what is *sweet*, and sometimes, also, *salt*.[1] Primitive peoples have highly developed the sensory side of their mental life, and their vocabularies bear witness to the intimate connection of sensations of taste and touch with emotional tone. There is, indeed, no occasion to

[1] There is no need to refer to the value of salt, and therefore the appreciation of the flavour of salt, to primitive people. Still to-day, in Spain, *sal* (salt) is popularly used for a more or less intellectual and moral quality which is highly admired.

go beyond our own European traditions to see that the
expression of moral qualities is based on fundamental
sensory qualities of taste. In Latin *suavis* is *sweet*, but
even in Latin it became a moral quality, and its
English derivatives have been entirely deflected from
physical to moral qualities, while *bitter* is at once a
physical quality and a poignantly moral quality. In
Sanskrit and Persian and Arabic *salt* is not only a
physical taste but the name for lustre and grace and
beauty.[1] It seems well in passing to point out that the
deeper we penetrate the more fundamentally we find
the æsthetic conception of morals grounded in Nature.
But not every one cares to penetrate any deeper and
there is no need to insist.

Shaftesbury held that human actions should have
a beauty of symmetry and proportion and harmony,
which appeal to us, not because they accord with any
rule or maxim (although they may conceivably be
susceptible of measurement), but because they satisfy
our instinctive feelings, evoking an approval which is
strictly an æsthetic judgment of moral action. This
instinctive judgment was not, as Shaftesbury understood it, a guide to action. He held, rightly enough,
that the impulse to action is fundamental and primary,
that fine action is the outcome of finely tempered
natures. It is a feeling for the just time and measure of

[1] Dr. C. S. Myers has touched on this point in *Reports of the Cam-
bridge Anthropological Expedition to Torres Straits*, vol. II, part II, chap.
IV; also "The Taste-Names of Primitive Peoples," *British Journal of
Psychology*, June, 1904.

human passion, and maxims are useless to him whose nature is ill-balanced. "Virtue is no other than the love of order and beauty in society." Æsthetic appreciation of the act, and even an ecstatic pleasure in it, are part of our æsthetic delight in Nature generally, which includes Man. Nature, it is clear, plays a large part in this conception of the moral life. To lack balance on any plane of moral conduct is to be unnatural; "Nature is not mocked," said Shaftesbury. She is a miracle, for miracles are not things that are performed, but things that are perceived, and to fail here is to fail in perception of the divinity of Nature, to do violence to her, and to court moral destruction. A return to Nature is not a return to ignorance or savagery, but to the first instinctive feeling for the beauty of well-proportioned affections. "The most natural beauty in the world is honesty and moral truth," he asserts, and he recurs again and again to "the beauty of honesty." "*Dulce et decorum est* was his sole reason," he says of the classical pagan, adding: "And this is still a good reason." In learning how to act, he thought, we are "learning to become artists." It seems natural to him to refer to the magistrate as an artist; "the magistrate, if he be an artist," he incidentally says. We must not make morality depend on authority. The true artist, in any art, will never act below his character. "Let who will make it for you as you fancy," the artist declares; "I know it to be wrong. Whatever I have made hitherto has been true work.

And neither for your sake or anybody's else shall I put my hand to any other." "This is virtue!" exclaims Shaftesbury. "This disposition transferred to the whole of life perfects a character. For there is a workmanship and a truth in actions."

Shaftesbury, it may be repeated, was an amateur, not only in philosophy, but even in the arts. He regarded literature as one of the schoolmasters for fine living, yet he has not been generally regarded as a fine artist in writing, though, directly or indirectly, he helped to inspire not only Pope, but Thomson and Cowper and Wordsworth. He was inevitably interested in painting, but his tastes were merely those of the ordinary connoisseur of his time. This gives a certain superficiality to his general æsthetic vision, though it was far from true, as the theologians supposed, that he was lacking in seriousness. His chief immediate followers, like Hutcheson, came out of Calvinistic Puritanism. He was himself an austere Stoic who adapted himself to the tone of the well-bred world he lived in. But if an amateur, he was an amateur of genius. He threw a vast and fruitful conception — caught from the "Poetics" of Aristotle, "the Great Master of Arts," and developed with fine insight — into our modern world. Most of the great European thinkers of the eighteenth and early nineteenth centuries were in some measure inspired, influenced, or anticipated by Shaftesbury. Even Kant, though he was unsympathetic and niggardly of appreciation, helped to develop the conception Shaftesbury first formulated. To-day we see it on every hand. It is slowly and subtly moulding the whole of our modern morality.

"The greatest Greek of modern times" — so he appears to those who study his work to-day. It is through Shaftesbury, and Shaftesbury alone that Greek morals, in their finest essence, have been a vivifying influence in our modern world. Georg von Gizycki, who has perhaps most clearly apprehended Shaftesbury's place in morals, indicates that place with precision and justice when he states that "he furnished the *elements* of a moral philosophy which fits into the frame of a truly scientific conception of the world." [1] That was a service to the modern world so great and so daring that it could scarcely meet with approval from his fellow countrymen. The more keenly philosophical Scotch, indeed, recognised him, first of all Hume, and he was accepted and embodied as a kind of founder by the so-called Scottish School, though so toned down and adulterated and adapted to popular tastes and needs, that in the end he was thereby discredited. But the English never even adulterated him; they clung to the antiquated and eschatological Paley, bringing forth edition after edition of his works whereon to discipline their youthful minds. That led naturally on to the English Utilitarians in morality, who would dis-

[1] Dr. Georg von Gizycki, *Die Philosophie Shaftesbury's* (1876); and the same author's *Die Ethik David Hume's* (1878).

dain to look at anything that could be called Greek.
Sir Leslie Stephen, who was the vigorous and capable
interpreter to the general public of Utilitarianism,
could see nothing good whatever in Shaftesbury; he
viewed him with contemptuous pity and could only
murmur: "Poor Shaftesbury!"

Meanwhile Shaftesbury's fame had from the first
been pursuing a very different course in France and
Germany, for it is the people outside a man's own
country who anticipate the verdict of posterity. Leibnitz, whose vast genius was on some sides akin (Shaftesbury has, indeed, been termed "the Leibnitz of morals"), admired the English thinker, and the universal
Voltaire recognised him. Montesquieu placed him on
a four-square summit with Plato and Montaigne and
Malebranche. The enthusiastic Diderot, seeing in
Shaftesbury the exponent of the naturalistic ethics of
his own temperament, translated a large part of his
chief book in 1745. Herder, who inspired so many of
the chief thinkers of the nineteenth century and even of
to-day, was himself largely inspired by Shaftesbury,
whom he once called "the virtuoso of humanity,"
regarding his writings as, even in form, well-nigh
worthy of Greek antiquity, and long proposed to make
a comparative study of the ethical conceptions of
Spinoza, Leibnitz, and Shaftesbury, but unfortunately
never carried out that happy idea. Rousseau, not only
by contact of ideas, but the spontaneous effort of his
own nature towards autonomous harmony, was in

touch with Shaftesbury, and so helped to bring his ideals into the general stream of modern life. Shaftesbury, directly or indirectly, inspired the early influential French Socialists and Communists. On the other hand he has equally inspired the moralists of individualism. Even the Spanish-American Rodó, one of the most delicately aristocratic of modern moralists in recent time, puts forth conceptions, which, consciously or unconsciously, are precisely those of Shaftesbury. Rodó believes that all moral evil is a dissonance in the æsthetic of conduct and that the moral task in character is that of the sculptor in marble: "Virtue is a kind of art, a divine art." Even Croce, who began by making a deep division between art and life, holds that there can be no great critic of art who is not also a great critic of life, for æsthetic criticism is really itself a criticism of life, and his whole philosophy may be regarded as representing a stage of transition between the old traditional view of the world and that conception towards which in the modern world our gaze is turned.[1]

As Shaftesbury had stated the matter, however, it was left on the whole vague and large. He made no very clear distinction between the creative artistic impulse in life and critical æsthetic appreciation. In the sphere of morals we must often be content to wait

[1] It should be added that Croce is himself moving in this direction, and in, for instance, *Il Carattere di Totalità della Espressione Artistica* (1917), he recognises the universality of art.

until our activity is completed to appreciate its beauty
or its ugliness.[1] On the background of general æsthetic
judgment we have to concentrate on the forces of
creative artistic activity, whose work it is painfully to
mould the clay of moral action, and forge its iron, long
before the æsthetic criterion can be applied to the final
product. The artist's work in life is full of struggle and
toil; it is only the spectator of morals who can assume
the calm æsthetic attitude. Shaftesbury, indeed, evidently recognised this, but it was not enough to say, as
he said, that we may prepare ourselves for moral
action by study in literature. One may be willing
to regard living as an art, and yet be of opinion
that it is as unsatisfactory to learn the art of living
in literature as to learn, let us say, the art of music in
architecture.

Yet we must not allow these considerations to lead
us away from the great fact that Shaftesbury clearly
realised — what modern psychology emphasises —
that desires can only be countered by desires, that
reason cannot affect appetite. "That which is of
original and pure nature," he declared, "nothing
besides contrary habit and custom (a second nature) is
able to displace. There is no speculative opinion,
persuasion, or belief, which is capable immediately or
directly to exclude or destroy it." Where he went

[1] Stanley Hall remarks in criticising Kant's moral æsthetics: "The
beauty of virtue is only seen in contemplating it and the act of doing
it has no beauty to the doer at the moment." (G. Stanley Hall, "Why
Kant is Passing," *American Journal of Psychology*, July, 1912.)

beyond some modern psychologists is in his Hellenic perception that in this sphere of instinct we are amid the play of art to which æsthetic criteria alone can be applied.

It was necessary to concentrate and apply these large general ideas. To some extent this was done by Shaftesbury's immediate successors and followers, such as Hutcheson and Arbuckle, who taught that man is, ethically, an artist whose work is his own life. They concentrated attention on the really creative aspects of the artist in life, æsthetic appreciation of the finished product being regarded as secondary. For all art is, primarily, not a contemplation, but a doing, a creative action, and morality is so preëminently.

Shaftesbury, with his followers Arbuckle and Hutcheson, may be regarded as the founders of æsthetics; it was Hutcheson, though he happened to be the least genuinely æsthetic in temperament of the three, who wrote the first modern treatise on æsthetics. Together, also, they may be said to have been the revivalists of Hellenism, that is to say, of the Hellenic spirit, or rather of the classic spirit, for it often came through Roman channels. Shaftesbury was, as Eucken has well said, the Greek spirit among English thinkers. He represented an inevitable reaction against Puritanism, a reaction which is still going on — indeed, here and there only just beginning. As Puritanism had achieved so notable a victory in England, it was natural that in England the first great champion of

Hellenism should appear. It is to Oliver Cromwell and Praise-God Barebones that we owe Shaftesbury.

After Shaftesbury it is Arbuckle who first deserves attention, though he wrote so little that he never attained the prominence he deserved.[1] He was a Dublin physician of Scottish ancestry, the friend of Swift, by whom he was highly esteemed, and he was a cripple from boyhood. He was a man of genuine artistic temperament, though the art he was attracted to was not, as with Shaftesbury, the sculptor's or the painter's, but the poet's. It was not so much intuition on which he insisted, but imagination as formative of a character; moral approval seemed to him thoroughly æsthetic, part of an imaginative act which framed the ideal of a beautiful personality, externalising itself in action. When Robert Bridges, the poet of our own time, suggests (in his "Necessity of Poetry") that "morals is that part of Poetry which deals with conduct," he is speaking in the spirit of Arbuckle. An earlier and greater poet was still nearer to Arbuckle. "A man to be greatly good," said Shelley in his "Defence of Poetry," "must imagine intensely and comprehensively. . . . The great instrument of moral good is the imagination." If, indeed, with Adam Smith and Schopenhauer, we choose to base morals on sympathy we really are thereby making the poet's imagination the great moral instrument. Morals was for Arbuckle a disinterested æsthetic harmony, and he had caught much of the genuine Greek spirit.

[1] See article on Arbuckle by W. R. Scott in *Mind*, April, 1899.

Hutcheson was in this respect less successful. Though he had occupied himself with æsthetics he had little true æsthetic feeling; and though he accomplished much for the revival of Greek studies his own sympathies were really with the Roman Stoics, with Cicero, with Marcus Aurelius, and in this way he was led towards Christianity, to which Shaftesbury was really alien. He democratised if not vulgarised, and diluted if not debased, Shaftesbury's loftier conception. In his too widely sympathetic and receptive mind the Shaftesburian ideal was not only Romanised, not only Christianised; it was plunged into a miscellaneously eclectic mass that often became inconsistent and incoherent. In the long run, in spite of his great immediate success, he injured in these ways the cause he advocated. He overemphasised the passively æsthetic side of morals; he dwelt on the term "moral sense," by Shaftesbury only occasionally used, as it had long previously been by Aristotle (and then only in the sense of "natural temper" by analogy with the physical senses), and this term was long a stumbling-block in the eyes of innocent philosophic critics, too easily befooled by words, who failed to see that, as Libby has pointed out, the underlying idea simply is, as held by Shaftesbury, that æsthetic notions of proportion and symmetry depend upon the native structure of the mind and only so constitute a "moral sense." [1] What Hutcheson, as distinct from Shaftes-

[1] See a helpful paper by F. Libby, "Influence of the Idea of Æsthetic

bury, meant by a "moral sense" — really a conative
instinct — is sufficiently indicated by the fact that he
was inclined to consider the conjugal and parental
affections as a "sense" because natural. He desired
to shut out reason, and cognitive elements, and that
again brought him to the conception of morality as
instinctive. Hutcheson's conception of "sense" was
defective as being too liable to be regarded as passive
rather than as conative, though conation was implied.
The fact that the "moral sense" was really instinct,
and had nothing whatever to do with "innate ideas,"
as many have ignorantly supposed, was clearly seen by
Hutcheson's opponents. The chief objection brought
forward by the Reverend John Balguy in 1728, in the
first part of his "Foundation of Moral Goodness,"
was precisely that Hutcheson based morality on instinct and so had allowed "some degree of morality to
animals." [1] It was Hutcheson's fine and impressive
personality, his high character, his eloquence, his
influential position, which enabled him to keep alive
the conception of morals he preached, and even to give
it an effective force, throughout the European world,
it might not otherwise easily have exerted. Philosophy

Proportion on the Ethics of Shaftesbury," *American Journal of Psychology*, May–October, 1901.

[1] We find fallacious criticism of the "moral sense" down to almost
recent times, in, for instance, McDougall's *Social Psychology*, even
though McDougall, by his insistence on the instinctive basis of morality,
was himself. carrying on the tradition of Shaftesbury and Hutcheson.
But McDougall also dragged in "some prescribed code of conduct,"
though he neglected to mention who is to "prescribe" it.

was to Hutcheson the art of living — as it was to the old Greek philosophers — rather than a question of metaphysics, and he was careless of consistency in thinking, an open-minded eclectic who insisted that life itself is the great matter. That, no doubt, was the reason why he had so immense an influence. It was mainly through Hutcheson that the more aristocratic spirit of Shaftesbury was poured into the circulatory channels of the world's life. Hume and Adam Smith and Reid were either the pupils of Hutcheson or directly influenced by him. He was a great personality rather than a great thinker, and it was as such that he exerted so much force in philosophy.[1]

With Schiller, whose attitude was not, however, based directly on Shaftesbury, the æsthetic conception of morals, which in its definitely conscious form had up till then been especially English, may be said to have entered the main stream of culture. Schiller regarded the identity of Duty and Inclination as the ideal goal of human development, and looked on the Genius of Beauty as the chief guide of life. Wilhelm von Humboldt, one of the greatest spirits of that age, was moved by the same ideas, throughout his life, much as in many respects he changed, and even shortly before his death wrote in deprecation of the notion that conformity to duty is the final aim of morality. Goethe, who was the intimate friend of both Schiller and Hum-

[1] See W. R. Scott, *Francis Hutcheson: His Life, Teaching and Position in the History of Philosophy.* (1900.)

boldt, largely shared the same attitude, and through him it has had a subtle and boundless influence. Kant, who, it has been said, mistook Duty for a Prussian drill-sergeant, still ruled the academic moral world. But a new vivifying and moulding force had entered the larger moral world, and to-day we may detect its presence on every side.

V

It has often been brought against the conception of morality as an art that it lacks seriousness. It seems to many people to involve an easy, self-indulgent, dilettante way of looking at life. Certainly it is not the way of the Old Testament. Except in imaginative literature — it was, indeed, an enormous and fateful exception — the Hebrews were no "æsthetic intuitionists." They hated art, for the rest, and in face of the problems of living they were not in the habit of considering the lilies how they grow. It was not the beauty of holiness, but the stern rod of a jealous Jehovah, which they craved for their encouragement along the path of Duty. And it is the Hebrew mode of feeling which has been, more or less violently and imperfectly, grafted into our Christianity.[1]

---

[1] It is noteworthy, however, that the æsthetic view of morals has had advocates, not only among the more latitudinarian Protestants, but in Catholicism. A few years ago the Reverend Dr. Kolbe published a book on *The Art of Life*, designed to show that just as the sculptor works with hammer and chisel to shape a block of marble into a form of beauty, so Man, by the power of grace, the illumination of faith, and the instrument of prayer, works to transform his soul. But this simile of the sculptor, which has appealed so strongly alike to Ch.istian and anti-

It is a complete mistake, however, to suppose that those for whom life is an art have entered on an easy path, with nothing but enjoyment and self-indulgence before them. The reverse is nearer to the truth. It is probably the hedonist who had better choose rules if he only cares to make life pleasant.[1] For the artist life is always a discipline, and no discipline can be without pain. That is so even of dancing, which of all the arts is most associated in the popular mind with pleasure. To learn to dance is the most austere of disciplines, and even for those who have attained to the summit of its art often remains a discipline not to be exercised without heroism. The dancer seems a thing of joy, but we are told that this famous dancer's slippers are filled with blood when the dance is over, and that one falls down pulseless and deathlike on leaving the stage, and the other must spend the day in darkness and silence. "It is no small advantage," said Nietzsche, "to have a hundred Damoclean swords suspended above one's head; that is how one learns to dance, that is how one attains 'freedom of movement.'" [2]

Christian moralists, proceeds, whether or not they knew it, from Plotinus, who, in his famous chapter on Beauty, bids us note the sculptor. "He cuts away here, he smooths there, he makes this line lighter, this other purer, until a living face has grown upon his work. So do you also cut away all that is excessive, straighten all that is crooked, bring light to all that is overcast, make all one glow of beauty, and never cease chiselling your statue until the godlike splendour shines on you from it, and the perfect goodness stands, surely, in the stainless shrine."

[1] "They who pitched the goal of their aspiration so high knew that the paths leading up to it were rough and steep and long," remarks A. W. Benn (*The Greek Philosophers*, 1914, p. 57); "they said 'the beautiful is hard' — hard to judge, hard to win, hard to keep."

[2] *Der Wille zur Macht*, p. 358.

For as pain is entwined in an essential element in
the perfect achievement of that which seems naturally
the most pleasurable of the arts, so it is with the whole
art of living, of which dancing is the supreme symbol.
There is no separating Pain and Pleasure without making the first meaningless for all vital ends and the
second turn to ashes. To exalt pleasure is to exalt
pain; and we cannot understand the meaning of pain
unless we understand the place of pleasure in the art of
life. In England, James Hinton sought to make that
clear, equally against those who failed to see that pain
is as necessary morally as it undoubtedly is biologically,
and against those who would puritanically refuse to
accept the morality of pleasure.[1] It is no doubt important to resist pain, but it is also important that it
should be there to resist. Even when we look at the
matter no longer subjectively but objectively, we
must accept pain in any sound æsthetic or metaphysical picture of the world.[2]

We must not be surprised, therefore, that this way
of looking at life as an art has spontaneously com-

[1] Mrs. Havelock Ellis, *James Hinton*, 1918.
[2] This has been well seen by Jules de Gaultier: "The joys and the
sorrows which fill life are, the one and the other," he says (*La Dépen-
dance de la Morale et l'Indépendance des Mœurs*, p. 340), "elements of
spectacular interest, and without the mixture of both that interest would
be abolished. To make of the representative worth of phenomena their
justification in view of a spectacular end alone, avoids the objection by
which the moral thesis is faced, the fact of pain. Pain becomes, on the
contrary, the correlative of pleasure, an indispensable means for its real-
ization. Such a thesis is in agreement with the nature of things, instead
of being wounded by their existence."

mended itself to men of the gravest and deepest character, in all other respects widely unlike. Shaftesbury was temperamentally a Stoic whose fragile constitution involved a perpetual endeavour to mould life to the form of his ideal. And if we go back to Marcus Aurelius we find an austere and heroic man whose whole life, as we trace it in his "Meditations," was a splendid struggle, a man who — even, it seems, unconsciously — had adopted the æsthetic criterion of moral goodness and the artistic conception of moral action. Dancing and wrestling express to his eyes the activity of the man who is striving to live, and the goodness of moral actions instinctively appears to him as the beauty of natural objects; it is to Marcus Aurelius that we owe that immortal utterance of æsthetic intuitionism: "As though the emerald should say: 'Whatever happens I must be emerald.'" There could be no man more unlike the Roman Emperor, or in any more remote field of action, than the French saint and philanthropist Vincent de Paul. At once a genuine Christian mystic and a very wise and marvellously effective man of action, Vincent de Paul adopts precisely the same simile of the moral attitude that had long before been put forth by Plotinus and in the next century was again to be taken up by Shaftesbury: "My daughters," he wrote to the Sisters of Charity, "we are each like a block of stone which is to be transferred into a statue. What must the sculptor do to carry out his design? First of all he must take the hammer and chip off all that he does not need. For this purpose he strikes the stone so violently that if you were watching him you would say he intended to break it to pieces. Then, when he has got rid of the rougher parts, he takes a smaller hammer, and afterwards a chisel, to begin the face with all the features. When that has taken form, he uses other and finer tools to bring it to that perfection he has intended for his statue." If we desire to find a spiritual artist as unlike as possible to Vincent de Paul we may take Nietzsche. Alien as any man could ever be to a cheap or superficial vision of the moral life, and far too intellectually keen to confuse moral problems with purely æsthetic problems, Nietzsche, when faced by the problem of living, sets himself — almost as instinctively as Marcus Aurelius or Vincent de Paul — at the standpoint of art. "Alles Leben ist Streit um Geschmack und Schmecken." It is a crucial passage in "Zarathustra": "All life is a dispute about taste and tasting! Taste: that is weight and at the same time scales and weigher; and woe to all living things that would live without dispute about weight and scales and weigher!" For this gospel of taste is no easy gospel. A man must make himself a work of art, Nietzsche again and again declares, moulded into beauty by suffering, for such art is the highest morality, the morality of the Creator.

There is a certain indefiniteness about the conception of morality as an artistic impulse, to be judged by ness of the criterion of moral action, falsely supposed to be a disadvantage, is really the prime condition for effective moral action. The academic philosophers of ethics, had they possessed virility enough to enter the field of real life, would have realised — as we cannot expect the moral reformers blinded by the smoke of their own fanaticism to realise — that the slavery to rigid formulas which they preached was the death of all high moral responsibility. Life must always be a great adventure, with risks on every hand; a clear-sighted eye, a many-sided sympathy, a fine daring, an endless patience, are for ever necessary to all good living. With such qualities alone may the artist in life reach success; without them even the most devoted slave to formulas can only meet disaster. No reasonable moral being may draw breath in the world without an open-eyed freedom of choice, and if the moral world is to be governed by laws, better to people it with automatic machines than with living men and women.

In our human world the precision of mechanism is for ever impossible. The indefiniteness of morality is a part of its necessary imperfection. There is not only room in morality for the high aspiration, the courageous decision, the tonic thrill of the muscles of the soul, but we have to admit also sacrifice and pain. The lesser good, our own or that of others, is merged in a larger good, and that cannot be without some rending of the heart. So all moral action, however in the end it may be justified by its harmony and balance, is in the making cruel and in a sense even immoral. Therein lies the final justification of the æsthetic conception of morality. It opens a wider perspective and reveals loftier standpoints; it shows how the seeming loss is part of an ultimate gain, so restoring that harmony and beauty which the unintelligent partisans of a hard and barren duty so often destroy for ever. "Art," as Paulhan declares, "is often more moral than morality itself." Or, as Jules de Gaultier holds, "Art is in a certain sense the only morality which life admits." In so far as we can infuse it with the spirit and method of art, we have transformed morality into something beyond morality; it has become the complete embodiment of the Dance of Life.

say, as a result of becoming urban, of living as a citizen in cities. We have to recognise, of course, that the idea of civilisation is relative; that any community and any age has its own civilisation, and its own ideals of civilisation. But, that assumed, we may provisionally assert — and we shall be in general accordance with Niceforo — that, in its most comprehensive sense, the art of civilisation includes the three groups of *material* facts, *intellectual* facts, and *moral* (with *political*) facts, so covering all the essential facts in our life.

Material facts, which we are apt to consider the most easily measurable, include quantity and distribution of population, production of wealth, the consumption of food and luxuries, the standard of life. Intellectual facts include both the diffusion and degree of instruction and creative activity in genius. Moral facts include the prevalence of honesty, justice, pity, and self-sacrifice, the position of women and the care of children. They are the most important of all for the quality of a civilisation. Voltaire pointed out that "pity and justice are the foundations of society," and, long previously, Pericles in Thucydides described the degradation of the Peloponnesians among whom every one thinks only of his own advantage, and every one believes that his own negligence of other things will pass unperceived. Plato in his "Republic" made justice the foundation of harmony in the outer life and the inner life, while in modern times various philosophers, like Shadworth Hodgson, have emphasised that doctrine of Plato's. The whole art of government comes under this head and the whole treatment of human personality.

The comparative prevalence of criminality has long been the test most complacently adopted by those who seek to measure civilisation on its moral and most fundamental aspect. Crime is merely a name for the most obvious, extreme, and directly dangerous forms of what we call immorality — that is to say, departure from the norm in manners and customs. Therefore the highest civilisation is that with the least crime. But is it so? The more carefully we look into the matter, the more difficult it becomes to apply this test. We find that even at the outset. Every civilised community has its own way of dealing with criminal statistics and the discrepancies thus introduced are so great that this fact alone makes comparisons almost impossible. It is scarcely necessary to point out that varying skill and thoroughness in the detection of crime, and varying severity in the attitude towards it, necessarily count for much. Of not less significance is the legislative activity of the community; the greater the number of laws, the greater the number of offences against them. If, for instance, Prohibition is introduced into a country, the amount of delinquency in that country is enormously increased, but it would be rash to assert that the country has thereby been sensibly lowered in the scale of civilisation. To avoid this difficulty, it has been proposed to take into consideration only what are called "natural crimes"; that is, those everywhere regarded as punishable. But, even then, there is a still more disconcerting consideration. For, after all, the criminality of a country is a by-product of its energy in business and in the whole conduct of affairs. It is a poisonous excretion, but excretion is the measure of vital metabolism. There are, moreover, the so-called evolutive social crimes, which spring from motives not lower but higher than those ruling the society in which they arise.[1] Therefore, we cannot be sure that we ought not to regard the most criminal country as that which in some aspects possesses the highest civilisation.

Let us turn to the intellectual aspect of civilisation. Here we have at least two highly important and quite fairly measurable facts to consider: the production of creative genius and the degree and diffusion of general instruction. If we consider the matter abstractly, it is highly probable that we shall declare that no civilisation can be worth while unless it is rich in creative genius and unless the population generally exhibits a sufficiently cultured level of education out of which such genius may arise freely and into which the seeds it produces may fruitfully fall. Yet, what do we find? Alike, whether we go back to the earliest civilisations we have definite information about or turn to the latest stages of civilisation we know to-day, we fail to see any correspondence between these two essential conditions of civilisation. Among peoples in a low state of culture,

[1] See e.g., Maurice Parmelee's *Criminology*, the sanest and most comprehensive manual on the subject we have in English.

292 THE DANCE OF LIFE

among savages generally, such instruction and education as exists really is generally diffused; every member of the community is initiated into the tribal traditions; yet, no observers of such peoples seem to note the emergence of individuals of strikingly productive genius. That, so far as we know, began to appear, and, indeed, in marvellous variety and excellence, in Greece, and the civilisation of Greece (as later the more powerful but coarser civilisation of Rome) was built up on a broad basis of slavery, which nowadays — except, of course, when disguised as industry — we no longer regard as compatible with high civilisation.

Ancient Greece, indeed, may suggest to us to ask whether the genius of a country be not directly opposed to the temper of the population of that country, and its "leaders" really be its outcasts. (Some believe that many, if not all, countries of to-day might serve to suggest the same question.) If we want to imagine the real spirit of Greece, we may have to think of a figure with a touch of Ulysses, indeed, but with more of Thersites.[1] The Greeks who interest us to-day were exceptional people, usually imprisoned, exiled, or slain by the more truly representative Greeks of their time. When Plato and the others set forth so persistently an ideal of wise moderation they were really putting up — and in vain — a supplication for mercy to a people who, as they had good ground for realising, knew noth-

[1] Élie Faure, with his usual incisive insight, has set out the real characters of the "Greek Spirit" ("Reflexions sur le Génie Grec," *Monde Nouveau*, December, 1922).

ing of wisdom, and scoffed at moderation, and were mainly inspired by ferocity and intrigue.

To turn to a more recent example, consider the splendid efflorescence of genius in Russia during the central years of the last century, still a vivifying influence on the literature and music of the world; yet the population of Russia had only just been delivered, nominally at least, from serfdom, and still remained at the intellectual and economic level of serfs. To-day, education has become diffused in the Western world. Yet no one would dream of asserting that genius is more prevalent. Consider the United States, for instance, during the past half-century. It would surely be hard to find any country, except Germany, where education is more highly esteemed or better understood, and where instruction is more widely diffused. Yet, so far as the production of high original genius is concerned, an old Italian city, like Florence, with a few thousand inhabitants, had far more to show than all the United States put together. So that we are at a loss how to apply the intellectual test to the measurement of civilisation. It would almost seem that the two essential elements of this test are mutually incompatible.

Let us fall back on the simple solid fundamental test furnished by the material aspect of civilisation. Here we are among elementary facts and the first that began to be measured. Yet our difficulties, instead of diminishing, rather increase. It is here, too, that we chiefly meet with what Niceforo has called "the paradoxical symptoms of superiority in progress," though I should prefer to call them ambivalent; that is to say, that, while from one point of view they indicate superiority, from another, even though some may call it a lower point of view, they appear to indicate inferiority. This is well illustrated by the test of growth of population, or the height of the birth-rate, better by the birth-rate considered in relation to the death-rate, for they cannot be intelligibly considered apart. The law of Nature is reproduction, and if an intellectual rabbit were able to study human civilisation he would undoubtedly regard rapidity of multiplication, in which he has himself attained so high a degree of proficiency, as evidence of progress in civilisation. In fact, as we know, there are even human beings who take the same view, whence we have what has been termed "Rabbitism" in men. Yet, if anything is clear in this obscure field, it is that the whole tendency of evolution is towards a diminishing birth-rate.[1] The most civilised countries everywhere, and the most civilised people in them, are those with the lowest birth-rate. Therefore, we have here to measure the height of civilisation by a test which, if carried to an extreme, would mean the disappearance of civilisation. Another such ambivalent test is the consumption of luxuries of which

[1] This tendency, on which Herbert Spencer long ago insisted, is in its larger aspects quite clear. E. C. Pell (*The Law of Births and Deaths*, 1921) has argued that it holds good of civilised man to-day, and that our decreasing birth-rate with civilisation is quite independent of any effort on Man's part to attain that evolutionary end.

alcohol and tobacco are the types. There is held to be
no surer test of civilisation than the increase per head
of the consumption of alcohol and tobacco. Yet alcohol and tobacco are recognisably poisons, so that their
consumption has only to be carried far enough to destroy civilisation altogether. Again, take the prevalence of suicide. That, without doubt, is a test of height
in civilisation; it means that the population is winding
up its nervous and intellectual system to the utmost
point of tension and that sometimes it snaps. We
should be justified in regarding as very questionable
a high civilisation which failed to show a high sui-
ciderate. Yet suicide is the sign of failure, misery,
and despair. How can we regard the prevalence
of failure, misery, and despair as the mark of high
civilisation?

Thus, whichever of the three groups of facts we attempt to measure, it appears on examination almost
hopelessly complex. We have to try to make our methods correspondingly complex. Niceforo had invoked
co-variation, or simultaneous and sympathetic changes
in various factors of civilisation; he explains the index
number, and he appeals to mathematics for aid out of
the difficulties. He also attempts to combine, with the
help of diagrams, a single picture out of these awkward
and contradictory tests. The example he gives is that
of France during the fifty years preceding the war. It is
an interesting example because there is reason to consider France as, in some respects, the most highly civil-

ised of countries. What are the chief significant measurable marks of this superiority? Niceforo selects about a dozen, and, avoiding the difficult attempt to compare France with other countries, he confines himself to the more easily practicable task of ascertaining whether, or in what respects, the general art of civilisation in France, the movement of the collective life, has been upward or downward. When the different categories are translated, according to recognised methods, into index numbers, taking the original figures from the official "Résumé" of French statistics, it is found that each line of movement follows throughout the same direction, though often in zigzag fashion, and never turns back on itself. In this way it appears that the consumption of coal has been more than doubled, the consumption of luxuries (sugar, coffee, alcohol) nearly doubled, the consumption of food per head (as tested by cheese and potatoes) also increasing. Suicide has increased fifty per cent; wealth has increased slightly and irregularly; the upward movement of population has been extremely slight and partly due to immigration; the death-rate has fallen, though not so much as the birth-rate; the number of persons convicted of offence by the courts has fallen; the proportion of illiterate persons has diminished; divorces have greatly increased, and also the number of syndicalist workers, but these two movements are of comparative recent growth.

This example well shows what it is possible to do by

the most easily available and generally accepted tests by which to measure the progress of a community in the art of civilisation. Every one of the tests applied to France reveals an upward tendency of civilisation, though some of them, such as the fall in the death-rate, are not strongly pronounced and much smaller than may be found in many other countries. Yet, at the same time, while we have to admit that each of these lines of movement indicates an upward tendency of civilisation, it by no means follows that we can view them all with complete satisfaction. It may even be said that some of them have only to be carried further in order to indicate dissolution and decay. The consumption of luxuries, for instance, as already noted, is the consumption of poisons. The increase of wealth means little unless we take into account its distribution. The increase of syndicalism, while it is a sign of increased independence, intelligence, and social aspiration among the workers, is also a sign that the social system is becoming regarded as unsound. So that, while all these tests may be said to indicate a rising civilisation, they yet do not invalidate the wise conclusion of Niceforo that a civilisation is never an exclusive mass of benefits, but a mass of values, positive and negative, and it may even be said that most often the conquest of a benefit in one domain of a civilisation brings into another domain of that civilisation inevitable evils. Long ago, Montesquieu had spoken of the evils of civilisation and left the question of the value of civilisation open, while Rousseau, more passionately, had decided against civilisation.

We see the whole question from another point, yet not incongruously, when we turn to Professor William McDougall's Lowell Lectures, "Is America Safe for Democracy?" since republished under the more general title "National Welfare and National Decay," for the author recognises that the questions he deals with go to the root of all high civilisation. As he truly observes, civilisation grows constantly more complex and also less subject to the automatically balancing influence of national selection, more dependent for its stability on our constantly regulative and foreseeing control. Yet, while the intellectual task placed upon us is ever growing heavier, our brains are not growing correspondingly heavier to bear it. There is, as Remy de Gourmont often pointed out, no good reason to suppose that we are in any way innately superior to our savage ancestors, who had at least as good physical constitutions and at least as large brains. The result is that the small minority among us which alone can attempt to cope with our complexly developing civilisation comes to the top by means of what Arsène Dumont called social capillarity, and McDougall the social ladder. The small upper stratum is of high quality, the large lower stratum of poor quality, and with a tendency to feeble-mindedness. It is to this large lower stratum that, with our democratic tendencies, we assign the political and other guidance of the community, and it is this lower stratum which has the higher birth-rate, since with all high civilisation the normal birth-rate is low.[1] McDougall is not concerned with the precise measurement of civilisation, and may not be familiar with the attempts that have been made in that direction. It is his object to point out the necessity in high civilisation for a deliberate and purposive art of eugenics, if we would prevent the eventual shipwreck of civilisation. But we see how his conclusions emphasise those difficulties in the measurement of civilisation which Niceforo has so clearly set forth.

McDougall is repeating what many, especially among eugenists, have previously said. While not disputing the element of truth in the facts and arguments brought forward from this side, it may be pointed out that they are often overstated. This has been well argued by Carr-Saunders in his valuable and almost monumental work, "The Population Problem," and his opinion is the more worthy of attention as he is himself a worker in the cause of eugenics. He points out that the social ladder is, after all, hard to climb, and that it only removes a few individuals from the lower social stratum, while among those who thus climb, even though they do not sink back, regression to the mean is ever in operation so that they do not greatly enrich in

[1] Professor McDougall refers to the high birth-rate of the lower stratum as more "normal." If that were so, civilisation would certainly be doomed. All high evolution *normally* involves a low birth-rate. Strange how difficult it is even for those most concerned with these questions to see the facts simply and clearly!

the end the class they have climbed up to. Moreover, as Carr-Saunders pertinently asks, are we so sure that the qualities that mark successful climbers — self-assertion, acquisition, emulation — are highly desirable? "It may even be," he adds, "that we might view a diminution in the average strength of some of the qualities which mark the successful at least with equanimity." Taken altogether, it would seem that the differences between social classes may mainly be explained by environmental influences. There is, however, ground to recognise a slight intellectual superiority in the upper social class, apart from environment, and so great is the significance for civilisation of quality that even when the difference seems slight it must not be regarded as negligible.[1]

More than half a century ago, indeed, George Sand pointed out that we must distinguish between the civilisation of *quantity* and the civilisation of *quality*. As the great Morgagni had said much earlier, it is not enough to count, we must evaluate; "observations are not to be numbered, they are to be weighed." It is not the biggest things that are the most civilised things. The largest structures of Hindu or Egyptian art are outweighed by the temples on the Acropolis of Athens, and similarly, as Bryce, who had studied the matter so thoroughly, was wont to insist, it is the smallest democracies which to-day stand highest in the scale. We have

[1] A. M. Carr-Saunders, *The Population Problem: A Study in Human Evolution* (1922), pp. 457, 472.

seen that there is much in civilisation which we may profitably measure, yet, when we seek to scale the last heights of civilisation, the ladder of our "metrology" comes to grief. "The methods of the mind are too weak," as Comte said, "and the Universe is too complex." Life, even the life of the civilised community, is an art, and the too much is as fatal as the too little. We may say of civilisation, as Renan said of truth, that it lies in a *nuance*. Gumplowicz believed that civilisation is the beginning of disease; Arsène Dumont thought that it inevitably held within itself a toxic principle, a principle by which it is itself in time poisoned. The more rapidly a civilisation progresses, the sooner it dies for another to arise in its place. That may not seem to every one a cheerful prospect. Yet, if our civilisation has failed to enable us to look further than our own egoistic ends, what has our civilisation been worth?

II

THE attempt to apply measurement to civilisation is, therefore, a failure. That is, indeed, only another way of saying that civilisation, the whole manifold web of life, is an art. We may dissect out a vast number of separate threads and measure them. It is quite worth while to do so. But the results of such anatomical investigation admit of the most diverse interpretation, and, at the best, can furnish no adequate criterion of the worth of a complex living civilisation.

Yet, although there is no precise measurement of the total value of any large form of life, we can still make an estimate of its value. We can approach it, that is to say, as a work of art. We can even reach a certain approximation to agreement in the formation of such estimates.

When Protagoras said that "Man is the measure of all things," he uttered a dictum which has been variously interpreted, but from the standpoint we have now reached, from which Man is seen to be preëminently an artist, it is a monition to us that we cannot to the measurement of life apply our instruments of precision, and cut life down to their graduated marks. They have, indeed, their immensely valuable uses, but it is strictly as instruments and not as ends of living or criteria of the worth of life. It is in the failure to grasp this that the human tragedy has often consisted, and for over two thousand years the dictum of Protagoras has been held up for the pacification of that tragedy, for the most part, in vain. Protagoras was one of those "Sophists" who have been presented to our contempt in absurd traditional shapes ever since Plato caricatured them — though it may well be that some, as, it has been suggested, Gorgias, may have given colour to the caricature — and it is only to-day that it is possible to declare that we must place the names of Protagoras, of Prodicus, of Hippias, even of Gorgias, beside those of Herodotus, Pindar, and Pericles. [1]

[1] Dupréel, *La Légende Socratique* (1922), p. 428. Dupréel considers

CONCLUSION

It is in the sphere of morals that the conflict has often been most poignant. I have already tried to indicate how revolutionary is the change which the thoughts of many have had to undergo. This struggle of a living and flexible and growing morality against a morality that is rigid and inflexible and dead has at some periods of human history been almost dramatically presented. It was so in the seventeenth century around the new moral discoveries of the Jesuits; and the Jesuits were rewarded by becoming almost until to-day a by-word for all that is morally poisonous and crooked and false — for all that is "Jesuitical." There was once a great quarrel between the Jesuits and the Jansenists — a quarrel which is scarcely dead yet, for all Christendom took sides in it — and the Jansenists had the supreme good fortune to entrap on their side a great man of genius whose onslaught on the Jesuits, "Les Provinciales,"

(p. 431) that the Protagorean spirit was marked by the idea of explaining the things of thought, and life in general, by the meeting, opposition, and harmony of individual activities, leading up to the sociological notion of *convention*, and behind it, of relativity. Nietzsche was a pioneer in restoring the Sophists to their rightful place in Greek thought. The Greek culture of the Sophists grew out of all the Greek instincts, he says (*The Will to Power*, section 428): "And it has ultimately shown itself to be right. Our modern attitude of mind is, to a great extent, Heraclitean, Democritean, and Protagorean. To say that it is Protagorean is even sufficient, because Protagoras was himself a synthesis of Heraclitus and Democritus." The Sophists, by realizing that many supposed objective ideas were really subjective, have often been viewed with suspicion as content with a mere egotistically individualistic conception of life. The same has happened to Nietzsche. It was probably an error as regards the greatest Sophists, and is certainly an error, though even still commonly committed, as regards Nietzsche; see the convincing discussion of Nietzsche's moral aim in Salter, *Nietzsche the Thinker*, chap. XXIV.

is even still supposed by many people to have settled the question. They are allowed so to suppose because no one now reads "Les Provinciales." But Remy de Gourmont, who was not only a student of unread books but a powerfully live thinker, read "Les Provinciales," and found, as he set forth in "Le Chemin de Velours," that it was the Jesuits who were more nearly in the right, more truly on the road of advance, than Pascal. As Gourmont showed by citation, there were Jesuit doctrines put forth by Pascal with rhetorical irony as though the mere statement sufficed to condemn them, which need only to be liberated from their irony, and we might nowadays add to them. Thus spake Zarathustra. Pascal was a geometrician who (though he, indeed, once wrote in his "Pensées": "There is no general rule") desired to deal with the variable, obscure, and unstable complexities of human action as though they were problems in mathematics. But the Jesuits, while it is true that they still accepted the existence of absolute rules, realised that rules must be made adjustable to the varying needs of life. They thus became the pioneers of many conceptions which are accepted in modern practice.[1] Their doctrine of invincible ignorance was a discovery of that kind, forecasting some of the opinions now held regarding responsibility. But in that age, as Gourmont

[1] I may here, perhaps, remark that in the General Preface to my *Studies in the Psychology of Sex* I suggested that we now have to lay the foundation of a new casuistry, no longer theological and Christian, but naturalistic and scientific.

pointed out, "to proclaim that there might be a sin or an offence without guilty parties was an act of intellectual audacity, as well as scientific probity." Nowadays the Jesuits (together, it is interesting to note, with their baroque architecture) are coming into credit, and casuistry again seems reputable. To establish that there can be no single inflexible moral code for all individuals has been, and indeed remains, a difficult and delicate task, yet the more profoundly one considers it, the more clearly it becomes visible that what once seemed a dead and rigid code of morality must more and more become a living act of casuistry. The Jesuits, because they had a glimmer of this truth, represented, as Gourmont concluded, the honest and most acceptable part of Christianity, responding to the necessities of life, and were rendering a service to civilisation which we should never forget.

There are some who may not very cordially go to the Jesuits as an example of the effort to liberate men from the burden of a subservience to rigid little rules, towards the unification of life as an active process, however influential they may be admitted to be among the pioneers of that movement. Yet we may turn in what direction we will, we shall perpetually find the same movement under other disguises. There is, for instance, Mr. Bertrand Russell, who is, for many, the most interesting and stimulating thinker to be found in England to-day. He might scarcely desire to be associated with the Jesuits. Yet he also seeks to unify life and even in an essentially religious spirit. His way of putting this, in his "Principles of Social Reconstruction," is to state that man's impulses may be divided into those that are creative and those that are possessive, that is to say, concerned with acquisition. The impulses of the second class are a source of inner and outer disharmony and they involve conflict; "it is preoccupation with possessions more than anything else that prevents men from living freely and nobly"; it is the creative impulse in which real life consists, and "the typical creative impulse is that of the artist." Now this conception (which was that Plato assigned to the "guardians" in his communistic State) may be a little too narrowly religious for those whose position in life renders a certain "preoccupation with possessions" inevitable; it is useless to expect us all to become, at present, fakirs and Franciscans, "counting nothing one's own, save only one's harp." But in regarding the creative impulses as the essential part of life, and as typically manifested in the form of art, Bertrand Russell is clearly in the great line of movement with which we have been throughout concerned. We must only at the same time — as we shall see later — remember that the distinction between the "creative" and the "possessive" impulses, although convenient, is superficial. In creation we have not really put aside the possessive instinct, we may even have intensified it. For it has been reasonably argued that it is precisely the deep urgency of the impulse to possess which stirs the

CONCLUSION

creative artist. He creates because that is the best way, or the only way, of gratifying his passionate desire to possess. Two men desire to possess a woman, and one seizes her, the other writes a "Vita Nuova" about her; they have both gratified the instinct of possession, and the second, it may be, most satisfyingly and most lastingly. So that — apart from the impossibility, and even the undesirability, of dispensing with the possessive instinct — it may be well to recognise that the real question is one of values in possession. We must needs lay up treasure; but the fine artist in living, so far as may be, lays up his treasure in Heaven.

In recent time some alert thinkers have been moved to attempt to measure the art of civilisation by less impossibly exact methods than of old, by the standard of art, and even of fine art. In a remarkable book on "The Revelations of Civilisation" — published about three years before the outbreak of that Great War which some have supposed to date a revolutionary point in civilisation — Dr. W. M. Flinders Petrie, who has expert knowledge of the Egyptian civilisation which was second to none in its importance for mankind, has set forth a statement of the cycles to which all civilisations are subject. Civilisation, he points out, is essentially an intermittent phenomenon. We have to compare the various periods of civilisation and observe what they have in common in order to find the general type. "It should be examined like any other action of Nature; its recurrences should be studied, and all the

principles which underlie its variations should be defined." Sculpture, he believes, may be taken as a criterion, not because it is the most important, but because
it is the most convenient and easily available, test. We
may say with the old Etruscans that every race has its
Great Year — it sprouts, flourishes, decays, and dies.
The simile, Petrie adds, is the more precise because
there are always irregular fluctuations of the seasonal
weather. There have been eight periods of civilisation,
he reckons, in calculable human history. We are now
near the end of the eighth, which reached its climax
about the year 1800; since then there have been merely
archaistic revivals, the value of which may be variously
interpreted. He scarcely thinks we can expect another
period of civilisation to arise for several centuries at
least. The average length of a period of civilisation is
1330 years. Ours Petrie dates from about A.D. 450. It
has always needed a fresh race to produce a new period
of civilisation. In Europe, between A.D. 300 and 600,
some fifteen new races broke in from north and east
for slow mixture. "If," he concluded, "the source of
every civilisation has lain in race mixture, it may be
that eugenics will, in some future civilisation, carefully
segregate fine races, and prohibit continual mixture,
until they have a distinct type, which will start a new
civilisation when transplanted. The future progress of
Man may depend as much on isolation to establish a
type as on fusion of types when established."

At the time when Flinders Petrie was publishing his

suggestive book, Dr. Oswald Spengler, apparently in complete ignorance of it, was engaged in a far more elaborate work, not actually published till after the War, in which an analogous conception of the growth and decay of civilisations was put forward in a more philosophic way, perhaps more debatable on account of the complex detail in which the conception was worked out.[1] Petrie had considered the matter in a summary empiric manner with close reference to the actual forces viewed broadly. Spengler's manner is narrower, more subjective, and more metaphysical. He distinguishes—though he also recognises eight periods—between "culture" and "civilisation." It is the first that is really vital and profitable; a "civilisation" is the decaying later stage of a "culture," its inevitable fate. Herein it reaches its climax. "Civilisations are the most externalised and artistic conditions of which the higher embodiment of Man is capable. They are a spiritual senility, an end which with inner necessity is reached again and again."[2] The transition from "culture" to "civilisation" in ancient times took place, Spengler holds, in the fourth century, and in the modern West in the nineteenth. But, like Petrie, though

[1] Oswald Spengler, *Der Untergang des Abendlandes*, vol. I (1918); vol. II (1922).

[2] In an interesting pamphlet, *Pessimismus?* Spengler has since pointed out that he does not regard his argument as pessimistic. The end of a civilisation is its fulfilment, and there is still much to be achieved (though not, he thinks, along the line of art) before our own civilisation is fulfilled. With Spengler's conception of that fulfilment we may, however, fail to sympathise.

more implicitly, he recognises the prominent place of the art activities in the whole process, and he explicitly emphasises the interesting way in which those activities which are generally regarded as of the nature of art are interwoven with others not so generally regarded.

III

HOWEVER we look at it, we see that Man, whether he works individually or collectively, may conveniently be regarded, in the comprehensive sense, as an artist, a bad artist, maybe, for the most part, but still an artist. His civilisation — if that is the term we choose to apply to the total sum of his group activities — is always an art, or a complex of arts. It is an art that is to be measured, or left immeasurable. That question, we have seen, we may best leave open. Another question that might be put is easy to deal with more summarily: What is Art?

We may deal with it summarily because it is an ultimate question and there can be no final answer to ultimate questions. As soon as we begin to ask such questions, as soon as we begin to look at any phenomenon as an end in itself, we are on the perilous slope of metaphysics, where no agreement can, or should be, possible. The question of measurement was plausible, and needed careful consideration. What is Art? is a question which, if we are wise, we shall deal with as Pilate dealt with that like question: What is Truth?

How futile the question is, we may realise when we

examine the book which Tolstoy in old age wrote to answer it. Here is a man who was himself, in his own field, one of the world's supreme artists. He could not fail to say one or two true things, as when he points out that "all human existence is full of art, from cradle songs and dances to the offices of religion and public ceremonial — it is all equally art. Art, in the large sense, impregnates our whole life." But on the main point all that Tolstoy can do is to bring together a large miscellaneous collection of definitions — without seeing that as individual opinions they all have their rightness — and then to add one of his own, not much worse, nor much better, than any of the others. Thereto he appends some of his own opinions on artists, whence it appears that Hugo, Dickens, George Eliot, Dostoievsky, Maupassant, Millet, Bastien-Lepage, and Jules Breton — and not always they — are the artists whom he considers great; it is not a list to treat with contempt, but he goes on to pour contempt on those who venerate Sophocles and Aristophanes and Dante and Shakespeare and Milton and Michelangelo and Bach and Beethoven and Manet. "My own artistic works," he adds, "I rank among bad art, excepting a few short stories." It seems a reduction of the whole question, What is Art? to absurdity, if one may be permitted to say so at a time when Tolstoy would appear to be the pioneer of some of our most approved modern critics.

Thus we see the reason why all the people who come

forward to define art — each with his own little measuring-rod quite different from everybody else's — inevitably make themselves ridiculous. It is true they are all of them right. That is just why they are ridiculous: each has mistaken the one drop of water he has measured for the whole ocean. Art cannot be defined because it is infinite. It is no accident that poetry, which has so often seemed the typical art, means a *making*. The artist is a maker. Art is merely a name we are pleased to give to what can only be the whole stream of action which — in order to impart to it selection and an unconscious or even conscious aim — is poured through the nervous circuit of a human animal or some other animal having a more or less similar nervous organisation. For a cat is an artist as well as a man, and some would say more than a man, while a bee is not only an obvious artist, but perhaps even the typical natural and unconscious artist. There is no defining art; there is only the attempt to distinguish between good art and bad art.

Thus it is that I find no escape from the Aristotelian position of Shakespeare that

> " Nature is made better by no mean
> But Nature makes that mean . . .
>   This is an art
> Which does mend Nature, change it rather, but
> The art itself is Nature."

And that this conception is Aristotelian, even the essential Greek conception, is no testimony to Shakespeare's scholarship. It is merely the proof that here

we are in the presence of one of these great ultimate
facts of the world which cannot but be sensitively perceived by the finest spirits, however far apart in time
and space. Aristotle, altogether in the same spirit as
Shakespeare, insisted that the works of man's making,
a State, for example, are natural, though Art partly
completes what Nature is herself sometimes unable to
bring to perfection, and even then that man is only
exercising methods which, after all, are those of Nature.
Nature needs Man's art in order to achieve many
natural things, and Man, in fulfilling that need, is
only following the guidance of Nature in seeming to
make things which are all the time growing by themselves.[1] Art is thus scarcely more than the natural
midwife of Nature.

There is, however, one distinguishing mark of Art
which at this stage, as we conclude our survey, must be
clearly indicated. It has been subsumed, as the acute
reader will not have failed to note, throughout. But it
has, for the most part, been deliberately left implicit.
It has constantly been assumed, that is to say, that
Art is the sum of all the active energies of Mankind.
We must in this matter of necessity follow Aristotle,
who in his "Politics" spoke, as a matter of course, of
all those who practice "medicine, gymnastics, and the
arts in general" as "artists." Art is the moulding
force of every culture that Man during his long course

[1] See, for instance, W. L. Newman, *The Politics of Aristotle*, vol. 1, p.
201, and S. H. Butcher, *Aristotle's Theory of Poetry and Fine Art*, p. 119.

has at any time or place produced. It is the reality of what we imperfectly term "morality." It is all human creation.

Yet creation, in the active visible constructive sense, is not the whole of Man. It is not even the whole of what Man has been accustomed to call God. When, by what is now termed a process of Narcissism, Man created God in his own image, as we may instructively observe in the first chapter of the Hebrew Book of Genesis, he assigned to him six parts of active creational work, one part of passive contemplation of that work. That one seventh part — and an immensely important part — has not come under our consideration. In other words, we have been looking at Man the artist, not at Man the æsthetician.

There was more than one reason why these two aspects of human faculty were held clearly apart throughout our discussion. Not only is it even less possible to agree about æsthetics, where the variety of individual judgment is rightly larger, than about art (ancient and familiar is the saying, *De gustibus* —), but to confuse art and æsthetics leads us into lamentable confusion. We may note this in the pioneers of the modern revival of what Sidgwick called "æsthetic Intuitionism" in the eighteenth century, and especially in Hutcheson, though Hutcheson's work is independent of consistency, which he can scarcely even be said to have sought. They never sufficiently emphasised the distinction between art and æsthetics, between, that is

to say, what we may possibly, if we like, call the dynamic and the static aspects of human action. Herein is the whole difference between work, for art is essentially work, and the spectacular contemplation of work, which æsthetics essentially is. The two things are ultimately one, but alike in the special arts and in that art of life commonly spoken of as morals, where we are not usually concerned with ultimates, the two must be clearly held apart. From the point of view of art we are concerned with the internal impulse to guide the activities in the lines of good work. It is only when we look at the work of art from the outside, whether in the more specialised arts or in the art of life, that we are concerned with æsthetic contemplation, that activity of vision which creates beauty, however we may please to define beauty, and even though we see it so widely as to be able to say with Remy de Gourmont: "Wherever life is, there is beauty," [1] provided, one may add, that there is the æsthetic contemplation in which it must be mirrored.

It is in relation with art, not with æsthetics, it may

[1] Beauty is a dangerous conception to deal with, and the remembrance of this great saying may, perhaps, help to save us from the degrading notion that beauty merely inheres in objects, or has anything to do with the prim and smooth conventions which make prettiness. Even in the fine art of painting it is more reasonable to regard prettiness as the negation of beauty. It is possible to find beauty in Degas and Cézanne, but not in Bouguereau or Cabanel. The path of beauty is not soft and smooth, but full of harshness and asperity. It is a rose that grows only on a bush covered with thorns. As of goodness and of truth, men talk too lightly of Beauty. Only to the bravest and skilfullest is it given to break through the briers of her palace and kiss at last her enchanted lips.

be noted in passing, that we are concerned with morals. That was once a question of seemingly such immense import that men were willing to spiritually slay each other over it. But it is not a question at all from the standpoint which has here from the outset been taken. Morals, for us to-day, is a species of which art is the genus. It is an art, and like all arts it necessarily has its own laws. We are concerned with the art of morals: we cannot speak of art *and* morals. To take "art" and "morals" and "religion," and stir them up, however vigorously, into an indigestible plum-pudding, as Ruskin used to do, is no longer possible.[1] This is a question which — like so many other furiously debated questions — only came into existence because the disputants on both sides were ignorant of the matter they were disputing about. It is no longer to be taken seriously, though it has its interest because the dispute has so often recurred, not only in recent days, but equally among the Greeks of Plato's days. The Greeks had a kind of æsthetic morality. It was instinctive with them, and that is why it is so significant for us. But they seldom seem to have succeeded in thinking æsthetic

[1] Ruskin was what Spinoza has been called, a God-intoxicated man; he had a gift of divine rhapsody, which reached at times to inspiration. But it is not enough to be God-intoxicated, for into him whose mind is disorderly and ignorant and ill-disciplined the Gods pour their wine in vain. Spinoza's mind was not of that kind, Ruskin's too often was, so that Ruskin can never be, like Spinoza, a permanent force in the world of thought. His interest is outside that field, mainly perhaps psychological in the precise notation of a particular kind of æsthetic sensibility. The admiration of Ruskin cherished by Proust, himself a supreme master in this field, is significant.

problems clearly out. The attitude of their philosophers towards many of the special arts, even the arts in
which they were themselves supreme, to us seem unreasonable. While they magnified the art, they often
belittled the artist, and felt an aristocratic horror for
anything that assimilated a man to a craftsman; for
craftsman meant for them vulgarian. Plato himself
was all for goody-goody literature and in our days
would be an enthusiastic patron of Sunday-school stories. He would forbid any novelist to represent a good
man as ever miserable or a wicked man as ever happy.
The whole tendency of the discussion in the third book
of the "Republic" is towards the conclusion that literature must be occupied exclusively with the representation of the virtuous man, provided, of course, that he
was not a slave or a craftsman, for to such no virtue
worthy of imitation should ever be attributed. Towards the end of his long life, Plato remained of the
same opinion; in the second book of "The Laws" it is
with the maxims of virtue that he will have the poet
solely concerned. The reason for this ultra-puritanical
attitude, which was by no means in practice that of the
Greeks themselves, seems not hard to divine. The very
fact that their morality was temperamentally æsthetic
instinctively impelled them, when they were thinking
philosophically, to moralise art generally; they had not
yet reached the standpoint which would enable them
to see that art might be consonant with morality without being artificially pressed into a narrow moral mould.

Aristotle was conspicuously among those, if not the first, who took a broader and saner view. In opposition to the common Greek view that the object of art is to teach morals, Aristotle clearly expressed the totally different view that poetry in the wide sense — the special art which he and the Greeks generally were alone much concerned to discuss — is an emotional delight, having pleasure as its direct end, and only indirectly a moral end by virtue of its cathartic effects. Therein he reached an æsthetic standpoint, yet it was so novel that he could not securely retain it and was constantly falling back towards the old moral conception of art.[1]

We may call it a step in advance. Yet it was not a complete statement of the matter. Indeed, it established the unreal conflict between two opposing conceptions, each unsound because incomplete, which loose thinkers have carried on ever since. To assert that poetry exists for morals is merely to assert that one art exists for the sake of another art, which at the best is rather a futile statement, while, so far as it is really accepted, it cannot fail to crush the art thus subordinated. If we have the insight to see that an art has its own part of life, we shall also see that it has its own intrinsic morality, which cannot be the morality of morals

[1] Butcher, *Aristotle's Theory of Poetry and Fine Art*, chap. v, "Art and Morals." Aristotle could have accepted the almost Freudian view of Croce that art is the deliverer, the process through which we overcome the stress of inner experiences by objectifying them (*Æsthetics as Science of Expression*, p. 35). But Plato could not accept Croce, still less Freud.

or of any other art than itself. We may here profitably
bear in mind that antinomy between morals and morality on which Jules de Gaultier has often insisted. The
Puritan's strait-jacket shows the vigour of his external
morals; it also bears witness to the lack of internal
morality which necessitates that control. Again, on
the other hand, it is argued that art gives pleasure.
Very true. Even the art of morals gives pleasure. But
to assert that therein lies its sole end and aim is an
altogether feeble and inadequate conclusion, unless
we go further and proceed to inquire what "pleasure"
means. If we fail to take that further step, it remains
a conclusion which may be said to merge into the conclusion that art is aimless; that, rather, its aim is to be
aimless, and so to lift us out of the struggle and tur-
moil of life. That was the elaborately developed argument of Schopenhauer: art — whether in music, in
philosophy, in painting, in poetry — is useless; "to be
useless is the mark of genius, its patent of nobility. All
other works of men are there for the preservation or al-
leviation of our existence; but this alone not; it alone is
there for its own sake; and is in this sense to be regarded as the flower, or the pure essence, of existence.
That is why in its enjoyment our heart rises, for we are
thereby lifted above the heavy earthen atmosphere of
necessity."[1] Life is a struggle of the will; but in art
the will has become objective, fit for pure contempla-

[1] Schopenhauer, *Die Welt als Wille und Vorstellung* (1859), vol. II,
p. 442. For a careful and detailed study of Schopenhauer's conception
of art, see A. Fauconnet, *L'Esthétique de Schopenhauer* (1913).

tion, and genius consists in an eminent aptitude for contemplation. The ordinary man, said Schopenhauer, plods through the dark world with his lantern turned on the things he wants; the man of genius sees the world by the light of the sun. In modern times Bergson adopted that view of Schopenhauer's, with a terminology of his own, and all he said under this head may be regarded as a charming fantasia on the Schopenhauerian theme: "Genius is the most complete objectivity." Most of us, it seems to Bergson, never see reality at all; we only see the labels we have fixed on things to mark for us their usefulness.[1] A veil is interposed between us and the reality of things. The artist, the man of genius, raises this veil and reveals Nature to us. He is naturally endowed with a detachment from life, and so possesses as it were a virginal freshness in seeing, hearing, or thinking. That is "intuition," an instinct that has become disinterested. "Art has no other object but to remove the practically useful symbols, the conventional and socially accepted generalities, so as to bring us face to face with reality itself."[2] Art would thus be fulfill-

[1] I find that I have here negligently ascribed to Bergson a metaphor which belongs to Croce, who at this point says the same thing as Bergson, though he gives it a different name. In *Æsthetics as Science of Expression* (English translation, p. 66) we read: "The world of which as a rule we have intuition [Bergson could not have used that word here] is a small thing. . . . 'Here is a man, here is a horse, this is heavy, this is hard, this pleases me,' etc. It is a medley of light and colour, which could not pictorially attain to any more sincere expression than a haphazard splash of colour, from among which would with difficulty stand out a few special distinctive traits. This and nothing else is what we possess in our ordinary life; this is the basis of our ordinary action. It is the index of a book. The labels tied to things take the place of things themselves."

[2] H. Bergson, *Le Rire*. For a clear, concise, and sympathetic exposi-

ing its function the more completely the further it removed us from ordinary life, or, more strictly, from any personal interest in life. That was also Remy de Gourmont's opinion, though I do not know how far he directly derived it from Schopenhauer. "If we give to art a moral aim," he wrote, "it ceases to exist, for it ceases to be useless. Art is incompatible with a moral or religious aim. It is unintelligible to the crowd because the crowd is not disinterested and knows only the principle of utility." But the difficulty of making definite affirmation in this field, the perpetual need to allow for *nuances* which often on the surface involve contradictions, is seen when we find that so great an artist as Einstein — for so we may here fairly call him — and one so little of a formal æsthetician, agrees with Schopenhauer. "I agree with Schopenhauer," he said to Moszkowski, "that one of the most powerful motives that attract people to science and art is the longing to escape from everyday life, with its painful coarseness and unconsoling barrenness, and to break the fetters of their own ever-changing desires. Man seeks to form a simplified synoptical view of the world conformable to his own nature, to overcome the world by replacing it with his picture. The painter, the poet, the philosopher, the scientist, each does this in his own way. He transfers the centre of his emotional life to his picture, to find a surer haven of peace than the

on of Bergson's standpoint, though without special reference to art, e Karin Stephen, *The Misuse of Mind*.

sphere of his turbulent personal experience offers." That is a sound statement of the facts, yet it is absurd to call such an achievement "useless."

Perhaps, however, what philosophers have really meant when they have said that art (it is the so-called fine arts only that they have in mind) is useless, is that *an art must not be consciously pursued for any primary useful end outside itself*. That is true. It is even true of morals, that is to say the art of living. To live in the conscious primary pursuit of a "useful" end — such as one of the fine arts — outside living itself is to live badly; to declare, like André Gide, that "outside the doctrine of 'Art for Art' I know not where to find any reason for living," may well be the legitimate expression of a personal feeling, but, unless understood in the sense here taken, it is not a philosophical statement which can be brought under the species of eternity, being, indeed, one of those confusions of substances which are, metaphysically, damnable. So, again, in the art of science: the most useful applications of science have sprung from discoveries that were completely useless for purposes outside pure science, so far as the aim of the discoverer went, or even so far as he ever knew. If he had been bent on "useful" ends, he would probably have made no discovery at all. But the bare statement that "art is useless" is so vague as to be really meaningless, if not inaccurate and misleading.

Therefore, Nietzsche was perhaps making a profound statement when he declared that art is th

CONCLUSION

great stimulus to life; it produces joy as an aid to life; it possesses a usefulness, that is to say, which transcends its direct aim. The artist is one who sees life as beauty, and art is thus fulfilling its function the more completely, the more deeply it enables us to penetrate into life. It seems, however, that Nietzsche insufficiently guarded his statement. Art for art's sake, said Nietzsche, is "a dangerous principle," like truth for truth's sake and goodness for goodness' sake. Art, knowledge, and morality are simply means, he declared, and valuable for their "life-promoting tendency." (There is here a pioneering suggestion of the American doctrine of Pragmatism, according to which how a thing "works" is the test of its validity, but Nietzsche can by no means be counted a Pragmatist.) To look thus at the matter was certainly, with Schopenhauer and with Gourmont, to put aside the superficial moral function of art, and to recognise in it a larger sociological function. It was on the sociological function of art that Guyau, who was so penetrating and sympathetic a thinker, insisted in his book, posthumously published in 1889, "L'Art au Point de Vue Sociologique." He argued that art, while remaining independent, is at the foundation one with morals and with religion. He believed in a profound unity of all these terms: life, morality, society, religion, art. "Art, in a word, is life." So that, as he pointed out, there is no conflict between the theory of art for art, properly interpreted, and the theory that assigns to art a moral and

social function. It is clear that Guyau was on the right
road, although his statement was confusingly awkward
in form. He deformed his statement, moreover, through
his perpetual tendency to insist on the spontaneously
socialising organisation of human groups — a tendency which has endeared him to all who adopt an an-
archist conception of society — and, forgetting that he
had placed morals only at the depth of art and not on
the surface, he commits himself to the supremely false
dictum: "Art is, above everything, a phenomenon of
sociability," and the like statements, far too closely resembling the doctrinary pronouncements of Tolstoy.
For sociability is an indirect end of art: it cannot be its
direct aim. We are here not far from the ambiguous
doctrine that art is "expression," for "expression" may
be too easily confused with "communication." [1]

All these eminent philosophers — though they meant
something which so far as it went was true — have
failed to produce a satisfying statement because they
have none of them understood how to ask the question
which they were trying to answer. They failed to understand that morals is just as much an art as any other
vital psychic function of man; they failed to see that,
though art must be free from the dominance of morals,

[1] This may seem to cast a critical reflection on Croce. Let me, therefore, hasten to add that it is merely the personal impression that Croce,
for all his virtuous aspirations after the concrete, tends to fall into verbal
abstraction. He so often reminds one of that old lady who used to find
(for she died during the Great War) such spiritual consolation in "that
blessed word Mesopotamia." This refers, however, to the earlier more
than to the later Croce.

it by no means followed that it has no morality of its own, if morality involves the organised integrity which all vital phenomena must possess; they failed to realise that, since the arts are simply the sum of the active functions which spring out of the single human organism, we are not called upon to worry over any imaginary conflicts between functions which are necessarily harmonious because they are all one at the root. We cannot too often repeat the pregnant maxim of Bacon that the right question is the half of knowledge. Here we might almost say that it is the whole of knowledge. It seems, therefore, unnecessary to pursue the subject further. He who cannot himself pursue it further had best leave it alone.

But when we enter the æsthetic sphere we are no longer artists. That, indeed, is inevitable if we regard the arts as the sum of all the active functions of the organism. Rickert, with his methodical vision of the world, — for he insists that we must have some sort of system, — has presented what he regards as a reasonable scheme in a tabular form at the end of the first volume of his "System." [1] He divides Reality into two great divisions: the monistic and asocial Contemplative and the pluralistic and social Active. To the first belong the spheres of Logic, Æsthetics, and Mysticism, with their values, truth, beauty, impersonal holiness; to the second, Ethics, Erotics, the Philosophy of Religion, with their values, morality, happiness, personal

[1] H. Rickert, *System der Philosophie*, vol. I (1921).

holiness. This view of the matter is the more significant as Rickert stands aside from the tradition represented by Nietzsche and returns to the Kantian current,
enriched, indeed, and perhaps not quite consistently,
by Goethe. It seems probable that all Rickert's active
attitudes towards reality may fairly be called Art, and
all the contemplative attitudes, Æsthetics.

There is in fact nothing novel in the distinction
which underlies this classification, and it has been
recognised ever since the days of Baumgarten, the
commonly accepted founder of modern æsthetics, not
to go further back.[1] Art is the active practical exercise
of a single discipline: æsthetics is the philosophic appreciation of any or all the arts. Art is concerned with
the more or less unconscious creation of beauty:
æsthetics is concerned with its discovery and contemplation. Æsthetics is the metaphysical side of all
productive living.

IV

THIS complete unlikeness on the surface between art
and æsthetics — for ultimately and fundamentally they

[1] Before Baumgarten this distinction seems to have been recognised,
though too vaguely and inconsistently, by Hutcheson, who is so often
regarded as the real founder of modern æsthetics. W. R. Scott (*Francis
Hutcheson*, p. 216) points out these two principles in Hutcheson's work,
"the Internal Senses, as derived from Reflection, representing the attitude of the 'Spectator' or observer in a picture gallery while, on the other
hand, as deduced from $\epsilon\nu\epsilon\rho\gamma\epsilon\iota\alpha$ they find a parallel in the artist's own
consciousness of success in his work; thus the former might be called
static and the latter dynamic consciousness, or, in the special case of
Morality, the first applies primarily to approval of the acts of others, the
second to each individual's approval of his own conduct."

are at one — has to be emphasised, for the failure to distinguish them has led to confusion and verbosity. The practice of morals, we must ever remember, is not a matter of æsthetics; it is a matter of art. It has not, nor has any other art, an immediate and obvious relationship to the creation of beauty.[1] What the artist in life, as in any other art, is directly concerned to express is not primarily beauty; it is much more likely to seem to him to be truth (it is interesting to note that Einstein, so much an artist in thought, insists that he is simply concerned with truth), and what he produces may seem at first to all the world, and even possibly to himself, to be ugly. It is so in the sphere of morals. For morals is still concerned with the possessive instinct, not with the creation of beauty, with the needs and the satisfaction of the needs, with the industrial and economic activities, with the military activities to which they fatally tend. But the æsthetic attitude, as Gaultier expresses it, is the radiant smile on the human face which in its primitive phases was anatomically built up to subserve crude vital needs; as he elsewhere more abstractly expresses it, "Beauty is an attitude of sensibility." It is the task of æsthetics, often a slow and painful task, to see art — including the art of Nature, some would insist — as beauty. That, it has

[1] This would probably be recognised even by those moralists who, like Hutcheson, in their anxiety to make clear an important relationship, have spoken ambiguously. "Probably Hutcheson's real thought," remarks F. C. Sharp (*Mind*, 1921, p. 42), "is that the moral emotion, while possessing many important affinities with the æsthetic, is in the last resort different in content."

to be added, is no mean task. It is, on the contrary, essential. It is essential to sweep away in art all that is ultimately found to be fundamentally ugly, whether by being, at the one end, distastefully pretty, or, at the other, hopelessly crude. For ugliness produces nausea of the stomach and sets the teeth on edge. It does so literally, not metaphorically. Ugliness, since it interferes with digestion, since it disturbs the nervous system, impairs the forces of life. For when we are talking æsthetics (as the word itself indicates) we are ultimately talking physiologically. Even our meta-physics — if it is to have any meaning for us — must have a physical side. Unless we hold that fact in mind, we shall talk astray and are likely to say little that is to the point.

Art has to be seen as beauty and it is the function of æsthetics so to see it. How slowly and painfully the function works every one must know by observing the æsthetic judgments of other people, if not by recalling his own experiences. I know in my own experience how hardly and subconsciously this process works. In the matter of pictures, for instance, I have found throughout life, from Rubens in adolescence to Cézanne in recent years, that a revelation of the beauty of a painter's work which, on the surface, is alien or repulsive to one's sensibility, came only after years of contemplation, and then most often by a sudden rev-elation, in a flash, by a direct intuition of the beauty of some particular picture which henceforth became the clue to all the painter's work. It is a process comparable to that which is in religion termed "conversion," and, indeed, of like nature.[1] So also it is in literature. And in life? We are accustomed to suppose that a moral action is much easier to judge than a picture of Cézanne. We do not dream of bringing the same patient and attentive, as it were æsthetic, spirit to life as we bring to painting. Perhaps we are right, considering what poor bungling artists most of us are in living. For "art is easy, life is difficult," as Liszt used to say. The reason, of course, is that the art of living differs from the external arts in that we cannot exclude the introduction of alien elements into its texture. Our art of living, when we achieve it, is of so high and fine a quality precisely because it so largely lies in harmoniously weaving into the texture elements that we have not ourselves chosen, or that, having chosen, we cannot throw aside. Yet it is the attitude of the spectators that helps to perpetuate that bungling.

It is Plotinus whom we may fairly regard as the founder of Æsthetics in the philosophic sense, and it was as formulated by Plotinus, though this we sometimes fail to recognise, that the Greek attitude in these matters, however sometimes modified, has come down

[1] Schopenhauer long ago pointed out that a picture should be looked at as a royal personage is approached, in silence, until the moment it pleases to speak to you, for, if you speak first (and how many critics one knows who "speak first"!), you expose yourself to hear nothing but the sound of your own voice. In other words, it is a spontaneous and "mystical" experience.

to us.[1] We may be forgiven for not always recognising it, because it is rather strange that it should be so. It is strange, that is to say, that the æsthetic attitude, which we regard as so emphatically Greek, should have been left for formulation until the Greek world had passed away, that it should not have been Plato, but an Alexandrian, living in Rome seven centuries after him, who set forth what seems to us a distinctively Platonic view of life.[2] The Greeks, indeed, seem to have recognised, apart from the lower merely "ethical" virtues of habit and custom, the higher "intellectual" virtues which were deliberately planned, and so of the nature of art. But Plotinus definitely recognised the æsthetic contemplation of Beauty, together with the One and the Good, as three aspects of the Absolute.[3] He thus at once placed æsthetics on the highest possible pedestal, beside religion and

[1] It is through Plotinus, also, that we realise how æsthetics is on the same plane, if not one, with mysticism. For by his insistence on Contemplation, which is æsthetics, we learn to understand what is meant when it is said, as it often is, that mysticism is Contemplation. (On this point, and on the early evolutions of Christian Mysticism, see Dom Cuthbert Butler, *Western Mysticism* (1922).

[2] Really, however, Plotinus was here a Neo-Aristotelian rather than a Neo-Platonist, for Aristotle (*Ethics*, book x, chap. 6) had put the claim of the Contemplative life higher even than Plato and almost forestalled Plotinus. But as Aristotle was himself here a Platonist that does not much matter.

[3] See Inge, *Philosophy of Plotinus*, p. 179. In a fine passage (quoted by Bridges in his *Spirit of Man*) Plotinus represents contemplation as the great function of Nature herself, content, in a sort of self-consciousness, to do nothing more than perfect that fair and bright vision. This "metaphysical Narcissism," as Palante might call it, accords with the conception of various later thinkers, like Schopenhauer, and like Gaultier, who, however, seldom refers to Plotinus.

morals; he placed it above art, or as comprehending art, for he insisted that Contemplation is an active quality, so that all human creative energy may be regarded as the by-play of contemplation. That was to carry rather far the function of æsthetic contemplation. But it served to stamp for ever, on the minds of all sensitive to that stamp who came after, the definite realisation of the sublimest, the most nearly divine, of human aptitudes. Every great spirit has furnished the measure of his greatness by the more or less completeness in which at the ultimate outpost of his vision over the world he has attained to that active contemplation of life as a spectacle which Shakespeare finally embodied in the figure of Prospero.

It may be interesting to note in passing that, psychologically considered, all æsthetic enjoyment among the ordinary population, neither artists in the narrow sense nor philosophers, still necessarily partakes to some degree of genuine æsthetic contemplation, and that such contemplation seems to fall roughly into two classes, to one or other of which every one who experiences æsthetic enjoyment belongs. These have, I believe, been defined by Müller-Freienfels as that of the "Zuschauer," who feels that he is looking on, and that of the "Mitspieler," who feels that he is joining in; on the one side, we may say, he who knows he is looking on, the *spectator*, and on the other he who imaginatively joins in, the *participator*. The people of the first group are those, it may be, in whom the sensory nervous apparatus is highly developed and they are able to adopt the most typical and complete æsthetic attitude; the people of the other group would seem to be most developed on the motor nervous side and they are those who themselves desire to be artists. Groos, who has developed the æsthetic side of "miterleben," is of this temperament, and he had at first supposed that every one was like him in this respect.[1] Plotinus, who held that contemplation embraced activity, must surely have been of this temperament. Coleridge was emphatically of the other temperament, *spectator haud particeps*, as he himself said. But, at all events in northern countries, that is probably not the more common temperament. The æsthetic attitude of the crowds who go to watch football matches is probably much more that of the imaginative participator than of the pure spectator.

There is no occasion here to trace the history of æsthetic contemplation. Yet it may be worth while to note that it was clearly present to the mind of the fine thinker and great moralist who brought the old Greek idea back into the modern world. In the "Philosophical Regimen" (as it has been named) brought to light a few years ago, in which Shaftesbury set down his self-communings, we find him writing in one place: "In the morning am I to see anew? Am I to be present yet longer and content? I am not weary, nor ever can

[1] R. Schmidt, *Deutsche Philosophie der Gegenwart im Selbstdarstellungen* (1921), vol. II.

be, of such a spectacle, such a theatre, such a presence, nor at acting whatever part such a master assigns me. Be it ever so long, I stay and am willing to see on whilst my sight continues sound; whilst I can be a spectator, such as I ought to be; whilst I can see reverently, justly, with understanding and applause. And when I see no more, I retire, not disdainfully, but in reverence to the spectacle and master, giving thanks. . . . Away, man! rise, wipe thy mouth, throw up thy napkin and have done. A bellyful (they say) is as good as a feast."

That may seem but a simple and homely way of stating the matter, though a few years later, in 1727, a yet greater spirit than Shaftesbury, Swift, combining the conception of life as æsthetic contemplation with that of life as art, wrote in a letter, "Life is a tragedy, wherein we sit as spectators awhile, and then act our own part in it." If we desire a more systematically philosophical statement we may turn to the distinguished thinker of to-day who in many volumes has most powerfully presented the same essential conception, with all its implications, of life as a spectacle. "Tirez le rideau; la farce est jouée." That Shakespearian utterance, which used to be attributed to Rabelais on his death-bed, and Swift's comment on life, and Shaftesbury's intimate meditation, would seem to be — on the philosophic and apart from the moral side of life — entirely in the spirit that Jules de Gaultier has so elaborately developed. The world is

a spectacle, and all the men and women the actors on
its stage. Enjoy the spectacle while you will, whether
comedy or tragedy, enter into the spirit of its manifold
richness and beauty, yet take it not too seriously, even
when you leave it and the curtains are drawn that
conceal it for ever from your eyes, grown weary at last.

Such a conception, indeed, was already to be seen in
a deliberately philosophical form in Schopenhauer
(who, no doubt, influenced Gaultier) and, later,
Nietzsche, especially the early Nietzsche, although he
never entirely abandoned it; his break with Wagner,
however, whom he had regarded as the typical artist,
led him to become suddenly rather critical of art and
artists, as we see in "Human-all-too-Human," which
immediately followed "Wagner in Bayreuth," and he
became inclined to look on the artist, in the narrow
sense, as only "a splendid relic of the past," not,
indeed, altogether losing his earlier conception, but
disposed to believe that "the scientific man is the
finest development of the artistic man." In his essay
on Wagner he had presented art as the essentially
metaphysical activity of Man, here following Schopenhauer. "Every genius," well said Schopenhauer, "is
a great child; he gazes out at the world as something
strange, a spectacle, and therefore with purely objective interest." That is to say that the highest attitude attainable by man towards life is that of æsthetic
contemplation. But it took on a different character in
Nietzsche. In 1878 Nietzsche wrote of his early essay

on Wagner: "At that time I believed that the world was created from the æsthetic standpoint, as a play, and that as a moral phenomenon it was a deception: on that account I came to the conclusion that the world was only to be justified as an æsthetic phenomenon."[1] At the end of his active career Nietzsche was once more reproducing this proposition in many ways. Jules de Gaultier has much interested himself in Nietzsche, but he had already reached, no doubt through Schopenhauer, a rather similar conception before he came in contact with Nietzsche's work, and in the present day he is certainly the thinker who has most systematically and philosophically elaborated the conception.[2]

Gaultier is most generally known by that perhaps not quite happily chosen term of "Bovarism," embodied in the title of his earliest book and abstracted from Flaubert's heroine, which stands for one of his most characteristic conceptions, and, indeed, in a large sense, for the central idea of his philosophy. In its primary psychological sense Bovarism is the tendency — the unconscious tendency of Emma Bovary and, more or less, all of us — to conceive of ourselves as other than we are. Our picture of the world, for good or for evil, is an idealised picture, a fiction, a waking

---

[1] E. Förster-Nietzsche, *Das Leben Nietzsches*, vol. II, p. 99.
[2] W. M. Salter in his *Nietzsche the Thinker* — probably the best and most exact study of Nietzsche's thought we possess — summarises Nietzsche's "æsthetic metaphysics," as he terms it (pp. 46–48), in words which apply almost exactly to Gaultier.

dream, an *als ob*, as Vaihinger would say. But when
we idealise the world we begin by first idealising ourselves. We imagine ourselves other than we are, and
in so imagining, as Gaultier clearly realises, we tend to
mould ourselves, so that reality becomes a prolonga-
tion of fiction. As Meister Eckhart long since finely
said: "A man is what he loves." A similar thought was
in Plato's mind. In modern times a variation of this
same idea has been worked out, not as by Gaultier
from the philosophic side, but from the medical and
more especially the psycho-analytic side, by Dr. Alfred Adler of Vienna.[1] Adler has suggestively shown
how often a man's or a woman's character is constituted by a process of fiction, — that is by making an
ideal of what it is, or what it ought to be, — and then
so far as possible moulding it into the shape of that
fiction, a process which is often interwoven with
morbid elements, especially with an original basis of
organic defect, the reaction being an effort, sometimes
successful, to overcome that defect, and even to transform it into a conspicuous quality, as when Demosthenes, who was a stutterer, made himself a great
orator. Even thinkers may not wholly escape this
tendency, and I think it would be easily possible to
show that, for instance, Nietzsche was moved by what
Adler calls the "masculine protest"; one remembers
how shrinkingly delicate Nietzsche was towards women

[1] See especially his book *Über den Nervösen Charakter* (1912). It has
been translated into English.

and how emphatically he declared they should never be approached without a whip. Adler owed nothing to Gaultier, of whom he seems to be ignorant; he found his first inspiration in Vaihinger's doctrine of the "as if"; Gaultier, however, owes nothing to Vaihinger, and, indeed, began to publish earlier, though not before Vaihinger's book was written. Gaultier's philosophic descent is mainly from Spinoza, Berkeley, Hume, Schopenhauer, and Nietzsche.

There is another deeper and wider sense, a more abstract esoteric sense, in which Jules de Gaultier understands Bovarism. It is not only the human being and human groups who are psychologically Bovaristic, the Universe itself, the Eternal Being (to adopt an accepted fiction), metaphysically partakes of Bovarism. The Universe, it seems to Gaultier, necessarily conceives itself as other than it is. Single, it conceives itself multiple, as subject and object. Thus is furnished the fundamental convention which we must grant to the Dramatist who presents the cosmic tragi-comedy.[1]

It may seem to some that the vision of the world which Man pursues on his course across the Universe becomes ever more impalpable and visionary. And so perhaps it may be. But even if that were an undesirable result, it would still be useless to fight against God. We are, after all, merely moulding the concep-

[1] Jules de Gaultier, *Le Bovarysme*, and various other of his works. Georges Palante has lucidly and concisely expounded the idea of Bovarism in a small volume, *La Philosophie du Bovarysme* (*Mercure de France*).

tions which a little later will become commonplaces
and truisms. For really — while we must hold physics
and metaphysics apart, for they cannot be blended —
a metaphysics which is out of harmony with physics
is negligible; it is nothing in the world. And it is our
physical world that is becoming more impalpable and
visionary. It is "matter," the very structure of the
"atom," that is melting into a dream, and if it may
seem that on the spiritual side life tends to be moulding itself to the conception of Calderon as a dream, it
is because the physical atom is pursuing that course.
Unless we hold in mind the analysis of the world
towards which the physicist is bringing us, we shall not
understand the synthesis of the world towards which
the philosopher is bringing us. Gaultier's philosophy
may not be based upon physics, but it seems to be in
harmony with physics.

This is the metaphysical scaffolding — we may if we
like choose to dispense with it — by aid of which Jules
de Gaultier erects his spectacular conception of the
world. He is by no means concerned to deny the
necessity of morality. On the contrary, morality is the
necessary restraint on the necessary biological instinct
of possession, on the desire, that is, by the acquisition
of certain objects, to satisfy passions which are most
often only the exaggeration of natural needs, but which
— through the power of imagination such exaggeration inaugurates in the world — lead to the development of civilisation. Limited and definite so long as

confined to their biological ends, needs are indefinitely elastic, exhibiting, indeed, an almost hysterical character which becomes insatiable. They mark a hypertrophy of the possessive instinct which experience shows to be a menace to social life. Thus the Great War of recent times may be regarded as the final tragic result of the excessive development through half a century of an economic fever, the activity of needs beyond their due biological ends producing suddenly the inevitable result.[1] So that the possessive instinct, while it is the cause of the formation of an economic civilised society, when pushed too far becomes the cause of the ruin of that society. Man, who begins by acquiring just enough force to compel Nature to supply his bare needs, himself becomes, according to the tragic Greek saying, the greatest force of Nature. Yet the fact that a civilisation may persist for centuries shows that men in societies have found methods of combating the exaggerated development of the possessive instinct, of retaining it within bounds which have enabled societies to enjoy a fairly long life. These methods become embodied in religions and moralities and laws. They react in concert to restrain the greediness engendered by the possessive instinct. They make virtues of Temperance and Sobriety and Abnegation. They invent Great Images which arouse human hopes and human fears. They prescribe im-

---

[1] Gaultier has luminously discussed the relations of War, Civilisation, and Art in the *Monde Nouveau*, August, 1920, and February, 1921.

peratives, with sanctions, in part imposed by the Great Images and in part by the actual executive force of social law. So societies are enabled to immunise themselves against the ravaging auto-intoxication of an excessive instinct of possession, and the services rendered by religions and moralities cannot be too highly estimated. They are the spontaneous physiological processes which counteract disease before medical science comes into play.

But are they of any use in those periods of advanced civilisation which they have themselves contributed to form? When Man has replaced flint knives and clubs and slings by the elaborate weapons we know, can he be content with methods of social preservation which date from the time of flint knives and clubs and slings? The efficacy of those restraints depends on a sensibility which could only exist when men scarcely distinguished imaginations from perceptions. Thence arose the credulity on which religions and moralities flourished. But now the Images have grown pale in human sensibility, just as they have in words, which are but effaced images. We need a deeper reality to take the place of these early beliefs which the growth of intelligence necessarily shows to be illusory. We must seek in the human ego an instinct in which is manifested a truly autonomous play of the power of imagination, an instinct which by virtue of its own proper development may restrain the excesses of the possessive instinct and dissipate the perils which threaten civilisation.

The æsthetic instinct alone answers to that double demand.

At this point we may pause to refer to the interesting analogy between this argument of Jules de Gaultier and another recently proposed solution of the problems of civilisation presented by Bertrand Russell, to which there has already been occasion to refer. The two views were clearly suggested by the same events, though apparently in complete independence, and it is interesting to observe the considerable degree of harmony which unites two such distinguished thinkers in different lands, and with unlike philosophic standpoints as regards ultimate realities.[1] Man's impulses, as we know, Bertrand Russell holds to be of two kinds: those that are possessive and those that are creative; the typical possessive impulse being that of property and the typical creative impulse that of the artist. It is in following the creative impulse, he believes, that man's path of salvation lies, for the possessive impulses necessarily lead to conflict while the creative

---

[1] These are problems concerning which innocent people might imagine that the wise refrained from speculating, but, as a matter of fact, the various groups of philosophic devotees may be divided into those termed "Idealists" and those termed "Realists," each assured of the superiority of his own way of viewing thought. Roughly speaking, for the idealist thought means the creation of the world, for the realist its discovery. But here (as in many differences between Tweedledum and Tweedledee for which men have slain one another these thousands of years) there seem to be superiorities on both sides. Each looks at thought in a different aspect. But the idealist could hardly create the world with nothing there to make it from, nor the realist discover it save through creating it afresh. We cannot, so to put it, express in a single formula of three dimensions what only exists as a unity in four dimensions.

impulses are essentially harmonious. Bertrand Russell seeks the unification of life. But consistency of action should, he holds, spring from consistency of impulse/ rather than from the control of impulse by will. Like Gaultier, he believes in what has been called, perhaps not happily, "the law of irony"; that is to say, that the mark we hit is never the mark we aimed at, so that, in all supreme success in life, as Goethe said of Wilhelm Meister, we are like Saul, the son of Kish, who went forth to seek his father's asses and found a kingdom. "Those who best promote life," Russell prefers to put it, "do not have life for their purpose. They aim rather at what seems like a gradual incarnation, a bringing into our human existence of something eternal." And, again like Gaultier, he invokes Spinoza and what in his phraseology he called "the intellectual love of God." "Take no thought, saying, What shall we eat? or, What shall we drink? or, Wherewithal shall we be clothed? Whosoever has known a strong creative impulse has known the value of this precept in its exact and literal sense; it is preoccupation with possession, more than anything else, that prevents men from living freely and nobly."[1]

This view of the matter seems substantially the same, it may be in an unduly simplified form, as the conception which Jules de Gaultier has worked out more subtly and complexly, seeking to weave in a large number of the essential factors, realising that the

[1] Bertrand Russell, *Principles of Social Reconstruction* (1916), p. 235.

harmony of life must yet be based on an underlying conflict.[2] The main difference would seem to be that Bertrand Russell's creative impulse seems to be fairly identical with the productive impulse of art in the large sense in which I have throughout understood it, while Jules de Gaultier is essentially concerned with the philosophic or religious side of the art impulse; that is to say, the attitude of æsthetic contemplation which in appearance forms the absolute antithesis to the possessive instinct. It is probable, however, that there is no real discrepancy here, for as we may regard æsthetic contemplation as the passive aspect of art, so art may be regarded as the active aspect of æsthetic contemplation, and Bertrand Russell, we may certainly believe, would include the one under art as Jules de Gaultier would include the other under æsthetics.

The æsthetic instinct, as Jules de Gaultier understands it, answers the double demand of our needs to-day, not, like religions and moralities, by evoking images as menaces or as promises, only effective if they can be realised in the world of sensation, and so merely constituting another attempt to gratify the possessive instinct, by enslaving the power of imagination to that alien master. Through the æsthetic instinct Man is enabled to procure joy, not from the things themselves and the sensations due to the possession of

[2] I may here be allowed to refer to another discussion of this point, Havelock Ellis, *The Philosophy of Conflict, and Other Essays*, pp. 57–68.

things, but from the very images of things. Beyond
the sense of utility bound up with the possession of
objects, he acquires the privilege, bound up with the
sole contemplation of them, of enjoying the beauty of
things. By the æsthetic instinct the power of imagination realises its own proper tendency and attains its
own proper end.

Such a process cannot fail to have its reaction on the
social environment. It must counteract the exaggeration of the possessive instinct. To that impulse, when it
transgresses the legitimate bounds of biological needs
and threatens to grow like a destructive cancer, the
æsthetic instinct proposes another end, a more human
end, that of æsthetic joy. Therewith the exuberance of
insatiable and ruinous cupidity is caught in the forms
of art, the beauty of the universe is manifested to all
eyes, and the happiness which had been sought in the
paradoxical enterprise of glutting that insatiable desire
finds its perpetual satisfaction in the absolute and
complete realisation of beauty.

As Jules de Gaultier understands it, we see that the
æsthetic instinct is linked on to the possessive instinct.
Bertrand Russell would sometimes seem to leave the
possessive instinct in the void without making any
provision for its satisfaction. In Gaultier's view, we
may probably say it is taken in charge by the æsthetic
instinct as soon as it has fulfilled its legitimate biological ends, and its excessive developments, what might
otherwise be destructive, are sublimated. The æs-

thetic instinct, Gaultier insists, like the other instincts, even the possessive instinct, has imperative claims; it is an appetite of the *ego*, developed at the same hearth of intimate activity, drawing its strength from the same superabundance from which they draw strength. Therefore, in the measure in which it absorbs force they must lose force, and civilisation gains.

The development of the æsthetic sense is, indeed, indispensable if civilisation — which we may, perhaps, from the present point of view, regard with Gaultier as the embroidery worked by imagination on the stuff of our elementary needs — is to pass safely through its critical period and attain any degree of persistence. The appearance of the æsthetic sense is then an event of the first order in the rank of natural miracles, strictly comparable to the evolution in the organic sphere of the optic nerves, which made it possible to know things clearly apart from the sensations of actual contact. There is no mere simile here, Gaultier believes: the faculty of drawing joy from the images of things, apart from the possession of them, is based on physiological conditions which growing knowledge of the nervous system may some day make clearer.[1]

[1] I may remark that Plato had long before attributed the same observation to the Pythagorean Timæus in the sublime and amusing dialogue that goes under that name: "Sight in my opinion is the source of the greatest benefit to us, for had we never seen the stars, and the sun, and the heavens, none of the words which we have spoken about the universe would ever have been uttered. But now the sight of day and night, and the months and the revolution of the years, have created Number, and have given us a conception of Time, and the powers of inquiring about

It is this specific quality, the power of enjoying things without being reduced to the need of possessing them, which differentiates the æsthetic instinct from other instincts and confers on it the character of morality. Based, like the other instincts on egoism, it, yet, unlike the other instincts, leads to no destructive struggles. Its powers of giving satisfaction are not dissipated by the number of those who secure that satisfaction. Æsthetic contemplation engenders neither hatred nor envy. Unlike the things that appeal to the possessive instinct, it brings men together and increases sympathy. Unlike those moralities which are compelled to institute prohibitions, the æsthetic sense, even in the egoistic pursuit of its own ends, becomes blended with morality, and so serves in the task of maintaining society.

Thus it is that, by aiming at a different end, the æsthetic sense yet attains the end aimed at by morality. That is the aspect of the matter which Gaultier would emphasise. There is implied in it the judgment that when the æsthetic sense deviates from its proper ends to burden itself with moral intentions — when, that is, it ceases to be itself — it ceases to realise morality. "Art for art's sake!" the artists of old cried. We laugh at that cry now. Gaultier, indeed, considers that the idea of pure art has in every age been a red rag in the eyes of the human bull. Yet, if we had possessed the

the Nature of the Universe, and from this source we have derived philosophy, than which no greater good ever was or will be given by the gods to mortal man."

necessary intelligence, we might have seen that it held a great moral truth. "The poet, retired in his Tower of Ivory, isolated, according to his desire, from the world of man, resembles, whether he so wishes or not, another solitary figure, the watcher enclosed for months at a time in a lighthouse at the head of a cliff. Far from the towns peopled by human crowds, far from the earth, of which he scarcely distinguishes the outlines through the mist, this man in his wild solitude, forced to live only with himself, almost forgets the common language of men, but he knows admirably well how to formulate through the darkness another language infinitely useful to men and visible afar to seamen in distress." [1] The artist for art's sake — and the same is constantly found true of the scientist for science's sake [2] — in turning aside from the common utilitarian aims of men is really engaged in a task none other can perform, of immense utility to men. The Cistercians of old hid their cloisters in forests and wildernesses afar from society, mixing not with men nor performing for them so-called useful tasks; yet they spent their days and nights in chant and prayer, working for the salvation of the world, and they stand as the symbol of all higher types of artists, not the less

[1] Jules de Gaultier, "La Guerre et les Destinées de l'Art," *Monde Nouveau*, August, 1920.

[2] Thus Einstein, like every true man of science, holds that cultural developments are not to be measured in terms of utilitarian technical advances, much as he has himself been concerned with such advances, but that, like the devotee of "Art for Art's sake," the man of science must proclaim the maxim, "Science for Science's sake."

so because they, too, illustrate that faith transcending sight, without which no art is possible.

The artist, as Gaultier would probably put it, has to effect a necessary Bovarism. If he seeks to mix himself up with the passions of the crowd, if his work shows the desire to prove anything, he thereby neglects the creation of beauty. Necessarily so, for he excites a state of combativity, he sets up moral, political, and social values, all having relation to biological needs and the possessive instinct, the most violent of ferments. He is entering on the struggle over Truth — though his opinion is here worth no more than any other man's — which, on account of the presumption of its universality, is brandished about in the most ferociously opposed camps.

The mother who seeks to soothe her crying child preaches him no sermon. She holds up some bright object and it fixes his attention. So it is the artist acts: he makes us see. He brings the world before us, not on the plane of covetousness and fears and commandments, but on the plane of representation; the world becomes a spectacle. Instead of imitating those philosophers who with analyses and syntheses worry over the goal of life, and the justification of the world, and the meaning of the strange and painful phenomenon called Existence, the artist takes up some fragment of that existence, transfigures it, shows it: There! And therewith the spectator is filled with enthusiastic joy, and the transcendent Adventure of

Existence is justified. Every great artist, a Dante or a
Shakespeare, a Dostoievsky or a Proust, thus furnishes
the metaphysical justification of existence by the
beauty of the vision he presents of the cruelty and the
horror of existence. All the pain and the madness, even
the ugliness and the commonplace of the world, he con-
verts into shining jewels. By revealing the spectacular character of reality he restores the serenity of its
innocence.[1] We see the face of the world as of a lovely
woman smiling through her tears.

How are we to expect this morality — if so we
may still term it — to prevail? Jules de Gaultier, as
we have seen, realising that the old moralities have
melted away, seems to think that the morality of art,
by virtue of its life, will take the place of that which is
dead. But he is not specially concerned to discuss in
detail the mechanism of this replacement, though he
looks to the social action of artists in initiation and
stimulation. That was the view of Guyau, and it fitted
in with his sociological conception of art as being one
with life; great poets, great artists, Guyau believed,
will become the leaders of the crowd, the priests of a
social religion without dogmas.[2] But Gaultier's conception goes beyond this. He cannot feel that the
direct action of poets and artists is sufficient. They

[1] In the foregoing paragraphs I have, in my own way, reproduced the
thought, occasionally the words, of Jules de Gaultier, more especially in
"La Moralité Esthétique" (*Mercure de France*, 15th December, 1921),
probably the finest short statement of this distinguished thinker's re-
flections on the matter in question.

[2] Guyau, *L'Art au Point de Vue Sociologique*, p. 163.

only reveal the more conspicuous aspects of the æsthetic sense. Gaultier considers that the æsthetic sense, in humbler forms, is mixed up with the most primitive manifestations of human life, wherein it plays a part of unsuspected importance.[1] The more thorough investigation of these primitive forms, he believes, will make it possible for the lawmaker to aid the mechanism of this transformation of morality.

Having therewith brought us to the threshold of the æsthetic revolution, Jules de Gaultier departs. It remains necessary to point out that it is only the threshold. However intimately the elements of the æsthetic sense may be blended with primitive human existence, we know too well that, as the conditions of human existence are modified, art seems to contract and degenerate, so we can hardly expect the æsthetic sense to develop in the reverse direction. At present,

---

[1] This diffused æsthetic sense is correlated with a diffused artistic instinct, based on craftsmanship, which the Greeks were afraid to recognise because they looked down with contempt on the handicrafts as vulgar. William Morris was a pioneer in asserting this association. As a distinguished English writer, Mr. Charles Marriott, the novelist and critic, clearly puts the modern doctrine: "The first step is to absorb, or re-absorb, the 'Artist' into the craftsman. . . . Once agree that the same æsthetic considerations which apply to painting a picture apply, though in a different degree, to painting a door, and you have emancipated labour without any prejudice to the highest meaning of art. . . . A good surface of paint on a door is as truly an emotional or æsthetic consideration as 'significant form,' indeed it *is* 'significant form.'" (*Nation and Athenæum*, 1st July, 1922.) Professor Santayana has spoken in the same sense: "In a thoroughly humanised society everything — clothes, speech, manners, government — is a work of art." (*The Dial*, June, 1922, p. 563.) It is, indeed, the general tendency to-day and is traceable in Croce's later writings.

in the existing state of civilisation, with the decay of the controlling power of the old morality, the æsthetic sense often seems to be also decreasing, rather than increasing, in the masses of the population.[1] One need not be troubled to find examples. They occur on every hand and whenever we take up a newspaper. One notes, for instance, in England, that the most widespread spectacularly attractive things outside cities may be said to be the private parks and the churches. (Cities lie outside the present argument, for their inhabitants are carefully watched whenever they approach anything that appeals to the possessive instinct.) Formerly the parks and churches were freely open all day long for those who desired to enjoy the spectacle of their beauty and not to possess it. The owners of parks and the guardians of churches have found it increasingly necessary to close them because of the alarmingly destructive or predatory impulses of a section of the public. So the many have to suffer for the sins of what may only be the few. It is common to speak of this as a recent tendency of our so-called civilisation. But the excesses of the possessive instinct cannot have been entirely latent even in remote times, though they seem to have been less in evidence. The Platonic Timæus attributed to the

[1] Thus it has often been pointed out that the Papuans are artists in design of the first rank, with a finer taste in some matters than the most highly civilised races of Europe. Professor R. Semon, who has some remarks to this effect (*Correspondenzblatt* of the German Anthropological Society, March, 1902), adds that their unfailing artistic sense is spread throughout the whole population and shown in every object of daily use.

spectacle of the sun and the moon and the stars the existence of philosophy. He failed to note that the sun and the moon and the stars would have disappeared long ago — as even their infinitely more numerous analogues on the earth beneath are likely to disappear — had they happened to be within the reach of predatory human hands. But the warps and strains of civilised life, with its excessive industrialism and militarism, seem to disturb the wholesome balance of even the humblest elements of the possessive and æsthetic instincts. This means, in the first and most important place, that the liberty of the whole community in its finest manifestations is abridged by a handful of imbeciles. There are infinite freedoms which it would be a joy for them to take, and a help to their work, and a benefit to the world, but they cannot be allowed to take them because there are some who can only take them and perish, damning others with themselves. Besides this supreme injury to life, there are perpetual minor injuries that the same incapable section of people are responsible for in every direction, while the actual cost of them in money, to the community they exert so pernicious an influence on, is so great and so increasing that it constitutes a social and individual burden which from time to time leads to outbursts of anxious expostulation never steady enough to be embodied in any well-sustained and coherent policy.

It is not, indeed, to be desired that the eugenic

CONCLUSION

action of society should be directly aimed at any narrowly æsthetic or moral end. That has never been the ideal of any of those whose conceptions of social life deserve to be taken seriously, least of all Galton, who is commonly regarded as the founder of the modern scientific art of eugenics. "Society would be very dull," he remarked, "if every man resembled Marcus Aurelius or Adam Bede." He even asserted that "we must leave morality as far as possible out of the discussion," since moral goodness and badness are shifting phases of a civilisation; what is held morally good in one age is held bad in another. That would hold true of any æsthetic revolution. But we cannot afford to do without the sane and wholesome persons who are so well balanced that they can adjust themselves to the conditions of every civilisation as it arises and carry it on to its finest issues. We should not, indeed, seek to breed them directly, and we need not, since under natural conditions Nature will see to their breeding. But it is all the more incumbent upon us to eliminate those ill-balanced and poisonous stocks produced by the unnatural conditions which society in the past had established.[1] That we have to do alike in the interests

[1] The presence of a small minority of abnormal or perverse persons — there will be such, we may be sure, in every possible society — affords no excuse for restricting the liberty of the many to the standard of the few. The general prevalence of an æsthetic morality in classic times failed to prevent occasional outbursts of morbid sexual impulse in the presence of objects of art, even in temples. We find records of Pygmalionism and allied perversities in Lucian, Athenæus, Pliny, Valerius Maximus. Yet supposing that the Greeks had listened to the proposals of some strayed Puritan visitor, from Britain or New England, to abolish nude statues,

of the offspring of these diseased stocks and in the interests of society. No power in Heaven or Earth can ever confer upon us the right to create the unfit in order to hang them like millstones around the necks of the fit. The genius of Galton enabled him to see this clearly afresh and to indicate the reasonable path of human progress. It was a truth that had long been forgotten by the strenuous humanitarians who ruled the nineteenth century, so anxious to perpetuate and multiply all the worst spawn of their humanity. Yet it was an ancient truth, carried into practice, however unconsciously and instinctively, by Man throughout his upward course, probably even from Palæolithic times, and when it ceased Man's upward course also ceased. As Carr-Saunders has shown, in a learned and comprehensive work which is of primary importance for the understanding of the history of Man, almost every people on the face of the earth has adopted one or more practices — notably infanticide, abortion, or severe restriction of sexual intercourse — adapted to maintain due selection of the best stocks and to limit the excess of fertility. They largely ceased to work because Man had acquired the humanity which was repelled by such methods and lost the intelligence to

or suppose that Plato, who wished to do away with imaginative literature as liable to demoralise, had possessed the influence he desired, how infinite the loss to all mankind! In modern Europe we not only propose such legal abolition; we actually, however in vain, carry it out. We seek to reduce all human existence to absurdity. It is, at the best, unnecessary, for we may be sure that, in spite of our efforts, a certain amount of absurdity will always remain.

see that they must be replaced by better methods. For the process of human evolution is nothing more than a process of sifting, and where that sifting ceases evolution ceases, becomes, indeed, devolution.[1]

When we survey the history of Man we are constantly reminded of the profound truth which often lay beneath the parables of Jesus, and they might well form the motto for any treatise on eugenics. Jesus was constantly seeking to suggest the necessity of that process of sifting in which all human evolution consists; he was ever quick to point out how few could be, as it was then phrased, "saved," how extremely narrow is the path to the Kingdom of Heaven, or, as many might now call it, the Kingdom of Man. He proclaimed symbolically a doctrine of heredity which is only to-day beginning to be directly formulated: "Every tree that bringeth not forth good fruit is hewn down and cast into the fire." There was no compunction at all in his promulgation of this radical yet necessary doctrine for the destruction of unfit stocks. Even the best stocks Jesus was in favour of destroying ruthlessly as soon as they had ceased to be the best: "Ye are the salt of the earth: but if the salt have lost his savour, . . . it is thenceforth good for nothing, but to be cast out, and to be trodden under foot of men." Jesus has been reproached by Nietzsche for founding a religion for slaves and plebeians, and so in the result it

[1] A. M. Carr-Saunders, *The Population Problem: A Study in Human Evolution* (Oxford Press, 1922).

may have become. But we see that, in the words of the Teacher as they have been handed down, the religion of Jesus was the most aristocratic of religions. Its doctrine embodied not even the permission to live for those human stocks which fall short of its aristocratic ideal. It need not surprise us to find that Jesus had already said two thousand years ago what Galton, in a more modern and — some would add — more humane way, was saying yesterday. If there had not been a core of vital truth beneath the surface of the first Christian's teaching, it could hardly have survived so long. We are told that it is now dead, but should it ever be revived we may well believe that this is the aspect by which it will be commended. It is a significant fact that at the two spiritual sources of our world, Jesus and Plato, we find the assertion of the principle of eugenics, in one implicitly, in the other explicitly.

Jules de Gaultier was not concerned to put forward an aristocratic conception of his æsthetic doctrine, and, as we have seen, he remained on the threshold of eugenics. He was content to suggest, though with no positive assurance, a more democratic conception. He had, indeed, one may divine, a predilection for that middle class which has furnished so vast a number of the supreme figures in art and thought; by producing a class of people dispensed from tasks of utility, he had pointed out, "a society creates for itself an organ fitted for the higher life and bears witness that it has passed beyond the merely biological stage to reach the human stage." But the middle class is not indispensable, and if it is doomed Gaultier saw ways of replacing it.[1] Especially we may seek to ensure that, in every social group, the individual task of utilitarian work shall be so limited that the worker is enabled to gain a leisure sufficiently ample to devote, if he has the aptitude, to works of intellect or art. He would agree with Otto Braun, the inspired youth who was slain in the Great War, that if we desire the enablement of the people "the eight-hours day becomes nothing less than the most imperative demand of culture." It is in this direction, it may well be, that social evolution is moving, however its complete realisation may, by temporary causes, from time to time be impeded. The insistent demand for increased wages and diminished hours of work has not been inspired by the desire to raise the level of culture in the social environment, or to inaugurate any æsthetic revolution, yet, by "the law of irony" which so often controls the realisation of things, that is the result which may be achieved. The new leisure conferred on the worker may be transformed into spiritual activity, and the liberated utilitarian energy into æsthetic energy. The road would thus be opened for a new human adventure, of anxious interest, which the future alone can reveal.

We cannot be sure that this transformation will take

[1] J. de Gaultier, "Art et Civilisation," *Monde Nouveau*, February, 1921.

place. We cannot be sure, indeed, that it is possible for it to take place unless the general quality of the population in whom so fine a process must be effected is raised by a more rigid eugenic process than there is yet any real determination among us to exert. Men still bow down before the fetish of mere quantity in population, and that worship may be their undoing. Giant social organisms, like the giant animal species of early times, may be destined to disappear suddenly when they have attained their extreme expansion.

Even if that should be so, even if there should be a solution of continuity in the course of civilisation, even then, as again Jules de Gaultier also held, we need not despair, for life is a fountain of everlasting exhilaration. No creature on the earth has so tortured himself as Man, and none has raised a more exultant Alleluia. It would still be possible to erect places of refuge, cloisters wherein life would yet be full of joy for men and women determined by their vocation to care only for beauty and knowledge, and so to hand on to a future race the living torch of civilisation. When we read Palladius, when we read Rabelais, we realise how vast a field lies open for human activity between the Thebaid on one side and Thelema on the other. Out of such ashes a new world might well arise. Sunset is the promise of dawn.

THE END

INDEX

INDEX

Abortion, once practised, 354.

Absolute, the, a fiction, 101.

Abyssian Church, dancing in worship of, 45.

Acting, music, and poetry, proceed in one stream, 36.

Adam, Villiers de l'Isle, his story *Le Secret de l'ancienne Musique*, 25.

Addison, Joseph, his style, 161–63, 184.

Adler, Dr. Alfred, of Vienna, 336, 337.

Adolescence, idealisation in, 107, 108.

Æschylus, developed technique of dancing, 56.

Æsthetic contemplation, 314, 315, 325, 326; recognised by the Greeks, 330, 331; two kinds of, that of spectator and that of participator, 331, 332; the Shaftesbury attitude toward, 332, 333; the Swift attitude toward, 333; involves life as a spectacle, 333, 334; and the systems of Gaultier and Russell, 343; engenders neither hatred nor envy, 346.

Æsthetic instinct, to replace moralities, religions, and laws, 340, 341, 343–45; differentiated from other instincts, 346; has the character of morality, 346.

Æsthetic intuitionism, 260, 276, 279, 314.

Æsthetic sense, development of, indispensable for civilisation, 345; realises morality when unburdened with moral intentions, 346; mixed with primitive manifestations of life, 350; correlated with diffused artistic instinct, 350 *n.*; seems to be decreasing, 350–52.

Æsthetics, and ethics, among the Greeks, 247; with us, 348; in the Greek sense, 263; the founders of, 271, 329; and art, the unlikeness of, 325–28; on same plane with mysticism, 330 *n.*

Africa, love-dance in, 46, 49, 50.

Akhenaten, 28.

Alaro, in Mallorca, dancing in church at, 44, 45.

Alberti, Leo, vast-ranging ideas of, 5.

Alcohol, consumption of, as test of civilisation, 295, 296.

Anatomy, studied by Leonardo da Vinci, 120.

Anaximander, 89.

Ancestry, the force of, in handwriting, 157, 158; in style, 158–61, 190.

Anna, Empress, 59.

Antisthenes, 249 *n.*

"Appearance," 219 *n.*

Aquinas, Saint Thomas, 202.

Arabs, dancing among, 38.

Arbuckle, one of the founders of æsthetics, 271; insisted on imagination as formative of character, 272.

Architecture. *See* Building.

Aristophanes, 311.

Aristotle, 89; on tragedy, 56; on the Mysteries, 242; on the moral quality of an act, 248; his use of the term "moral sense," 273; on Art and Nature in the making of the State, 313; his use of the term "artists," 313; his view of poetry, 318; and the contemplative life, 330 *n.*

Art, life as, more difficult to realise than to act, 1, 2; universe conceived as work of, by the primitive philosopher, 1; life as, views of finest thinkers of China and Greece on, 2–6, 247–52; whole conception of, has been narrowed and debased, 6, 7; in its proper sense, 7, 8; as the desire for beautification, 8; of living, has been decadent during the last two thousand years, 8 *n.*; Napoleon in the sphere of, 10; of living, the Lifuan, 13–18; of living, the Chinese, 27; Chinese civilisation shows that human life is, 30; of living, T'ung's story the embodiment of the Chinese symbol of, 33; life identical with, 33–35; of dancing, 36, 51–67, *see* Dancing; of life, a dance, 66, 67; science and, no distinction between, in classic times, 68; science and, distinction between, in modern times, 68–70; science is of the nature of, 71; represented by Pythagoras as source of science, 74; Greek, 76 *n.*; of thinking, 68–140, *see* Thinking; the solution of the conflicts of philosophy in, 82, 83; philosophy and, close relationship of, 83–85; impulse of, transformed sexual instinct, 108–12; and mathematics, 138–40; of writing, 141–190, *see* Writing; Man added to Nature, is the task in, 153; the freedom and the easiness of, do not necessarily go together, 182; of religion, 191–243, *see* Religion; of morals, 244–84, *see* Morals; the critic of, a critic of life, 269; civilisation is an, 301, 310; consideration of the question of the definition of, 310–12; Nature and, 312, 313; the sum of the active energies of mankind, 313; and æsthetics, the unlikeness of, 314, 315, 325-28; a genus, of which morals is a species, 316; each, has its own morality, 318; to assert that it gives pleasure a feeble conclusion, 319; on the uselessness of, according to Schopenhauer and others, 319-21; meaninglessness of the statement that it is useless, 322; sociological function of, 323, 324; philosophers have failed to see that it has a morality of its own, 324, 325; for art's sake, 346, 347.

Artist, partakes of divine nature of creator of the world, 2; Napoleon as an, 10-12; the true scientist as, 72, 73, 112; the philosopher as, 72, 73, 85; explanation of, 108-12; Bacon's definition of, Man added to Nature, 153; makes all things new, 153; in words, passes between the plane of new vision and the plane of new creation, 170, 178; life always a discipline for, 277; lays up his treasure in Heaven, 307; Man as, 310; is a maker, 312; Aristotle's use of the term, 313; reveals Nature, 320; has to effect a necessary Bovarism, 348, 349.

Artistic creation, the process of its birth, 108, 109.

Arts, sometimes classic and sometimes decadent, 8 n.; and sciences, 68-70; Master of, 69.

"Arty" people, 6, 7.

"As if," germs of doctrine of, in Kant, 87; world of, and Plato's "Ideas," 88; source of the phrase, 88, 89; seen in play, 89; the doctrine of, not immune from criticism, 102; fortifying influence of the doctrine, 102, 103. See Fiction, Vaihinger.

Asceticism, has nothing to do with normal religion, 222, 223; among the Greeks, traced, 249 n.; and Christianity, 249 n.

Asclepios, the cult of, 197 n.

Atavism, in handwriting, 157, 158; in style, 158-61, 190.

Athenæus, 55, 353 n.; his book about the Greeks, 76 n.

Atom, a fiction or an hypothesis, 97, 338; the structure of, 97 n.

Attraction, force of, a fiction, 98.

Aurelius, Marcus, regarded art of life as like the dancer's art, 66; his statement of the mystical core of religion, 207; adopted æsthetic criterion of moral action, 279.

Australians, religious dances among, 40.

Auto-erotic activities, 110, 111.

Axioms, akin to fiction, 94, 95.

Babies, 105.

Bach, Sebastian, 62, 311.

Bacon, Francis, his definition of the artist, Man added to Nature, 153; his style compared with that of Shakespeare, 160; the music of his style, 163; heavy and formal letters of, 184; his axiom, the right question is half the knowledge, 325.

Bacon, Roger, on the sciences, 68.

Balguy, Rev. John, 274.

Ballad, a dance as well as song, 62.

Ballet, the, chief form of Romantic dancing, 53; the germ of, to be found in ancient Rome, 56; origin of the modern, 56; the Italian and the French, 56-58; decline of, 58; the Russian, 58-60; the Swedish, 60.

Bantu, the question of the, 38, 45.

Baptism, 242.

"Barbarians," the classic use of the term, 285.

Barebones, Praise-God, 272.

Baretti, G. M. 50.

Bastien-Lepage, Jules, 311.

Baudelaire, Charles, on vulgar locutions, 151.

Baumgarten, A. G., the commonly accepted founder of æsthetics, 326.

Bayaderes, 52.

Bayle, G. L., 261.

"Beautiful," the, among Greeks and Romans, 247, 252.

Beauty, developed by dancing, 47; as an element of literary style, 176-78; and the good, among the Greeks, 247; Plotinus's doctrine of, 250, 251; of virtue, 270 n.; æsthetic contemplation creates, 315, 327, 328; and prettiness, 315 n.; revelation of, sometimes comes as by a process of "conversion," 328, 329.

Bee, the, an artist, 312.

Beethoven, 311; his Seventh Symphony, 62, 63.

Beggary in China, 31.

Benn, A. W., his The Greek Philosophers, 6, 252, 277 n.

Bentham, Jeremy, adopted a fiction for his system, 99.

Berenson, Bernhard, critic of art, 114; his attitude toward Leonardo da Vinci, 114, 117.

Bergson, Henri Louis, pyrotechnical allusions frequent in, 23; regards philosophy as an art, 83, 84; on clarity in style, 176, 177; his idea of intuition, 232 n.; on reality, 320.

Berkeley, George, 95.

Bernard, Claude, personality in his Leçons de Physiologie Expérimentales, 144.

Bible, the, the source of its long life, 179. See Old Testament, Revelation.

Birds, dancing of, 36 n., 45; the attitude of the poet toward, 168.

Birth-rate, as test of civilisation, 294, 296, 299 n.

"Bitter," a moral quality, 264.

Blackguard, the, 244, 245.

Blake, William, on the Dance of Life, 66; on the golden rule of life, 281.

Blasco Ibañez, 171.

Blood, Harvey's conception of circulation of, nearly anticipated by Leonardo da Vinci, 120.

Boisguillebert, Pierre Le Pesant, sieur de, his "barometer of prosperity," 287.

Botany, studied by Leonardo da Vinci, 119.

Botticelli, Sandro, 56.

Bouguereau, G. A., 315 n.

Bovarism, explanation of, 335; applied to the Universe, 337; a necessary, effected by the artist, 348, 349.

Brantôme, Pierre de B., his style, 161.

Braun, Otto, 357.

Breton, Jules, 311.

Bridges, Robert, 272.

Browne, Sir Thomas, his style, 161, 175, 176, 178.

Browning, Robert, 113; too clumsy to influence others, 184.

Brunetière, Ferdinand, a narrow-minded pedagogue, 125.

Bruno, Giordano, 207.

Bruno, Leonardo, 207.

Bryce, James, on democracies, 300.

Bücher, Karl, on work and dance, 61, 62.

Buckle, H. T., 99.

Buddhist monks, 224 n.

Building, and dancing, the two primary arts, 36; birds' nests, the chief early form of, 36 n.

Bunyan, John, 79.

Burton, Robert, as regards his quotations, 152.

Bury, J. B., 287 n.

Cabanel, 315 n.

Cadiz, the dancing-school of Spain, 54.

Camargo, innovations of, in the ballet, 57.

Carlyle, Thomas, revelation of family history in his style, 158, 159; compared to Aristophanes, 159 n.; too clumsy to influence others, 184.

Carpenter, the, sacred position of, in some countries, 2.

Carr-Saunders, A. M., on the social ladder and the successful climbers, 299, 300; on selecting the best stock of humanity, 354.

Cassirer, Ernest, on Goethe, 137 n.

Castanets, 54.

Casuistry, 304 n., 305.

Categories, are fictions, 94.

Cathedrals, dancing in, 44, 45.

Ceremony, Chinese, 22, 29; and music, Chinese life regulated by, 24-26.

Cézanne, artist, 153, 315 n.

Chanties, of sailors, 61, 62.

Cheetham, Samuel, on the Pagan Mysteries, 241 n.

Chemistry, analogy of, to life, 33-35.

Chess, the Chinese game of, 23.

Chiaroscuro, method of, devised by Leonardo da Vinci, 117.

Chidley, Australian philosopher, 79-82.

China, finest thinkers of, perceived significance in life of conception of art, 3; art animates the whole of life in, 27, 28; beggary in, 31.

Chinese, the, the accounts of, 18-21; their poetry, 21, 22, 29, 32; their etiquette of politeness, 22; the quality of play in their character, 22-24; their life regulated by music and ceremony, 24-26, 29; their civilisation shows that life is art, 27, 28, 30; the æsthetic supremacy of, 28-30; endurance of their civilisation, 28, 30; their philosophic calm, 29 n.; decline in civilisation of, in last thousand years, 30; their pottery, 32, 33; embodiment of their symbol of the art of living, 33.

Chinese life, the art of balancing æsthetic temperament and guarding against its excesses, 29.

Choir, the word, 42.

Christian Church, supposed to have been originally a theatre, 42.

Christian ritual, the earliest known, a sacred dance, 42.

Christian worship, dancing in, 42-45; central function of, a sacred drama, 43.

Christianity, Lifuan art of living undermined by arrival of, 18; dancing in, 40-45; the ideas of, as dogmas, hypotheses, and fictions, 99; and the Pagan Mysteries, 242; and asceticism, 249 n.; the Hebrew mode of feeling grafted into, 276.

Chrysostom, on dancing at the Eucharist, 43.

Church, and religion, not the same, 228 n.

Church Congress, at Sheffield in 1922, ideas of conversion expressed at, 220 n.

Churches, 351.

Cicero, 73, 252.

Cinema, educational value of, 138.

Cistercian monks, 43.

Cistercians, the, 347.

Civilisation, develops with conscious adhesion to formal order, 172; standards for measurement of, 285; Niceforo's measurement of, 286; on meaning of, 287; the word, 288; the art of, includes three kinds of facts, 289; criminality as a measure of, 290, 291; creative genius and general instruction in connection with, 291–93; birth-rate as test of, 294; consumption of luxuries as test of, 294, 295; suicide rate as test of, 295; tests of, applied to France by Niceforo, 295–97; not an exclusive mass of benefits, but a mass of values, 297; becoming more complex, 298; small minority at the top of, 298; guidance of, assigned to lower stratum, 298, 299; art of eugenics necessary to save, 299, 300; of quantity and of quality, 300; not to be precisely measured, 301; the more rapidly it progresses, the sooner it dies, 301; an art, 301, 310; an estimate of its value possible, 302; meaning of Protagoras's dictum with relation to, 302; measured by standard of fine art (sculpture), 307, 308; eight periods of, 307, 308; a fresh race needed to produce new period of, 308; and culture, 309; æsthetic sense indispensable for, 345; possible break-up of, 358.

Clarity, as an element of style, 176–78.

Clichés, 149–51.

Cloisters, for artists, 358.

Cochez, of Louvain, on Plotinus, 249 *n.*

Coleridge, S. T., his "loud bassoon," 169; of the spectator type of the contemplative temperament, 332.

Colour-words, 164 *n.*

Colvin, Sir Sidney, on science and art, 70.

Commandments, tables of, 253, 255.

Communists, French, inspired by Shaftesbury, 269.

Community, the, 244.

Comte, J. A., 301.

Confucian morality, the, 29.

Confucianism, outward manifestation of Taoism, 26.

Confucius, consults Lao-tze, 25, 26.

Conrad, Joseph, his knowledge of the sea, 171.

Contemplation. *See* Æsthetic contemplation.

Convention, and Nature, Hippias makes distinction between, 5.

Conventions. *See* Traditions.

Conversion, a *questionnaire* on, 210 *n.*; the process of, 218; the fundamental fact of, 218, 218 *n.*; essential outlines of, have been obscured, 220 *n.*; Churchmen's ideas of, 220 *n.*; not the outcome of despair or a retrogression, 221, 222; nothing ascetic about it, 222; among the Greeks, 240; revelation of beauty sometimes comes by a process of, 328, 329.

Cooper, Anthony, 261.

Cornish, G. Warre, his article on "Greek Drama and the Dance," 56.

Cosmos. *See* Universe.

Courtship, dancing a process of, 46.

Cowper, William, 184; influence of Shaftesbury on, 266.

Craftsman, the, partakes of divine nature of creator of the world, 2.

Creation, not the whole of Man, 314.

Creative impulses. *See* Impulses.

Crime, an effort to get into step, 245 *n.*; defined, 290; natural, 290; evolutive social, 291.

Criminality, as a measure of civilisation, 290, 291.

Critics, of language, 141–51; difficulty of their task, 153 *n.*

Croce, Benedetto, his idea of art, 84; tends to move in verbal circles, 84; on judging a work of art, 153 *n.*; on mysticism and science, 191 *n.*; tends to fall into verbal abstraction, 324 *n.*; his idea of intuition, 232 *n.*, 320 *n.*; on the critic of art as a critic of life, 269; on art the deliverer, 318 *n.*; on union of æsthetic sense with artistic instinct, 350 *n.*

Croiset, Maurice, on Plotinus, 249 *n.*

Cromwell, Oliver, 272.

Cruz, Friar Gaspar de, on the Chinese, 31.

Culture, and civilisation, 309.

Curiosity, the sexual instinct a reaction to the stimulus of, 104, 112.

Custom, 245.

Cuvier, Georges, 181.

Cymbal, the, 53.

Dance, love, among insects, birds, and mammals, 45, 46; among savages, 46; has gained influence in the human world, 48; various forms of, 48, 49; the complete, 49, 50; the seductiveness of, 50; prejudice against, 50, 51; choral, Plotinus compares the moral life of the soul to, 251, 252.

Dance of Life, the, 66, 67.

Dancing, and building, the two primary acts, 36; possibly accounts for origin of birds' nests, 36 *n.*; supreme manifestation of physical life and supreme symbol of spiritual life, 36; the significance of, 37; the primitive expression of religion and of love, 37, 38, 45; entwined with human tradition of war, labour, pleasure, and education, 37; the expression of the whole man, 38, 39; rules the life of primitive men, 39 *n.*; religious importance of, among primitive men, 39, 40; connected with all religions, 40; ecstatic and pantomimic, 41, 42; survivals of, in religion, 42; in Christian worship, 42–45; in cathedrals, 44, 45; among birds and insects, 45; among mammals, 45, 46; a process of courtship and novitiate for love, 46, 47; double function of, 47; different forms of, 48–51; becomes an art, 51;

INDEX

professional, 52; Classic and Romantic, 52–60; the ballet, 53, 56–60; solo, 53; Egyptian and Gaditanian, 53, 54; Greek, 55, 56, 60; as morals, 60, 61, 63; all human work a kind of, 61, 62; and music, 61–63; social significance of, 60, 61, 63, 64; and war, allied, 63, 64; importance of, in education, 64, 65; Puritan attack on, 65; is life itself, 65; always felt to possess symbolic significance, 66; the learning of, a severe discipline, 277.

Dancing-school, the function of, process of courtship, 47.

D'Annunzio, Gabriele, 178.

Danse du ventre, the, 49 n.

Dante, 311, 349; dancing in his "Paradiso," 43; intellectual life of, largely guided by delight in beauty of rhythmic relation between law and instance, 73.

Darwin, Charles, 88; poet and artist, 128, 129; and St. Theresa, 198.

Darwin, Erasmus, 181.

David, Alexandra, his book, *Le Philosophe Meh-ti et l'Idée de Solidarité*, 26 n.

Decadence, of art of living, 8 n.; rigid subservience to rule a mark of, 173.

Degas, 315 n.

Democracies, the smallest, are highest, 300.

Demography, 285.

Demosthenes, 336.

De Quincey, Thomas, the music of his style, 164.

Descartes, René, on arts and sciences, 69; represents in France new impetus to sciences, 180; religious, though man of science, 208.

Design, the arts of, 36.

Devadasis, the, sacred dancing girls, 51, 52.

Diaghilev, 59.

Dickens, Charles, 311.

Dickinson, G. Lowes, his account of the Chinese, 20, 21; his account of Chinese poetry, 21, 22.

Diderot, Denis, wide-ranging interests of, 5; translated Shaftesbury, 268.

"Dieta Salutis," the, 43.

Discipline, definition of a, 71 n.

"Divine command," the, 255.

"Divine malice," of Nietzsche, 155 n.

Diving-bell, constructed by Leonardo da Vinci, 119.

Divorces, as test of civilisation, 296.

Doctor, and priest, originally one, 197 n., 203.

Dogma, hypothesis, and fiction, 98, 99.

Dogmas, shadows of personal experience, 217.

Dostoievsky, F. M., 311, 349; his master-piece, "*The Brothers Karamazov*," 135, 136.

Drama, Greek, origin of, 55, 56; the real Socrates possibly to be seen in, 78.

Driesch, Hans, on his own mental development, 216 n.

Drum, the influence of the, 63.

Dryden, John, 148.

Dujardin, Edouard, his story of Huysmans, 166; on Bergson's style, 177.

Dumont, Arsène, on civilisation, 298, 301.

Duncan, Isadora, 60.

Duprat, G. L., on morality, 34.

Dupréel, Professor, on Hippias, 6 n.; his *La Légende Socratique*, 82 n.; on the Protagorean spirit, 302 n.

Duty, 275, 276.

Easter, dancing of priests at, 44.

Eckhart, Meister, 234, 336.

Education, importance of dancing in, 64, 65; Einstein's views on, 137; and genius, as tests of civilisation, 291–93.

Egypt, ancient, dancing in, 42; Classical dancing originated in, 52; the most influential dancing-school of all time, 53; musical instruments associated with dancing, originated or developed in, 53; modern, dancing in, 54 n.; importance of its civilisation, 307.

Eight-hours day, the, 357.

Einstein, Albert, 2, 69 n., 72; substitutes new axioms for old, 95; casts doubts on Leonardo da Vinci's previsions of modern science, 120 n.; seems to have won a place beside Newton, 133; an imaginative artist, 134; his fondness for music, 134, 135; his other artistic likings and dislikings, 135, 136; an artist also in his work, 136; his views on science, 137; his views on education, 137, 138; on the motives that attract people to science and art, 138, 321; feels harmony of religion and science, 207; concerned with truth, 327; and "science for science's sake," 347 n.

Eleusinian Mysteries, the, 240–43.

Eliot, George, her knowledge of the life of country people, 171; Tolstoy's opinion of, 311.

Ellis, Havelock, childhood of, 210, 211; his period of emotional and intellectual expansion, 211; loses faith, 212; influence of Hinton's "*Life in Nature*" on, 215–18.

Els Cosiers, dancing company, 45.

Emerson, R. W., his style and that of Bacon, 161.

Emmanuel, his book on Greek dancing, 55.

Empathy, 66.

Engineering, professional, Leonardo da Vinci called the founder of, 118, 119.

English laws, 98.

English prose style, Cartesian influence on, 180 n.

English speech, licentiousness of, in the sixteenth century, 148; the best literary prose, 155, 156.

Enjoyment, without possession, 343–46.

Epictetus, 249 n.

Epicurus, 207.

Erosian, river, importance of, realised by Leonardo da Vinci, 120.

Eskimos, 255.

Este, Isabella d', 123.

Ethics, and æsthetics, among the Greeks, 247.

Etruscans, the, 56, 308.

Eucharist, dancing at the, 43.

Eucken, Rudolf, on Shaftesbury, 271.

Eugenics, art of, necessary for preservation of civilisation, 299; Galton the founder of the modern scientific art of, 353; assertion of principle of, by Jesus, 355, 356; question of raising quality of population by process of, 358.

Eusebius, on the worship of the Therapeuts, 42.

Evans, Sir Arthur, 112.

Evolution, theory of, 88, 104; a process of sifting, 355; and devolution, 355; social, 357, 358.

Existence, totality of, Hippias's supreme ideal, 6.

Existing, and thinking, on two different planes, 101.

"Expression," 324.

Facts, in the art of civilisation, material, intellectual, and moral (with political), 289.

Fandango, the, 50.

Faraday, Michael, characteristics of, trust in facts and imagination, 130–32; his science and his mysticism, 208.

Farnell, L. R., on religion and science, 197 n.

Farrer, Reginald, on the philosophic calm of the Chinese, 29 n.

Faure, Élie, his conception of Napoleon, 10; on Greek art, 76 n.; has faith in educational value of cinema, 137; on knowledge and desire, 154; on the Greek spirit, 292 n.

Ferrero, Guglielmo, on the art impulse and the sexual instinct, 109.

Fiction, germs of doctrine of, in Kant, 87; first expression of doctrine of, found in Schiller, 89; doctrine of, in F. A. Lange's History of Materialism, 93; Vaihinger's doctrine of, 94–103; hypothesis, and dogma, 98, 99; of Bovarism, 335, 336; character constituted by process of, 336.

Fictions, the variety of, 94–100; the value of, 96, 97; summatory, 98; scientific and æsthetic, 102; may always be changed, 103; good and bad, 103.

Fiji, dancing at, 49.

Fijians, the, 13 n.

Fine arts, the, 70; civilisation measured by standard of, 307; not to be pursued for useful end outside themselves, 322.

Fireworks, 22, 23.

Flaubert, Gustave, is personal, 144; sought to be most objective of artists, 182.

Flowers, the attitude of the poet toward, 168, 169.

Flying-machines, 72 n.; designed by Leonardo da Vinci, 119.

Foch, Ferdinand, quoted, 103.

Fokine, 59.

Folk-dances, 62.

Force, a fiction, 96.

Fossils, significance of, discovered by Leonardo da Vinci, 120.

Fox, George, 237.

France, tests of civilization applied to, by Niceforo, 295–97.

Francis of Assisi, 237.

Franck, César, mysticism in music of, 237.

Frazer, J. G., on magic and science, 195, 196.

Freedom, a fiction, 100.

French ballet, the, 57, 58.

French speech, its course, 148, 149.

Freud, Sigmund, 111, 318 n.; regards dreaming as fiction, 103; on the probability of the disappearance of religion, 228 n.

Frobisher, Sir Martin, his spelling, 173, 174.

Galen, 120.

Galton, Francis, a man of science and an artist, 126–28; founder of the modern scientific art of eugenics, 353; and Jesus's assertion of the principle of eugenics, 356.

Games, the liking of the Chinese for, 23.

Gaultier, Jules de, 330 n.; on Buddhist monks, 224 n.; on pain and pleasure in life, 278 n.; on morality and reason, 281; on morality and art, 284; on the antinomy between morals and morality, 319; on beauty, 327; on life as a spectacle, 333; the Bovarism of, 335–37; his philosophic descent, 337; applies Bovarism to the Universe, 337; his philosophy seems to be in harmony with physics, 338; the place of morality, religion, and law in his system, 338–40; place of the æsthetic instinct in his system, 341, 343–45; system of, compared with Russell's, 342, 343; im-

INDEX

portance of development of æsthetic sense to, 345; and the idea of pure art, 346, 347; considers æsthetic sense mixed in manifestations of life, 349, 350; had predilection for middle class, 356, 357; sees no cause for despair in break-up of civilisation, 358.

Gauss, C. F., religious, though man of science, 208.

Genesis, Book of, the fashioning of the cosmos in, 1, 314.

Genius, the birth of, 109; and education, as tests, of civilisation, 291-93; of country, and temper of the population, 292, 293.

Geology, founded by Leonardo da Vinci, 120.

Geometry, Protagoras's studies in, 3; a science or art, 68.

Gibbon, Edward, 162.

Gide, André, 322.

Gizycki, Georg von, on Shaftesbury, 260, 267.

God, a fiction, 100, 337.

Goethe, J. W., 342; representative of ideal of totality of existence, 6; called architecture "frozen music," 135; his power of intuition, 137; his studies in mathematical physics, 137 n.; use of word "stamped" of certain phrases, 149; mistook birds, 168; felt harmony of religion and science, 207; and Schiller and Humboldt, 275.

Gomperz, Theodor, his *Greek Thinkers*, 4, 5, 6 n., 75, 78.

Goncourt, Jules de, his style, 182, 183.

Goncourts, the, 183.

Good, the, and beauty, among the Greeks, 247.

Goodness, and sweetness, in Shaftesbury's philosophy, 262; and sweetness, originally the same, 263; moral, originally expressed in terms of taste, 263.

Gorgias, 302.

Gourmont, Remy de, 65; his remark about pleasure, 24; on personality, 144; on style, 177; on civilisation, 298; on the Jesuits, 304, 305; on beauty, 315; on art and morality, 321; on sociological function of art, 323.

Government, as art, 3.

Grace, an element of style in writing, 155, 156.

Grammar, Protagoras the initiator of modern, 4; a science or art, 68; writing not made by the laws of, 172, 173.

Grammarian, the, the formulator, not the lawgiver, of usage, 148.

Great Wall of China, the, 28.

Great War, the, 339.

Greece, ancient, genius built upon basis of slavery in, 292; the spirit of, 292.

Greek art, 76 n.

Greek dancing, 55, 56, 60.

Greek drama, 55, 56, 78.

Greek morality, an artistic balance of light and shade, 260.

Greek speech, the best literary prose, 155.

Greek spirit, the, 76 n.

Greeks, attitude of thinkers of, on life as art, 3, 247-53; the pottery of, 32; importance of dancing and music in organisation of some states of, 64; books on, written by barbarians, 76 n.; mysticism of, 205-07, 240-43; spheres of ethics and æsthetics not distinguished among, 247; had a kind of æsthetic morality, 316-18; recognised destruction of ethical and intellectual virtues, 330; a small minority of abnormal persons among, 353 n.

Greenslet, Ferris, on the Cartesian influence on English prose style, 180 n.

Groos, Karl, his "the play of inner imitation," 66; has developed æsthetic side of *miterleben*, 332.

Grosse, on the social significance of dancing, 63, 64.

Grote, George, his chapter on Socrates, 76.

Grotius, Hugo, 261.

Guitar, the, an Egyptian instrument, 53.

Gumplowicz, Ludwig, on civilisation, 301.

Gunpowder, use made of, by Chinese, 22, 23.

Guyau, insisted on sociological function of art, 323, 324; believes that poets and artists will be priests of social religion without dogmas, 349, 350.

Gypsies, possible origin of the name "Egyptians" as applied to them, 54 n.

Hadfield, Emma, her account of the life of the natives of the Loyalty Islands, 13-18.

Hakluyt, Richard, 143; his picture of Chinese life, 19.

Hall, Stanley, on importance of dancing, 64, 65; on the beauty of virtue, 270 n.

Handel, G. F., 62.

Handwriting, partly a matter of individual instinct, 156, 157; the complexity and mystery enwrapping, 157; resemblances in, among members of the same family, 157, 158; atavism in, 157, 158.

Hang-Chau, 20.

Hardy, Thomas, his lyrics, 170 n.; his sensitivity to the sounds of Nature, 171; his genius unquestioned, 187 n.

Hawaii, dancing in, 51.

Hawthorne, Nathaniel, his style, 161.

Hebrews, their conception of the fashioning of the universe, 1; ancient, their priests and their prophets, 203; never conceived of the art of morals, 253; were no æsthetic intuitionists, 276.

Hegel, G. W. F., 90; poetic quality of his philosophy, 84; his attempt to transform subjective processes into objective world-processes, 101.

Heine, Heinrich, 155 n.

Hellenism, the revivalists of, 271.

Helmholtz, H. L. F., science and art in, 72.

Hemelverdeghem, Salome on Cathedral at, 49 n.

Heraclitus, 74.

Herder, J. G. von, his *Ideen zur Geschichte der Menschheit*, 88; inspired by Shaftesbury, 268.

Heredity, in handwriting, 157, 158; in style, 158–61, 190; tradition the corporeal embodiment of, 161.

Hincks, Marcella Azra, on the art of dancing in Japan, 42 n.

Hindu dance, 41.

Hinton, James, on thinking as an art, 86 n.; on the arts, 111; the universe according to, 215, 216; Ellis's copy of his book, 220; on pleasure and pain in the art of life, 278; on methods of arts and moral action, 281, 282.

Hippias, 302; significance of his ideas, in conception of life as an art, 4–6; his ideal, 4, 6; the Great Logician, 6 n.

Hobbes, Thomas, on space, 95; his dictum *Homo homini lupus*, 262.

Hodgson, Shadworth, 289.

Hoffman, Bernhard, his *Guide to the Bird-World*, 168.

Horace, the popularity of, in modern times, 92.

Hovelaque, Émile, on the Chinese, 27, 28.

Howell, James, his "Familiar Letters," 184.

Hugo, Victor, 149, 311.

Hula dance, the, 51.

Humboldt, Wilhelm von, 275.

Hume, David, took up fictional point of view, 96; recognised Shaftesbury, 267; influenced by Hutcheson, 275.

Hunt, Leigh, sensitively acute critic of Keats, 167.

Hunter, John, 181.

Hutcheson, Francis, æsthetic moralist, 251; came out of Calvinistic Puritanism, 266; one of the founders of æsthetics, 271, 326 n.; wrote the first modern treatise on æsthetics, 271; represented reaction against Puritanism, 271; Shaftesbury's ideas as developed by, 273; his use of the term "moral sense," 273, 274; his impressive personality, 274; philosophy was art of living to, 274, 275; inconsistent, 314; on distinction between art and æsthetics, 326 n.;

his idea of the æsthetic and the moral emotion, 327 n.

Huysmans, J. K., his vocabulary, 165; at Wagner concert, 166; fascinated by concert programmes, 166, 167.

"Hymn of Jesus," the, 42.

Hypothesis, dogma, and fiction, 98, 99.

I and *me*, 147.

Idealisation, in adolescence, 107, 108.

Idealism, 83.

Idealists, 70, 341 n.

Ideals, are fictions, 100.

Imagination, a constitutive part of thinking, 102; man lives by, 102; guarded by judgment and principles, 130–32; part performed by, in morals, 272; and the æsthetic instinct, 344.

Imbeciles, 352–55.

Imitation, in the productions of young writers, 164.

Immoral, significance of the word, 246.

Immortality, a fiction, 100.

Impulses, creative and possessive, 306, 307, 341–43.

Inclination, 275.

India, dancing in, 51, 52; the Todas of, 203 n.

Indians, American, religious dances among, 40, 42.

Infanticide, 255, 354.

Infinite, the, a fiction, 95.

Infinitive, the split, 145–47.

Inge, Dean, on Plotinus, 223 n., 249 n.; on Pagan Mysteries, 241 n.

Innate ideas, 274.

Insects, dancing among, 45.

Instinct, the part it plays in style, 163; imitation a part of, 164; and tradition, mould morals, 254–59; the possessive, 338–40, 344, 345, 351, see Possessive instinct; the æsthetic, 341, 343–46, 350, see Æsthetic instinct.

Instincts, 234, 235.

Intelligence, the sphere of, 233, 234.

Intuition, the starting point of science, 137; meaning of, 232 n.; of the man of genius, 320.

Intuitionism, æsthetic, 260, 276, 279, 314.

Intuitionists, the, 232–34.

Invention, necessary in science, 137.

Invincible ignorance, doctrine of, 304.

Irony, Socratic, 78, 83.

Irrationalism, of Vaihinger, 90.

Isocrates, on beauty and virtue, 247.

Italy, Romantic dancing originated in, 53, 56; the ballet in, 56–58.

Jansenists, the, 303.

Japan, dancing in, 42, 49.

Java, dancing in, 49.

Jehovah, in the Book of Genesis, 1.

Jeremiah, the prophet, his voice and instrument, 178, 179.

Jeres, cathedral of, dancing in, 44.

Jesuits, the, 303-05.

Jesus, and Napoleon, 10, 11; and the Platonic Socrates, 82, 83; asserts principle of eugenics, 353, 356; and Plato, 356.

Joël, Karl, on the Xenophontic Socrates, 78; on the evolution of the Greek philosophic spirit, 206.

John of the Cross, 237.

Johnson, Samuel, the pedantry of, 156; Latin-French element in, 162; his idea of "matter," 230.

Johnston, Sir H. H., on the dancing of the Pygmies, 51.

Jones, Dr. Bence, biographer of Faraday, 130.

Jonson, Ben, 184.

Joyce, James, 172, 184; his Ulysses, 185, 186.

Kant, Immanuel, 89; germs of the doctrine of the "as if" in, 87; his idea of the art of morals, 253, 254; influenced by Shaftesbury, 253, 254, 266; anecdote about, 257 n., 276; rationalises morality, 281.

Keats, John, concerned with beautiful words in "The Eve of St. Agnes," 167.

Kepler, Johann, his imagination and his accuracy in calculation, 132, 133.

Keyserling, Count Hermann, his Philosophie als Kunst, 83 n.

"Knowing," analysis of, 70, 71.

Kolbe, Rev. Dr., illustrates æsthetic view of morals, 276 n.

Lamb, Charles, 184.

Landor, W. S., 149; on vulgarisms in language, 151 n.; on the poet and poetry, 154, 172; on style, 163.

Lange, F. A., his The History of Materialism, 73 n., 83; sets forth conception of philosophy as poetic art, 83; the Neo-Kantism of, 87; his influence on Vaihinger, 92, 93.

Language, critics of present-day, 141-51; of our forefathers and of to-day, 143; things we are told to avoid in, 145-51; is imagery and metaphor, 165; reaction of thought on, 179-81; progress in, due to flexibility and intimacy, 183.

Languages, the Yo-heave-ho theory of, 61.

Lankester, Sir E. Ray, 70.

Lao-tze, and Confucius, 25, 26; the earliest of the great mystics, 204; harmony of religion and science in his work, 204, 205.

Law, a restraint placed upon the possessive instinct, 339, 340; to be re-

placed by æsthetic instinct, 340, 341.

Laycock, on handwriting, 158 n.

Leibnitz, Baron S. W. von, 6 n.; on space, 95; on music, 135; admired Shaftesbury, 268.

"L'Esprit Nouveau," 179.

Libby, F., on Shaftesbury, 273.

Lie, Jonas, 163.

Life, more difficult to realise it as an art than to act it so, 1, 2; as art, view of highest thinkers of China and Greece on, 2-6, 247-52; ideal of totality of, 6; art of, has been decadent during last two thousand years, 8 n.; of the Loyalty Islanders, 13-18; the Lifuan art of, 13-18; the Chinese art of, 27, 28; Chinese civilization proves that it is art, 30; embodiment of the Chinese symbol of the art of, 33; identical with art, 33-35; the art of, a dance, 66, 67; mechanistic explanation of, 216; viewed in its moral aspect, 244; the moralist the critic of the art of, 247; as art, attitude of Romans toward, 252; as art, attitude of Hebrews toward, 253; the art of, both pain and pleasure in, 277, 278; as art, a conception approved by men of high character, 278, 279; not to be precisely measured by statistics, 302; as a spectacle, 333, 334.

Lifu. See Loyalty Islands.

Lifuans, the, the art of living of, 13-18.

Limoges, 44.

Linnæan system, the, a fiction, 99.

Liszt, Franz, 329.

Livingstone, David, 38.

Locke, John, and Shaftesbury, 261, 262.

Locomotive, the, 72 n.

Lodge, Sir Oliver, his attempt to study religion, 201.

Logic, a science or art, 68; and fiction, 94; of thought, inescapable, 183.

Loret, on dancing, 54 n.

Love, dancing the primitive expression of, 37, 45; curiosity one of the main elements of, 112.

Love-dance, 45-51. See Dance, Dancing.

Loyalty Islands, the, customs of the natives of, 13-18.

Lucian, 353 n.; on dancing, 40, 45.

Lucretius, 207.

Lull, Ramon, 237.

Lulli, J. B., brought women into the ballet, 57.

Luxuries, consumption of, as test of civilisation, 294-97.

Machinery of life, 216.

Madagascar, dancing in, 49.

Magic, relation of, to science and religion, 193-96.

Magna Carta, 98.

Malherbe, François de, 148.

Mallarmé, Stéphane, music the voice of the world to, 166.

Mallorca, dancing in church in, 44, 45.

Mammals, dancing among, 45, 46.

Man, has found it more difficult to conceive life as an art than to act it so, 1; his conception less that of an artist, as time went on, 2; in Protagoras's philosophy, 3, 4, 302; ceremony and music, his external and internal life, 25; added to Nature, 153; has passed through stages of magic, religion, and science, 196; an artist of his own life, 271; is an artist, 310; as artist and as æsthetician, 314; becomes the greatest force in Nature, 339; practices adopted by, to maintain selection of best stock, 354.

Mandeville, Sir John, on Shaftesbury, 262.

Manet, 311.

Marco Polo, his picture of Chinese life, 19, 20; noticed absence of beggars in China, 31; on public baths in China, 32.

Marett, on magic and science, 195.

Marlowe, Christopher, 170, 184.

Marquesans, the, 13 n.

Marriott, Charles, on the union of æsthetic sense with artistic instinct, 350 n.

Martial, 54.

Mass, dancing in ritual of, 43–45; analogy of Pagan Mysteries to, 242.

Master of Arts, 69.

Materialism, 97, 230.

Materialistic, the term, 229.

Mathematical Renaissance, the, 69.

Mathematics, false ideas in, 94, 95; and art, 138–40.

Matter, a fiction, 97, 229, 338; and spirit, 229, 230.

Maupassant, Guy de, 311.

McDougall, William, accepts magic as origin of science, 195; his criticism of the "moral sense," 274 n.; his study of civilisation, 298; on birth-rate, 298 n.

Me and I, 147.

Mead, G. R., his article The Sacred Dance of Jesus, 44.

Measurement, Protagoras's saying concerning, 3, 302.

Mechanics, beginning of science of, 74; theories of, studied by Leonardo da Vinci, 120.

Medici, Catherine de', brought Italian ballet to Paris, 57.

Medicine, and religion, 197 n., 203.

Medicine-man, the, 192–95.

Meh-ti, Chinese philosopher, 26, 27.

Men, of to-day and of former days, their comparative height, 142.

"Men of science," 125, 126. See Scientist.

Meteorological Bureau, the, 203.

Metre, poetic, arising out of work, 62.

Michelangelo, 311.

Milan, the ballet in, 58.

Mill, J. S., on science and art, 70; criticism of Bentham, 99.

Millet, J. F., 311.

Milton, John, his misuse of the word "eglantine," 169; Tolstoy's opinion of, 311.

Mirandola, Pico della, 6 n.

Mittag-Lefler, Gustav, on mathematics, 139.

Möbius, Paul Julius, German psychologist, 109.

Moissac, Salome capital in, 49 n.

Montaigne, M. E. de, his style flexible and various, 148; his quotations moulded to the pattern of his own mind, 152; his style and that of Renan, 161; the originality of his style found in vocabulary, 165.

Montesquieu, Baron de, his admiration for Shaftesbury, 268; on the evils of civilisation, 297.

Moral, significance of the term, 246.

Moral maxims, 254, 258.

Moral reformer, the, 282.

"Moral sense," the term as used by Hutcheson and Shaftesbury, 273, 274; in McDougall's Social Psychology, 274 n.

Moral teaching, 246 n.

Moral World-Order, the, a fiction, 100.

Morand, Paul, 170 n.

Moreau, Gustave, 167.

Morgagni, G. B., 300.

Morris, William, 350 n.

Moses, 253, 282.

Moszkowski, Alexander, his book on Einstein, 134 n.

Moralist, the critic of the art of life, 247.

Morality, Greek, an artistic balance of light and shade, 260; a matter of taste, 263; the æsthetic quality of, evidenced by language, 263, 264; Shaftesbury's views on, 264–66; the influence of Shaftesbury on our modern, 266, 267; imagination in, 272; instinctive, according to Hutcheson, 274; conception of, as an art, does not lack seriousness, 276; the æsthetic view of, advocated by Catholics, 276 n.; the æsthetic view of, repugnant to two classes of minds, 280–82; indefiniteness of criterion of, an advantage, 282, 283; justification of æsthetic conception of, 283, 284; flexible and inflexible, illustrated by Jesuits and Pascal, 303–05; art the reality of, 314; æsthetic, of the Greeks, 316–18; the antinomy between morals and, 319; a restraint placed upon the possessive instinct, 338–40; to be replaced by æsthetic instinct, 340, 341; æsthetic instinct has the character of, 346.

Morals, dancing as, 61, 63, 66; books on, 244; defined, 245; means *custom*, 245; Plotinus's conception of, 250–52; as art, views of the Greeks and the Romans on, differ, 252. Hebrews never conceived of the art of, 253; as art, modern conception of, 253; the modern feeling about, is Jewish and Roman, 253; Kant's idea of the art of, 253, 254; formed by instinct, tradition and reason, 254–59; Greek, have come to modern world through Shaftesbury, 267; the æsthetic attitude possible for spectator of, 270; art and æsthetics to be kept apart in, 314, 315, 325–28; a species of the genus art, 316; the antinomy between morality and, 319; philosophers have failed to see that it is an art, 324.

Morisco, the, 49 *n.*

Mozart, Wolfgang, his interest in dancing, 62.

Müller-Freienfels, Richard, two kinds of æsthetic contemplation defined by, 331.

Multatuli, quoted on the source of curiosity, 112.

Music, and ceremony, 24–26; and acting, and poetry, 36; and singing, and dancing, their relation, 62; a science or art, 68; discovery of Pythagoras in, 74; philosophy the noblest and best, 81 *n.*; the most abstract, the most nearly mathematical of the arts, 135; of style, 163, 164; of philosophy and religion, 179.

Musical forms, evolved from similar dances, 62.

Musical instruments, 53, 54.

Musset, Alfred de, his *Confession d'un Enfant du Siècle*, 144.

Mysteries, the Eleusinian, 240–43.

Mystic, the genuine, 202; Lao-tze, the earliest great, 204.

Mystics, the great, 236, 237.

Mysticism, the right use and the abuse of the word, 191; and science, supposed difference between, 191–203; what is meant by, 192; and science, the harmony of, as revealed in human history, 203–08; of the Greeks, 205–07, 240–43; and science, the harmony of, as supported by personal experience of Havelock Ellis, 209–18; and science, how they came to be considered out of harmony, 226–35; and science, harmony of, summary of considerations confirming, 235, 236; the key to much that is precious in art and Nature in, 237, 238; is not science, 238–40; æsthetics on same plane as, 330 *n. See* Religion.

Napoleon, described as unmitigated scoundrel by H. G. Wells, 8–10; described as lyric artist by Élie Faure, 10.

Nature, and convention, Hippias made distinction between, 5; comes through an atmosphere which is the emanation of supreme artists, 166; the attitude of the poet in the face of, 168, 169; the object of Leonardo da Vinci's searchings, 114, 117, 125; Man added to, 153; communion with, 227; in Shaftesbury's system, 265; and art, 312, 313.

Neo-Platonists, the, 237; asceticism in, 249 *n.*

Nests, birds', and dancing, 36 *n.*

Newell, W. W., 41 *n.*

Newman, Cardinal J. H., the music of his style, 164.

Newton, Sir Isaac, his wonderful imagination, 72; his force of attraction a summatory fiction, 98; represents in England new impetus to sciences, 180; his attempt to study religion, 199–201; religious, though a man of science, 208.

Niceforo, Alfred, his measurement of civilisation, 286, 293, 297; tests of civilisation applied to France by, 295–97.

Nietzsche, Friedrich, 111; conceived the art of life as a dance, 66, 67; poetic quality of his philosophy, 84; Vaihinger's opinion of, 94; on Leonardo da Vinci, 115; the "divine malice" of, 155 *n.*; laboured at his prose, 182; demolished D. F. Strauss's ideas, 215; on learning to dance, 277; his gospel of taste, 280; on the Sophists, 302 *n.*; on art as the great stimulus of life, 322, 323; on the world as a spectacle, 334, 335; moved by the "masculine protest," 336; Jesus reproached by, 355.

Novelists, their reservoirs of knowledge, 171.

Noverre, and the ballet, 57.

Ockham, William of, 96.

Old Testament, the, and the conception of morality as an art, 276. *See* Bible, Genesis.

Omahas, the, 46.

Onions, C. T., 146 *n.*

Optimism, and pessimism, 90–92.

Origen, on the dancing of the stars, 43.

Orpheus, fable of, 61.

Osler, Sir William, 72.

Pacific, the, creation as conceived in, 2; dancing in, 49. *See* Lifuans.

Pain, and pleasure, united, 278.

Painting, Chinese, 29, 32; and sculpture, and the arts of design, 36; of Leonardo da Vinci, 113, 114, 117, 118.

Palante, Georges, 337 *n.*

Paley, William, 267.

Palladius, 358.

Pantomime, and pantomimic dancing, 41, 42, 49, 56.

Papuans, the, are artistic, 351 *n.*

Parachute, constructed by Leonardo da Vinci, 119.

Paris, dancing in choir in, 44; the ballet at, 57.

Parker, Professor E. H., his book *China: Past and Present*, 23 *n.*; his view of Chinese vermin and dirt, 31, 32.

Parks, 351.

Parmelee, Maurice, his *Criminology*, 291 *n.*

Parsons, Professor, 142.

Pascal, Blaise, and the Jesuits, 303, 304.

Pater, W. H., the music of his style, 164.

Pattison, Pringle, his definition of mysticism, 192 *n.*

Paul, Vincent de, his moral attitude, 279, 280.

Paulhan, on morality, 284.

Pell, E. C., on decreasing birth-rate, 294 *n.*

Pepys, Samuel, the accomplishment of his "Diary," 176.

Perera, Galeotto, his picture of Chinese life, 19; noticed absence of beggars in China, 31.

Pericles, 289.

Personality, 144.

Pessimism, and optimism, 90–92.

Petrie, Dr. W. M. Flinders, his attempt to measure civilisation by standard of sculpture, 307, 308.

Peyron, traveller, 50.

Phenomenalism, Protagoras the father of, 3.

Philosopher, the primitive, usually concluded that the universe was a work of art, 1; a creative artist, 72, 73, 85; curiosity the stimulus of, 104, 105.

Philosophy, of the Chinese, 32; solution of the conflicts of, in art, 82, 83; and art, close relationship of, 83–85; and poetry, 83, 85; is music, 179.

Physics, and fiction, 95.

Pictures, revelation of beauty in, 328, 329; should be looked at in silence, 329 *n.*

Pindar, calls Hellas "the land of lovely dancing," 55.

Planck, Max, physicist, 136.

Plato, Protagoras calumniated by, 3; made fun of Hippias, 4; his description of a good education, 64; a creative artist, 73; his picture of Socrates, 75, 78; the biographies of, 76, 77; his irony, 78, 83; a marvellous artist, 82; a supreme artist in philosophy, 83; a supreme dramatist, 83; his "Ideas"

and the "As-If world," 88; the myths, as fictions, hypotheses, and dogmas, 99; represents the acme of literary prose speech, 155; and Plotinus, 222; on the Mysteries, 242; asceticism, traced in, 249 *n.*; on justice, 289; his ideal of wise moderation addressed to an immoderate people, 292; Sophists caricatured by, 302; his "guardians," 306; the ultrapuritanical attitude of, 317, 318 *n.*; and Bovarism, 336; on the value of sight, 345 *n.*; wished to do away with imaginative literature, 353 *n.*; and Jesus, 356.

Pleasure, a human creation, 24; and pain, united, 278.

Pliny, 353 *n.*

Plotinus, 222; Greek moral spirit reflected in, 249; his doctrine of Beauty, 250, 251; his idea that the moral life of the soul is a dance, 251, 252; his simile of the sculptor, 276 *n.*; founder of æsthetics in the philosophic sense, 329; recognised three aspects of the Absolute, 330; insisted on contemplation, 330 *n.*, 331; of the participating contemplative temperament, 332.

Poet, the type of all thinkers, 102; Landor on, 154; his attitude in the presence of Nature, 168, 169; the great, does not describe Nature minutely, but uses his knowledge of, 170, 171.

Poetry, Chinese, 21, 22, 29, 32; and music, and acting, 36; and dancing, 56; and philosophy, 83, 85; and science, no sharp boundary between, 102, 128, 129; Landor on, 154; a *making*, 312; Aristotle's view of, 318; does not exist for morals, 318.

Polka, origin of the, 60.

Polynesia, dancing in, 49.

Polynesian islanders, 255.

Pontiff, the Bridge-Builder, 2.

Pope, Alexander, influence of Shaftesbury on, 266.

Porphyry, 167.

Possessive impulses, 306, 307, 341–43.

Possessive instinct, restraints placed upon, 338–40; in Gaultier and Russell, 344; excesses of, 351.

Pottery, of the Chinese, 32, 33; of the Greeks and the Minoan predecessors of the Greeks, 32.

Pound, Miss, on the origin of the ballad, 62 *n.*

Pragmatism, 323.

Pragmatists, the, 93, 231, 232.

Precious stones, attitude of the poet toward, 169.

Preposition, the post-habited, 146, 147, 162.

Prettiness, and beauty, 315 *n.*

Priest, cultivated science in form of

magic, 195; and doctor, originally one, 197 n., 203.

Prodicus, 302; the Great Moralist, 6 n.

Progress, 143, 149; on meaning of, 287.

Prophecy, 204.

Prophet, meaning of the word, 203, 204.

Propriety, 24–26.

Protagoras, significance of his ideas, in conception of life as an art, 3, 4; his interest for us to-day, 3; his dictum "Man is the measure of all things," 3, 302; concerned to regard living as an art, 248.

Proust, Marcel, 172, 184; his art, 170 n., 186, 187; his *A la Recherche du Temps Perdu*, 171, 187; admiration of, for Ruskin, 316 n.

Puberty, questions arising at time of, 105–07.

Puritanism, reaction against, represented by Hutcheson, 271.

Pygmalionism, 353 n.

Pygmies, the dancing of the, 51.

Pythagoras, represents the beginning of science, 73, 74; fundamentally an artist, 74, 75; founded religious brotherhoods, 206, 207.

Quatelet, on social questions, ^88.

Quoting, by writers, 152.

Rabbitism, 294.

Rabelais, François, 148, 165, 358.

Race mixture, 308.

Raleigh, Sir Walter, his literary style, 143.

Ramedjenis, the, street dancers, 52.

Rank, Dr. Otto, his essay on the artist, 111.

Realism, 83.

Realists, 70, 341 n.

Reality, a flux of happening, 101.

Reason, helps to mould morals, 255–59.

Reid, Thomas, influenced by Hutcheson, 275.

Relativism, Protagoras the father of, 3.

Religion, as the desire for the salvation of the soul, 8; origin of dance in, 38; connection of dance with, among primitive men, 39; in music, 179; and science, supposed difference between, 191–203; its quintessential core, 191; control of Nature through oneness with Nature, at the heart of, 194; relation of, to science and magic, 194–96; the man of, studying science, 202; and science, the harmony of, as revealed in human history, 203–08; and science, the harmony of, as supported by personal experience of Havelock Ellis, 209–18; asceticism has nothing to do with normal, 222; and science, how they came to be considered out of harmony,

226–35; the burden of the traditions of, 227; and church, not the same, 228 n.; the instinct of, 234; and science, harmony of, summary of considerations confirming, 235, 236; is not science, 238–40; an act, 243; a restraint placed upon the possessive instinct, 339, 340; to be replaced by æsthetic instinct, 340, 341. *See* Mysticism.

Religions, in every case originally salatory, 40.

Religious dances, ecstatic and pantomimic, 41; survivals of, 42; in Christianity, 42–45.

Renan, J. E., his style, 161; his *Life of Jesus*, 212; on truth, 301.

"Resident in Peking, A," author of *China as it Really Is*, 21, 22.

Revelation, Book of, 153.

Revival, the, 241, 243.

Rhythm, marks all the physical and spiritual manifestations of life, 37; in work, 61.

Rickert, H., his twofold division of Reality, 325, 326.

Ridgeway, William, his theory of origin of tragedy, 56.

Roberts, Morley, ironical over certain "men of science," 126 n.

Robinson, Dr. Louis, on apes and dancing, 46; on the influence of the drum, 63.

Rodó, his conceptions those of Shaftesbury, 269.

Roman law, 98.

Romans, the ancient, dancing and war allied among, 63, 64; did not believe that living is an art, 252.

Romantic spirit, the, 206.

Romantics, the, 149, 156.

Rome, ancient, dancing in, 49; genius built upon basis of slavery in, 292.

Rops, Félicien, 167.

Ross, Robert, 150.

Rouen Cathedral, Salome on portal of, 49 n.

Rousseau, J. J., Napoleon before grave of, 11; felt his lapses, 79; grace of, 149; love of Nature developed through, 238; and Shaftesbury, 268, 269; decided against civilisation, 298.

Roussillon, 44.

Rule, rigid subserviency to, mark of decadence, 173; much lost by rigid adherence to, in style, 175.

Rules for Compositors and Readers, on spelling, Oxford University Press, 174 n.

Ruskin, John, 316; a God-intoxicated man, 316 n.

Russell, Bertrand, on the Chinese, 23; on mathematics, 139, 140; on the creative and the possessive impulses, 305–07,

341, 342; system of, compared with Gaultier's, 342, 343.

Russia, the genius of, compared with the temper of the population, 293.

Russian ballet, the, 58–60.

Rutherford, Sir Ernest, on the atomic constitution, 97 n.

St. Augustine, 79, 202; on the art of living well, 252.

St. Basil, on the dancing of the angels, 43.

St. Bonaventura, said to have been author of "Dieta Salutis," 43.

St. Denis, Ruth, 60.

St. Theresa, and Darwin, 198, 199.

Salome, the dance of, 49.

Salt, intellectual and moral suggestion of the word, 263, 263 n., 264.

Salt, Mr., 169.

Salter, W. M., his Nietzsche the Thinker, 335 n.

Samoa, sacred position of carpenter in, 2.

Sand, George, on civilisation, 300.

Santayana, Professor George, on union of æsthetic sense with artistic instinct, 350 n.

Schelling, F. W. J. von, 90; on philosophy and poetry, 83.

Schiller, Friedrich von, influence on Vaihinger, 89; and the æsthetic conception of morals, 275.

Schleiermacher, Friedrich, 90.

Schmidt, Dr. Raymund, 93 n.

Schopenhauer, Arthur, 330 n.; his influence on Vaihinger, 90; as regards his quotations, 152; morals based on sympathy, according to, 272; on the uselessness of art, 319; on the man of genius, 320; on sociological function of art, 323; on the proper way of looking at pictures, 329 n.; on the world as a spectacle, 334.

Science, spirit of modern, in Protagoras, 4; as the search for the reason of things, 8; and poetry, no sharp boundary between, 102, 128, 129; impulse to, and the sexual instinct, 112; intuition and invention needed by, 137; and mysticism, supposed difference between, 191–203; what is meant by, 192; and art, no distinction between, in classic times, 68; and art, distinction between, in modern times, 68–70; definitions of, 70, 71; is of the nature of art, 71; the imaginative application of, 72; Pythagoras represents the beginning of, 74; control of Nature through oneness with Nature, at the heart of, 194; relation of, to magic and religion, 194–96; and pseudo-science, 199–202; and mysticism, the harmony of, as revealed in human history, 203–08; and mysticism, the harmony of,

as supported by personal experience of Havelock Ellis, 209–18; and mysticism, how they came to be considered out of harmony, 226–35; traditions of, 228; the instinct of, 234; and mysticism, harmony of, summary of considerations confirming, 235, 236; is not religion, 238–40; not pursued for useful ends, 322; for science's sake, 347.

Sciences, and arts, 68–70. biological and social, fiction in, 99; mathematical impetus given to, toward end of seventeenth century, 180; biological, awakening of, 181; mathematical, renaissance of, 181.

Scientist, the true, an artist, 72, 73, 112, 126; curiosity the stimulus of, 104, 105; the false, 125, 126; who turns to religion, 199–201.

Scott, W. R., on art and æsthetics, 326 n.

Scottish School, the, 267.

Sculpture, painting, and the arts of design, 36; civilisation measured by standard of, 308.

Seises, the, the dance of, 44 n.

Selous, Edmund, 36 n.

Semon, Professor, R., 351 n.

"Sense," Hutcheson's conception of, 274.

Seville, cathedral of, dancing in, 44.

Sex, instinct of, a reaction to the stimulus of curiosity, 104; early questions concerning, 105–07; source of art impulse, 108–12; and the scientific interest, 112; not absolutely essential, 234.

Sexual imagery, strain of, in thought, 113.

"Shadow," 219 n.

Shaftesbury, Earl of, influence on Kant, 254; illustrated unsystematic method of thinking, 259; his book, 260; his theory of Æsthetic Intuitionism, 260; his affinity to the Greeks, 260; his early life, 261; his idea of goodness, 262; his principles expounded, 264–66; his influence on later writers and thinkers, 266; his influence on our modern morality, 266, 267; the greatest Greek of modern times, 267, 271; his service to the modern world, 267; measure of his recognition in Scotland and England, 267; recognition of, abroad, 268, 269; made no clear distinction between creative artistic impulse and critical æsthetic appreciation, 270; realised that reason cannot affect appetite, 270; one of the founders of æsthetics, 271; his use of the term "moral sense," 273, 274; temperamentally a Stoic, 279; of the æsthetic contemplative temperament, 332, 333.

Shakespeare, William, 148; his style compared with that of Bacon, 160; affected by the intoxication of words, 167; stored up material to be used freely later, 170, 171; the spelling of his name by himself, 173; surpasses contemporaries in flexibility and intimacy, 184; Tolstoy's opinion of, 311; on Nature and art, 312, 313; his figure of Prospero, 331.

Shamans, the, religious dances among, 40, 41; their wills brought into harmony with the essence of the world, 193; double attitude of, 194.

Sharp, F. C., on Hutcheson, 327 n.

Shelley, P. B., mysticism in poetry of, 237; on imagination and morality, 372.

Sidgwick, Henry, 255, 314.

Singer, Dr. Charles, his definition of science, 70, 71.

Singing, relation to music and dancing, 62.

Silberer, Herbert, on magic and science, 195.

Simcox, Edith, her description of conversion, 218 n.

Skene, on dances among African tribes, 38.

Slezakova, Anna, the polka extemporised by, 60.

Smith, Adam, his "economic man," 99; morals based on sympathy, according to, 272; influenced by Hutcheson, 275.

Smith, Arthur H., his book Chinese Characteristics, 23 n.

Social capillarity, 298.

Social ladder, 298, 299.

Social statistics, 286–88.

Socialists, French, inspired by Shaftesbury, 269.

Socrates, the Platonic, 75, 78; Grote's chapter on, 76; the real and the legendary, 76, 79, 82; three elements in our composite portrait of, 77–79; the Platonic, and the Gospel Jesus, 82, 83; on philosophy and music, 179; his view of the moralist, 248.

Solidarity, socialistic, among the Chinese, 26, 27.

Solmi, Vincian scholar, 114.

Sophists, the, 4, 302, 302 n.

Sophocles, danced in his own dramas, 56; beauty and moral order in, 247; Tolstoy's opinion of, 311.

Soul, a fiction, 100; in harmony with itself, 219; the moral life of, as a dance, 251, 252.

South Sea Islands, dancing in, 49.

Space, absolute, a fiction, 95.

Spain, dancing in, 44, 50, 54.

Speech, the best literary prose, 155; in Greece, 155; in England, 155, 156; the artist's, 156; a tradition, 161.

Spelling, and thinking, 127 n.; has little to do with style, 173; now uniform and uniformly bad, 174, 175.

Spencer, Herbert, on science and art, 68; on use of science in form of magic, 195; the universe according to, 215; on the harmlessness of moral teaching, 246 n.; on diminishing birth-rate, 294 n.

Spengler, Dr. Oswald, on the development of music, 135 n.; argues on the identity of physics, mathematics, religion, and great art, 138; his theory of culture and civilisation, 309, 310.

Spinoza, Baruch, 89; has moved in sphere where impulses of religion and science spring from same source, 207; transforms ethics into geometry, 281; has been called a God-intoxicated man, 316 n.; his "intellectual love of God," 342.

Spirit, and matter, 229, 230.

Statistics, uncertainty of, 286; for measurement of civilisation, 286–88; applied to France to test civilisation, 295–97.

Steele, Dr. John, on the Chinese ceremonial, 29 n.

Stephen, Sir Leslie, on poetry and philosophy, 85; could see no good in Shaftesbury, 268.

Stevenson, R. L., 188.

Stocks, eradication of unfit, by Man, 354; recommended by Jesus, 355, 356.

Stoics, the, 207.

Strauss, D. F., his The Old Faith and the New, 214.

Style, literary, of to-day and of our forefathers' time, 143; the achievement of, 155; grace seasoned with salt, 155; atavism in, in members of the same family, 158, 190; atavism in, in the race, 160, 190; much that is instinctive in, 163; the music of, 163, 164; vocabulary in, 164, 165; the effect of mere words on, 165–67; familiarity with author's, necessary to understanding, 171, 172; spelling has little to do with, 173; much lost by slavish adherence to rules in, 75; must have clarity and beauty, 176–78; English prose, Cartesian influence on, 180 n.; personal and impersonal, 182, 183; progress in, lies in casting aside accretions and exuberances, 183; founded on a model, the negation of style, 188; the task of breaking the old moulds of, 188, 189; summary of elements of, 190. See Writing.

Suicide, rate of, as test of civilisation, 295, 296.

Swahili, dancing among, 38.

Swedenborg, Emanuel, his science and his mysticism, 208.

Swedish ballet, the, 60.

Sweet (suavis), referring to moral qualities, 264.

Sweetness, and goodness, in Shaftesbury's philosophy, 262; originally the same, 263.

Swift, Jonathan, laments "the corruption of our style," 142; beauty of his style, rests on truth to logic of his thought, 183; utterance of, combining two conceptions of life, 333.

Swimming-belt, constructed by Leonardo da Vinci, 119.

Swinburne, C. A., on writing poetry to a tune, 62; his *Poems and Ballads*, 172; his *Songs before Sunrise*, 212.

Sylvester, J. J., on mathematics, 139.

Symphony, the development of a dance suite, 62.

Syndicalism, as test of civilisation, 296, 297.

Taglioni, Maria, 58.

Tahiti, dancing at, 50.

Tambourine, the, 53.

Tao, the word, 204.

Taste, the gospel of, 280.

Telegraph, the, 72 *n.*

Telephone, the, 72 *n.*

Tell-el-Amarna, 28.

Theology, 227.

Therapeuts, the worship of, 42.

Thing-in-Itself, the, a fiction, 101.

Things, are fictions, 98.

Thinking, of the nature of art, 85, 86; and existing, on two different planes, 101; the special art and object of, 101; is a comparison, 102; is a regulated error, 103; abstract, the process of its birth, 108, 109.

Thompson, Silvanus, on Faraday, 132.

Thomson, James, influence of Shaftesbury on, 266.

Thomson, Sir Joseph, on matter and weight, 230.

Thoreau, H. D., on morals, 282.

Thought, logic of, inescapable, 183.

Tobacco, consumption of, as test of civilisation, 295.

Todas, the, of India, 203 *n.*

Toledo, cathedral of, dancing in, 44.

Tolstoy, Count Leo, his opinions on art, 311.

Tonga, sacred position of carpenter in, 2.

Tooke, Horne, 151 *n.*

Townsend, Rev. Joseph, on the fandango, 50.

Tradition, the corporeal embodiment of heredity, 161; and instinct, mould morals, 254–59.

Traditions, religious, 227; scientific, 228.

Triangles, 53.

Truth, the measuring-rod of, 230–32.

Tunisia, Southern, dancing in, 49.

T'ung, the story of, 33.

Turkish dervishes, dances of, 41.

Tuscans, the, 56. *See* Etruscans.

Tyndall, John, on Faraday, 130–32.

Tyrrells, the, the handwriting of, 157.

Ugliness, 328.

Ulysses, representative of ideal of totality of existence, 6.

United States, the genius of, compared with the temper of the population, 293.

Universe, conceived as work of art by primitive philosopher, 1; according to D. F. Strauss, 214; according to Spencer, 215; according to Hinton, 216; according to Sir James Frazer, 219 *n.*; according to Bertrand Russell, 219 *n.*; conception of, a personal matter, 219 *n.*; the so-called materialistic, 229, 230; Bovarism of, 337.

Utilitarians, the, 267, 268.

Uvea, 15. *See* Loyalty Islands.

Vaihinger, Hans, his *Philosophie des Als Ob*, 86; English influence upon, 86, 87; allied to English spirit, 87, 88; his origin, 88; his training, and vocation, 88–93; influence of Schiller on, 89; philosophers who influenced, 89, 90; his pessimisms, irrationalism, and voluntarism, 90; his view of military power of Germany, 90, 91; his devouring appetite for knowledge, 92; reads F. A. Lange's *History of Materialism*, 92, 93; writes his book at about twenty-five years of age, 93; his book published, 94; the problem he set out to prove, 94; his doctrine of fiction, 94–102; his doctrine not immune from criticism, 102; the fortifying influence of his philosophy, 102, 103; influenced Adler, 337.

Valencia, cathedral of, dancing in, 44.

Valerius, Maximus, 353 *n.*

Van Gogh, mysticism in pictures of, 237.

Varnhagen, Rahel, 66.

Verbal counters, 149, 150.

Verlaine, Paul, the significance of words to, 168.

Vesalius, 120.

Vasari, Giorgio, his account of Leonardo da Vinci, 115, 123.

Vestris, Gaetan, and the ballet, 57.

Vinci, Leonardo da, man of science, 113, 125; as a painter, 113, 114, 117, 118; his one aim, the knowledge and mastery of Nature, 114, 117, 125; an Overman, 115; science and art joined in, 115–17; as the founder of professional engineering, 118, 119; the extent of his studies and inventions, 119, 120; a supreme master of language, 121; his appearance, 121; his parentage, 121; his youthful accomplishments, 122; his sexual temperament, 122, 123; the man, woman, and child in, 123, 124; a figure for awe rather than love, 124.

Vinci, Ser Piero da, father of Leonardo da Vinci, 121.

Virtue, and beauty, among the Greeks, 247; the art of living well, 252; in Shaftesbury's system, 265, 266; beauty of, 270 *n.*

Virtues, ethical and intellectual, 330.

Visconti, Galeazzo, spectacular pageants at marriage of, 57.

Vocabulary, each writer creates his own, 164, 165.

Voltaire, F. M. A. de, recognised Shaftesbury, 268; on the foundations of society, 289.

Wagner, Richard, on Beethoven's Seventh Symphony, 62, 63.

Wallas, Professor Graham, on Plato and Dante, 73.

War, and dancing, allied, 63, 64.

Wealth, as test of civilisation, 296, 297.

Weight, its nature, 230.

Weismann, and the study of heredity, 127.

Wells, H. G., his description of Napoleon, 8–10, 12.

Whitman, Walt, his *Leaves of Grass*, 172; words attributed to him on what is right, 254.

Woman, the question, what she is like, 106.

Words, have a rich content of their own, 166; the intoxication of, 167–69; their arrangement chiefly studied by young writer, 172.

Wordsworth, William, 184; influence of Shaftesbury on, 266.

Work, a kind of dance, 61, 62.

World, becoming impalpable and visionary, 337, 338. *See* Universe.

Writers, the great, have observed decorum instinctively, 181, 182; the great, learn out of themselves, 188, 189; the great, are heroes at heart, 189.

Writing, personality in, 144, 190; a common accomplishment to-day, 144, 145; an arduous intellectual task, 151, 153, 190; good and bad, 154; the achievement of style in, 155; machine-made, 156; not made by the laws of grammar, 172, 173; how the old method gave place to the new, 179–81; summary of elements of, 190. *See* Handwriting, Style.

Wundt, Wilhelm, on the dance, 38, 39 *n.*

Xavier, Francis, 123, 237.

Xenophon, his portrait of Socrates, 77.

Zeno, 249 *n.*